Canyonlands
National Park

Favorite Jeep Roads & Hiking Trails

WARNING:
HIKING INVOLVES RISK!

Hiking is a sport, not a pastime, and like all sports it involves an element of risk. There have been several instances in recent years of people suffering injury while hiking in Utah's backcountry and then filing a lawsuit against a person or organization that gave them information about the hike. This is a disturbing trend with serious implications for everyone involved in the sport.

The author and publisher of this book will not assume responsibility for any mishap that may occur as a result of information present or not present in this book. It is assumed that anyone attempting any of the hikes described in the following pages is already aware of the potential risks, has made all the necessary preparations, and has had sufficient experience to assume responsibility for himself.

Furthermore, while the author has done his best to assure that the information herein presented is accurate, he cannot guarantee its accuracy. Hikers using the information in this book should make allowance for the possibility that it may not be correct.

Canyonlands
National Park

Favorite Jeep Roads & Hiking Trails

written and illustrated by J. David Day

Rincon Publishing Company
1465 West 1700 North
Provo, Utah 84604
www.UtahTrails.com

first printing: 2004

All of the photographs in this book were taken by the author.
Leasing agreements are available on request.

front cover: Elephant Canyon, Needles District
back cover: Millard Canyon Road, Maze District
    page 1: Green River and White Rim Road, Island District
    page 3: Big Spring Canyon, Needles District
    page 5: Handprints in Devils Lane Canyon, Needles District

Library of Congress Control Number: 2003095191
ISBN: 0-9660858-2-5

Printed by Art Printing Works, Kuala Lumpur, Malaysia

Published by:

Rincon Publishing Company
1465 West 1700 North
Provo, Utah 84604

(801) 377-7657
www.UtahTrails.com

To the ancient ones
who came before.

I have often
felt your presence
as I walk alone
through your canyons.

Contents

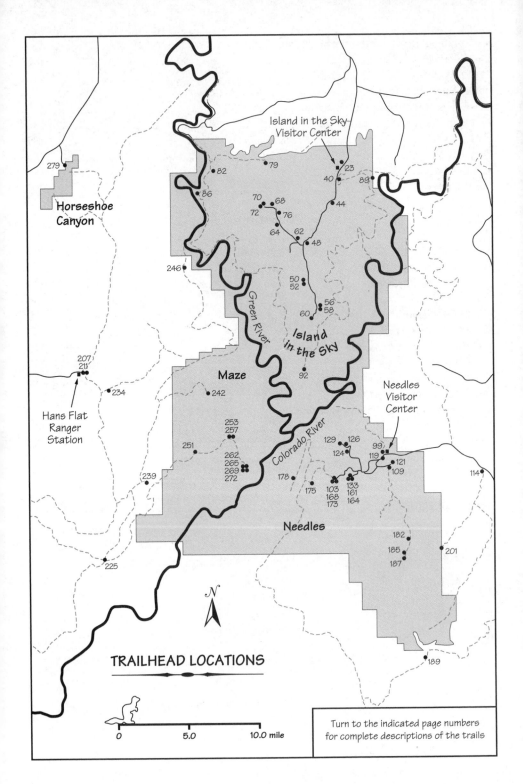

279

Horseshoe
Canyon

82   79   Island in the Sky
              Visitor Center

86   40 23
              89

70 68
72 76   44

64 62

48

246

50
52

56
58

60

Green River

Island
in the
Sky

207
211   92

234

Hans Flat
Ranger
Station

242

Maze

Needles
Visitor
Center

253
257

251   129 126
                124   99
262   119 121
265   109
269   178
272   175   103 133   114
                   168 161
Colorado River   173 164

239

Needles

225   182
           185
           187 201

N

189

TRAILHEAD LOCATIONS

0   5.0   10.0 mile

Turn to the indicated page numbers
for complete descriptions of the trails

8

Preface

Vast, rugged, and remote are the words that best describe Canyonlands National Park. The 527-square-mile park contains no lodges, no restaurants, and very few paved roads. What it does offer is a wilderness experience unlike any other in Utah. It is a place where time has stood still for centuries, and where treasures from the past lie hidden and protected from the excesses of our modern world. Towering buttes, sunken valleys, orange cliffs, and huge sandstone arches await your discovery, as do ancient Indian ruins, long abandoned cowboy camps, and unexpected desert springs. You may even discover a forgotten part of yourself in the solitude of the canyons. But don't expect Canyonlands to yield its rewards easily. To its credit the Park Service has made a concerted effort to preserve the wild nature of the park, so you can expect many miles of rocky trails and rough roads.

The Green and Colorado Rivers divide Canyonlands National Park into three separate districts, Island in the Sky, Needles, and Maze, with the confluence of the rivers being in the center. There is no way to cross from one district to another without leaving the park, and the distances involved make it unfeasible to visit more than one district on a single trip. This book has been divided into three major sections, each covering one district. The relevant jeep trails are discussed at the beginning of each section, followed by the hiking trails. You will note that many of the hiking trailheads are accessed via the jeep roads, so combination jeep and hiking trips are the most practical way to see the park.

About half of the hiking trails can be accessed with an ordinary car. Mountain biking is also popular on the park's jeep roads, but there is no substitute for a 4WD vehicle. The Maze District in particular is almost impossible to explore without a 4WD vehicle. Several of the jeep roads are too long to be completed in a single day, so you will need to carry extra food, water, and camping gear. The Park Service has strict rules regarding overnight camping in the park and reservations are required, so be sure to contact them before finalizing your plans. You can read more about the rules and regulations and the reservation system in the introduction.

As with my other books, I have rated each of the hiking and jeep trails on a scale of one to five stars according to how much I personally enjoy that trail. The best rating is five stars ☆ ☆ ☆ ☆ ☆, which means that that trail is one of the five most enjoyable in the park. These ratings are only my personal opinion, however, and I am sure many of you will disagree with my assessments. If you have been on a particular trail and agree or disagree with my rating I hope you will post your comments on our website at *www.UtahTrails.com* and let us all know what you think.

May the wilderness remain forever wild!

David Day
Provo, Utah
davidday@utahtrails.com

Introduction

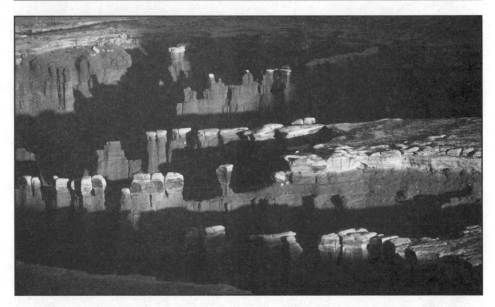

...here all is exposed and naked, dominated by the monolithic formations of sandstone which stand above the surface of the ground and extend for miles, sometimes level, sometimes tilted or warped by pressures from below, carved by erosion and weathering into an intricate maze of glens, grottoes, fissures, passageways, and deep narrow canyons.

Edward Abbey[1]

Canyonlands truly is a wilderness of exposed and naked rock. It is as if God had cut open the earth's outer cover and peeled back a thin layer to reveal the inner beauty of His creation. On one level of understanding the splendor is stark and simple, a tapestry of deeply shaded canyons filled with pinnacles and spires and distant flat-topped buttes. But like all masterpieces, there is something even more compelling about Canyonlands than its visual grandeur. The geological wonderland frequently brings forth an irresistible urge to explore—to learn more about how the canyons were formed and

about the ancient peoples who once called them home.

With its 527 square miles of rocky wilderness Canyonlands is, by far, Utah's largest national park, and it is in large part the vast expanse of the rugged terrain that makes it so appealing. There are only 32 miles of paved roads within the park, but a large network of jeep roads and hiking trails make the back country reasonably accessible to anyone willing to leave the asphalt behind. The paved roads can provide a brief introduction to the wonders of this fascinating area, but the fun really begins in the

[1] Edward Abbey, *Desert Solitaire, a Season in the Wilderness*, Simon & Schuster, New York, 1968. (with permission)

backcountry.

Most of what we see in Canyonlands today is the result of 30 million years of erosive action by two of the West's great rivers: the Green and the Colorado. The two rivers join at a point roughly in the center of the national park, dividing it into three distinctly separate districts commonly referred to as the Maze, the Needles, and the Island in the Sky. One might reasonably expect the three adjacent parts to be pretty much the same, but, as you will see, they are actually quite different. The three parts of the national park are also very much isolated from one another. In order to get from one district to another one must drive out of the park to Moab, Green River, or Hite, where there are bridges across the rivers.

Because of the isolation between its three districts, Canyonlands is almost like three separate national parks. Each district has its own rangers and its own visitor center, and there are even subtle differences in how the three districts are managed. The Island in the Sky, with its paved roads, its dramatic mesa-top viewpoints, and its close proximity to Moab, has a special appeal for tourists who want to see some spectacular scenery without a lot of walking or driving. The Needles District, on the other hand, is more geared to hiking. Here it is possible to chose from a wide variety of trails that meander through an intriguing landscape of heavily eroded sandstone pinnacles. The Maze District is different in yet another way. This area is being managed as a remote, undeveloped wilderness where little has changed in the last thousand years. There are no paved roads in the Maze; if you want to explore this area you must have a 4WD vehicle.

Season

Canyonlands, like most of Southern Utah, is in a dry desert environment, and it can get very hot in the summer. The park is open all year round, but the best time for a visit is during the spring months of March, April and May. The Easter weekend is probably the single busiest time, and visitation drops off markedly after Memorial Day. Fall is also a pleasant time to spend some time in Canyonlands National Park, and visitation generally picks up again after Labor Day. There are a fair number of desert rats (like me) who keep coming back even in the heat of midsummer, but winter visitors are few.

Canyonlands receives a third of its annual rainfall in the two months between mid-July and mid-September, so if you are planning a trip during that time be sure to pack some rain gear. At other times rain is rarely a problem; on average Canyonlands receives only 6-10 inches of precipitation each year. Insects can be troublesome near the rivers and in some shaded canyons in late spring and early summer, but in general they are

Colorado River, from Gooseneck Trail

not a serious bother. If you plan to be near the rivers in May or June you can easily solve this problem by wearing long pants and a long sleeved shirt.

Getting There from Nearby Towns

Moab, with a population of 5,400, is the largest town in southeastern Utah, and its proximity to both Canyonlands and Arches National Parks makes it a favorite base for people visiting these areas. It has a wide variety of restaurants and motels, as well as river rafting, bicycling, and jeep touring agencies. Call the Moab Visitor Center at (435) 259-8825 for more information.

The Island in the Sky Visitor Center is only 32 miles from Moab; consequently this pleasant town is often used as a base for trips into that district of Canyonlands. To get there drive north of Moab on Highway 191 for 11 miles to the junction with Highway 313. Turn left at the sign and drive another 20

miles to the Canyonlands National Park entrance gate. The visitor center is located on the north side of the road 1.2 miles beyond the gate.

5.5 miles before reaching the Island in the Sky entrance gate you will pass a well-marked road that leads to Dead Horse Point State Park. This state park is also worth a visit if you have the time. Its main attraction is the Dead Horse Point Overlook which offers a marvelous view of the Colorado River Gooseneck just east of Canyonlands National Park (see page 89). This overlook point is 7.5 miles from Highway 313, at the end of the Dead Horse Point Road.

Moab is also often used as a base for trips into the Needles District of Canyonlands. To get to the Needles Visitor Center you must drive south of the town for 40 miles to the junction with Highway 211. Turn right onto Highway 211 and drive another 34 miles to the Needles entrance gate. The visitor cen-

The Sentinels, near Dollhouse Rock

ter is 0.8 miles beyond the gate.

Montecello, the county seat of San Juan County, is the closest town to the Needles District of Canyonlands. Only about 2000 people live in this small farming community, but it does have a half-dozen motels and a limited selection of restaurants. It is about a half-hour closer to the Needles than Moab; hence it is sometimes used as a base for trips into that area. To get to the Needles from Montecello you must drive 13 miles north on Highway 191 to the junction with Highway 211. Turn west there and drive another 35 miles to the Needles Visitor Center.

Green River, a small farming town famous for its watermelon production, is situated north of Canyonlands National Park on the west side of the Green River. Only 1000 people live in Green River, but because the town is on Interstate Highway 70 it is well equipped for the tourist trade. It has a nice selection of motels and restaurants and, as a bonus, it is also the home of Utah's John Wesley Powell Museum. More information about accommodations in the town can be obtained from the Green River Travel Council at (435) 564-3526.

Green River can be used as a possible base for trips into both the Island in the Sky and the Maze Districts of Canyonlands. To get to the Island in the Sky you must drive east on I-70 to the junction with Highway 191. Then turn south toward Moab and drive another 20 miles to Highway 313. Finally, turn right onto Highway 313 and drive the last 21 miles to the Island in the Sky Visitor Center.

If you are going to the Maze you must drive west from Green River on I-70 for 13 miles to the junction with Highway 24. Turn south on Highway 24 and drive toward Hanksville for 25 miles. 0.6 mile after passing the road to Goblin Valley State Park you will see a well marked gravel road leaving the east side of the highway for Roost Flats

Unnamed Arch, Lavender Canyon

and Hans Flat Ranger Station. Turn left at this point and follow the signs for the next 45 miles to the Hans Flat Ranger Station. The ranger station is actually located in the Orange Cliffs District of Glen Canyon National Recreation Area, but it nevertheless serves as the visitor center for the adjacent Maze District as well. The Orange Cliffs and the Maze are managed together and, for all practical purposes, the Orange Cliffs can be considered to be part of the national park.

Hanksville is the town closest to the Hans Flat Ranger Station; consequently it is a possible base for trips into the Maze. It is just a small crossroads town of about 400 people, but it does have a few motels and restaurants. The best place to get general information is the local BLM office, which can be reached at (435) 542-3461. To get into the Maze from Hanksville you must drive north on Highway 24 for 19 miles to

South Butte, Buttes of the Cross, from Anderson Bottom

the gravel road that goes to Roost Flats and the Hans Flat Ranger Station. (The Hans Flat turnout is on the right side of the road 0.6 mile before the turnout to Goblin Valley State Park) Turn east on the Hans Flat Road and continue the last 45 miles from Highway 24 to the ranger station/visitor center.

The **Hite Marina** is the only settlement near the southern access road into the Maze District. There are no motels in Hite, but there is a gas station and a convenience store. To get into the Maze from Hite you must Drive north from the Hite turnoff on Highway 95 for 1.1 miles to the bridge across Lake Powell. After you cross this bridge drive another 1.0 mile until you see an unmarked gravel road departing on the right. This is the road to Waterhole Flat. The distance to the flat is 34 miles along a road that can usually be driven by most cars. There are numerous side roads along the way, mostly built by local ranchers, but if you just stay on the best-traveled road you should

have no trouble.

You will know you have arrived at Waterhole Flat when you come to a 4-way intersection with signs indicating the way to the Dollhouse, Flint Trail, and Hatch Canyon. If you turn right at this junction you will be starting on the Dollhouse Road to the Land of Standing Rocks (described on page 225). If you go straight for 6.9 miles you will join the jeep road to the Flint Trail and the Green River (described on page 211). You will need a 4WD vehicle to go beyond Waterhole Flat.

Campgrounds

There are only two small developed campgrounds in Canyonlands National Park, one at Squaw Flat in the Needles District and one at Willow Flat in the Island in the Sky. Both campgrounds are operated on a first-come-first-served basis only and they fill up quickly during the peak season from mid-March through May, so if you are planning a stay during those months you had better arrive early. It is also possible to camp just outside the park boundary in any of the three districts without a permit, and many people choose to do that—especially during the busy season.

Willow Flat Campground is the smaller and more primitive of the two campgrounds. It has only 12 sites, no water, and costs only $5.00/night. The Squaw Flat Campground in the Needles District has 26 sites and drinking water is available, but the cost is $10.00/night. Most of the campsites have an upper limit of 10 people and 2 vehicles, but in the Needles District there are three additional group sites that can accommodate as many as 50 people. These sites can be reserved in advance at a cost of $3.00/person.

Backcountry Permits

Permits are required for all overnight trips into the backcountry of Canyonlands National Park, whether by foot, motor vehicle, mountain bike, or boat. Permits are also required to take vehicles, bicycles, or horses on day trips into Horse/Salt Creek Canyon and Lavender Canyon in the Needles District. All other day use of allowed trails and roads in other areas does not require a permit. It should also be noted that all vehicles in Canyonlands National Park must be street legal. Dirt motorcycles and ATVs are not allowed.

A backpacking permit allows a group of 5-7 people to stay up to 7 consecutive nights in an assigned site or zone. The cost is $15.00/group. A vehicle or bicycle permit allows up to 15 people with no more than 3 vehicles to stay a maximum of 3 consecutive nights at a designated backcountry vehicle camp. The cost is $30.00/group. A day use vehicle or bicycle permit for the Needles District allows one vehicle or bicycle to enter Horse/Salt Creek Canyon or Lavender Canyon. The cost is $5.00/vehicle.

Labyrinth Canyon, Green River

Reservations

It is sometimes possible to obtain last minute backcountry permits and campsite assignments from the visitor centers with no prior reservations. But only a limited number of permits are issued each day, so to avoid disappointment it is best to make reservations in advance. Reservation requests for all backcountry permits are accepted by mail or fax no earlier than the second Monday in July for the following calendar year and no later than two weeks before your departure date.

Last minute backcountry permits and campsite assignments can usually be obtained only in person at the visitor centers. However the road into the Maze from the Hite Marina does not pass the Maze Visitor Center (Hans Flat Ranger Station); consequently it is sometimes possible to get permits and campsite assignments for the Maze

District by telephone. If you are entering the Maze from Hite and do not already have an overnight permit call the Hans Flat Ranger Station at (435) 259-2652. Have a credit card ready and if there is space available in the area in which you want to camp they will issue you a permit over the telephone. Do not attempt to enter the Maze without an overnight permit; the distances involved are too great for day trips.

Office staff are available to answer questions by telephone and assist with trip planning during mornings, Monday through Friday, 8:00 a.m.-12:30 p.m. Mountain Time. You can also get reservation information on the internet, but the actual advance reservations can only be made by mail or fax.

Canyonlands National Park
2282 S. West Resource Blvd.
Moab, Utah 84532
website: www.nps.gov/cany/
e-mail: canyinfo@nps.gov

General information:	(435) 719-2313
Administration:	(435) 719-2100
Backcountry info:	(435) 259-4351
FAX for reservations:	(435) 259-4285
FAX administration:	(435) 719-2300
Island Visitor Center:	(435) 259-4712
Needles Visitor Center:	(435) 259-4711
Hans Flat Ranger Station	
(Maze Visitor Center):	(435) 259-2652

Tips for 4WD drivers

Other than the requirement that your vehicle must be street legal, the Park Service has no restrictions on what kind of vehicles are allowed in Canyonlands. But don't underestimate the importance of making sure your car or truck is compatible with the trip you are planning. Many of the jeep roads in Canyonlands can be driven by any high clearance vehicle, but some of them are definitely for 4WD vehicles only. Furthermore, some

of the trails will lead you into areas that may be more than 50 miles from the pavement, and a breakdown in such an area would be disastrous. It can cost several thousand dollars to hire someone to tow you out, and even if your old car is not worth that much the Park Service will not allow you to abandon it.

There are challenging 4WD sections of road in all three districts of Canyonlands, but the Maze District deserves special mention. The Park Service has made a deliberate effort to keep this part of Canyonlands as wild and unspoiled as possible; consequently there is no way to get into the Maze without a good 4WD vehicle. Furthermore it is virtually impossible to see the Maze as a day trip. It takes at least 5 hours of off-highway driving to get into the Maze, and the roads are often rough enough to knock the fillings out of your teeth. Be sure you

Shot Canyon

Bagpipe Butte, near Golden Stairs Camp

are prepared before you enter this area.

Gasoline: Depending on how much exploring you do you, some jeep trips in Canyonlands can be well over a hundred miles plus the distance to and from the nearest town with a gas station. Also, bear in mind that while you are creeping along in 4-wheel-drive you may get only 5 miles/gallon. Be sure to fill your tank just before entering the park, and carry an extra 5-10 gallons of fuel for emergencies.

Tires: Your old, worn tires may work just fine on pavement, but not on the rocky jeep trails of Canyonlands. The roads are littered with sharp and pointed rocks that can play havoc with your treads, and new tires can withstand the punishment much better than old tires. Double-check the condition of your spare tire before you start, and make sure you have the tools to change it. You should also note that it is not wise to over-inflate your tires while driving on rough roads. First, if the tires are too hard they can be more easily punctured by the sharp rocks. And second, your car will handle much better in loose sand if the tires are slightly under inflated.

Battery: It has been my experience that dead batteries are even more common than flat tires, especially in cars that are driven on rough roads. Most people don't realize how fragile the lead plates inside a lead-acid battery are, but they can be easily bent or broken with the shaking they receive on a rough road, causing the battery to short and become useless. This has happened to me so many times that I now have a piece of foam rubber under my battery to help cushion it from shocks. Also, I always carry a fully charged spare battery in my jeep whenever I venture into remote areas.

Water: The importance of carrying extra water in your car cannot be overemphasized. Not only do you need it for cooking, drinking, and cleaning up, but there is always the possibility that you might have to replace the liquid in a leaky radiator. Water is generally unavailable in the park, particularly in the backcountry, so be sure to carry plenty.

Tips for Bicyclists

Bicycling is very popular in the Island in the Sky and Needles Districts of Canyonlands. Most of the bicycle trips are multiday journeys done with the help of a support vehicle; however there are a few interesting rides in the Needles District that can be done in one day. The rules for bicycling are basically the same as the rules for driving motor vehicles: backcountry permits are required for overnight camping (in assigned sites), and off-road riding is not allowed. Bicycling on the hiking trails is also not allowed.

You will be thankful if your bike has spring suspension, both in the front and back, since most of the jeep roads in Canyonlands are very rocky. The roads are also frequently sandy, so your bike tires should be as wide as possible. Punctures from thorns are common with bikes that don't have thorn-proof tubes. But the biggest challenge bikers face in Canyonlands is the problem of carrying enough water; the environment is generally hot and dry, and there is very little shade.

Tips for hikers

Cars are a necessity for getting to the trailheads, but really the best way to see Canyonlands is on foot. There are so many notable places in the park where cars and bicycles cannot go, and so many interesting things along the trails that need time to appreciate. But desert hiking is not the same as walking in a shaded forest, so before you set out take a little time to consider what the hike entails.

Probably the most common mistake hikers make is not carrying enough water. If you are planning to be gone for more than

an hour or two a typical 1-liter water bottle is not enough. The Park Service recommends a minimum of one gallon of water a day for hiking and backpacking during the summer months, and I suggest you follow their advice. Nothing can ruin an otherwise pleasant walk faster than running out of water on a hot summer day.

Another problem unique to desert hiking is insufficient salt retention. Sweating and drinking large amounts of water quickly leaches salt out of the body, and the nervous system does not work very well without salt. The first sign of salt deficiency is fatigue. You may think your exhaustion is simply the result of being out of shape, but a salt deficiency is often part of the problem. If you increase your intake of sodium and potassium while you are in the desert you will find that you have a lot more energy.

White Rim Road, near Murphy Camp

It is important to protect yourself from the sun in Canyonlands, which means wearing a hat and using sunblock on those parts of the body that can't be easily covered. Personally, I am one of those odd people who prefer to wear long pants and long-sleeved cotton shirts while hiking in the desert. I sometimes get strange looks, but I have my reasons. When my hiking companions in shorts and T-shirts return from a trip with sunburned arms and welts on their legs from brush scratches and insect bites I can always say I told you so.

Sneakers are just fine for many trails, but it you are going on a long hike or if the trail is very rocky you should wear boots. The sharp rocks will quickly destroy a good pair of sneakers, and boots will give you much better protection against a twisted ankle. High-topped boots are also a good defense against rattlesnake bites, although snakebites are rare in Canyonlands.

Anasazi ruin, Salt Creek Canyon

Minimum Impact

There was a time in the West when there were so few people using the backcountry that human impact was not a problem, and people did not think much about their affect on the environment. But population pressure has changed all of that. Places like Canyonlands National Park now receive hundreds of thousands of visitors every year, and if we want to preserve these places we must all make a special effort to protect them.

Utah's desert areas require special consideration from backcountry hikers and drivers. Most people don't realize how fragile the arid ecosystems are, but it can take years for the desert to recover from the impact of a careless act. Old campfire sites, tire tracks, and even footprints seem never to go away.

Desert soils are filled with an array of dry, thread-like microscopic plants that nitrogenate the soil and bind it together, and once these plants are crushed or burned it can take

decades for them to recover. Without this component of the soil, called the cryptobiotic crust, the desert would be a barren place indeed; most shrubs and grasses could not survive without it. So when hiking or driving in Canyonlands try to stay on the established trails as much as possible, and when doing off-trail hiking try to walk on the slickrock or in the sandy bottoms of washes where there is no ground cover.

Another area of concern is garbage. There is nothing more disheartening to a nature lover than to walk through a pristine wilderness area that has been littered with trash. The slogan "pack it in, pack it out" is a good one to follow. Some organic material, such as unwanted food or body wastes can be buried, but only if it is deposited at least six inches below the surface and covered with well packed dirt. But do not bury your toilet paper; it takes forever for it to decompose in the dry soil.

Candlestick Tower, from the Wilhite Trail

Some of Canyonlands' greatest treasures are the archeological sites that were left behind by prehistoric Indians that lived in the area from 700 to 9,000 years ago. They include pictograph panels, granaries, cliff dwellings, and scattered fields of flint chips where the ancient peoples manufactured stone tools. It is impossible to describe the thrill of discovering one of these archeological gems, often far from any road in a wild desert canyon, yet these precious remnants of the past have received a great deal of abuse in recent years. Most of the damage was inflicted long before Canyonlands became a national park, but even today the ancient artifacts are still being damaged. Occasionally they are intentionally vandalized; more often damage is inflicted as a result of carelessness. If you visit one of these sites be careful not to damage it in any way. Do not touch the rock paintings, do not climb on the granaries and buildings, and do not remove any pottery shards, corncobs, flint chips, or other objects from the sites. Treat them just as you would treat an exhibit in a museum, because that is exactly what they are.

In addition to Indian artifacts, there are also many areas in Canyonlands National Park where you can see the remnants of habitation by Utah's early European settlers. Beginning in the 1880s many settlers attempted to establish homesteads along the Green River in the northern part of the park, but none stayed more than a few years. During the early and mid-1900s the park was widely used as a summer pasture by cattle and sheep ranchers. Then in the 1950s uranium was discovered in Canyonlands, and the entire area was scoured over by prospectors. Many of the trails described in this book were originally built by these early settlers and explorers, and they often pass by the old corrals, cabins, cowboy camps, uranium mines and mining equipment that was left behind. Again, please do not remove or deface any of the historic artifacts. Lets keep them as they are, so that future visitors can enjoy them as much as we do.

Maps

There is no substitute for a good map of the place you are exploring. The maps provided in this book should be sufficient to complete the described trips, but if possible you should take along a more detailed map of the area you plan to visit—especially if you are traveling on foot. Part of the joy of hiking is exploring and taking side trips that may not have been part of the original plan, and it is much easier to do this if you have a good map. Also, it is sometimes useful to know exactly where you are on the trail. A good map will help you plot your course with greater accuracy.

The best topographic maps available are the 7.5-minute series, published by the United States Geological Survey. They are large scale, about 2.6 inches per mile, with contour lines at 40 foot intervals, but unfortunately they do not show many of the trails. Alternatively, National Geographic publishes two Trails Illustrated maps of Canyonlands that show nearly all of the park's hiking and jeep trails. Although the Trails Illustrated maps are smaller scale than the USGS maps they are very popular. Both the USGS maps and the National Geographic maps are available in the visitor centers.

You will find your map much more useful if you also carry a compass and a watch. The watch will help you estimate how far you have gone since the last landmark (most people walk about 2 miles per hour on level ground). When using your compass to determine a direction, bear in mind that the magnetic declination in Canyonlands National Park is about 13 degrees east. In other words, your compass needle will always point 13 degrees east of the direction of true north.

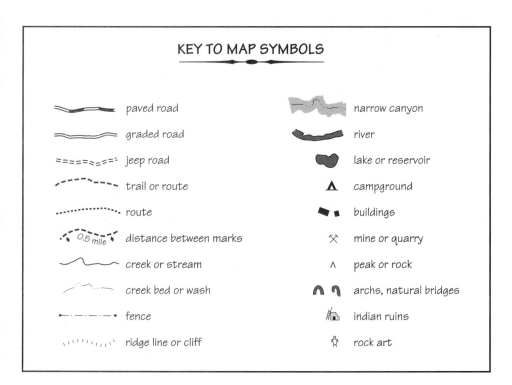

KEY TO MAP SYMBOLS

paved road		narrow canyon	
graded road		river	
jeep road		lake or reservoir	
trail or route		campground	
route		buildings	
0.5 mile distance between marks		mine or quarry	
creek or stream		peak or rock	
creek bed or wash		archs, natural bridges	
fence		indian ruins	
ridge line or cliff		rock art	

Island in the Sky District

There is no better introduction to Canyonlands National Park than the panoramic roadside vistas in the Island in the Sky District. This section of the park is dominated by a long, narrow promontory of land called the Island in the Sky Mesa that protrudes into the canyons from the north. A paved road follows the mesa top all the way to its southern end, and along the way it passes several remarkable viewpoints that should not be missed. The air is so clean that mountains fifty miles away appear as jagged purple cutouts on the distant horizon. The Green and Colorado Rivers wind through deep gorges 2000 feet below the mesa, while the intervening canyons are filled with a profusion of buttes, pinnacles, and plateaus.

From Grandview Point, on the southern tip of Island in the Sky Mesa, you can see many prominent landmarks in all three districts of the park. This is also a good place to study the geology of the area and gain some appreciation for the forces that created the canyons. Directly below the mesa is a sheer 600-foot cliff of Wingate Sandstone. Beneath that you will see a sloping layer of shale and mudstone, after which the land levels off onto a wide bench called the White Rim Plateau.

The White Rim Plateau figures prominently in the history of Canyonlands. This benchland was a popular winter grazing pasture for both sheep and cattle from the 1890s until the early 1960s, and many of the trails described on the following pages were originally built by ranchers in order to gain access to the plateau. Local cowboys originally called this area Between the Rivers, and the top of the mesa was usually referred to as Grays Pasture. It was only after the national park was created that it was renamed the Island in the Sky.

The White Rim Plateau was also used as an access corridor by prospectors during the uranium boom of the early 1950s. Most of the prospecting was done just above the White Rim Plateau in the Chinle Formation, and it was the uranium miners and prospectors that built the White Rim Road. Today the White Rim Road is one of the most popular jeep trails in Utah. It can clearly be seen winding across the White Rim Plateau from most of the Island in the Sky viewpoints.

In most places the White Rim Sandstone, which supports the White Rim Plateau, lies a thousand feet above the Colorado and Green Rivers. But in the northwest corner of the park the White Rim Formation actually dips below the Green River, causing the nature of the river canyon to change drastically. Upstream from that point the river is much more approachable, with many wide fertile soil deposits, called bottoms, along its shores.

These river bottoms played an important role in the history of Canyonlands. They were frequently used by early cattle ranchers, and many of the bottoms were homesteaded by early settlers. The prehistoric Anasazi and Fremont Indians also had settlements on some of the river bottoms, as evidenced by the granaries and other artifacts they left behind.

White Rim Road

☆ ☆ ☆ ☆

4WD vehicle required
3-day jeep ride

Distance:	111.8 miles (including all points of interest)
Road conditions:	Most of the road could be driven by an ordinary car, but there are a few brief sections where a 4WD, high clearance vehicle is a necessity.
Campsites:	The Park Service maintains nineteen campsites along this route, but camping elsewhere is not permitted. The sites are all equipped with composting toilets, although none of them have water. See pages 15-16 for more information on how reserve the sites and obtain camping permits.
Vicinity:	Starts near the Island in the Sky Visitor Center
USGS Maps:	Musselman Arch, Monument Basin, Turks Head, Upheaval Dome, Horsethief Canyon, Bowknot Bend, Mineral Canyon, The Knoll

The drive begins at the junction of Highway 313 and the Shafer Trail, 1.0 mile north of the Island in the Sky Visitor Center. It ends is at the junction of Highway 313 and Horsethief Road, 9.0 miles north of the Visitor Center.

Before driving this road you should be sure to spend some time at the overlook points on the Island in the Sky Mesa south of the visitor center. The thread of the White Rim Road can clearly be seen from all of these vantage points, as it winds its way across the White Rim Plateau 1,200 feet below the mesa. The views are extremely impressive, and few observers will not feel a pang of excitement at the prospect of following the road through the canyon below. The views are particularly striking from the Grandview and White Rim Overlooks at the south end of the

see color photos, pages 137-139

Grandview Point, where the White Rim Road skirts around Monument Basin and Gooseberry Canyon above the western side of the Colorado River.

The White Rim Road and the White Rim Plateau were both named after a thin but very hard layer of White Rim Sandstone that was deposited some 225 million years ago at the top of a geologic layer called the Cutler Formation. Millions of years later new layers of shale, mudstone, and sandstone were deposited over the White Rim Sandstone; then, after the Green and Colorado Rivers were formed, these softer overlying layers began to erode away. This action re-

Shafer Trail

sulted in the formation of a wide, flat bench of desert, the White Rim Plateau, that now lies between the river gorges below and the mesa tops above.

In the early 1950s uranium was discovered in the shales overlying the White Rim Sandstone, and the flat bench became a natural access route for building roads to the mining claims. Thus the White Rim Road was born. The uranium boom lasted for only 3-4 years, however, and the primitive road was never improved. After the mid-1950s new discoveries in more accessible places caused the price of the yellow ore to plunge, and by the end of the decade the mines in Canyonlands were abandoned.

When Canyonlands National Park was formed in 1964 there was some talk of improving the White Rim Road into a scenic loop drive, but fortunately that never happened. Today, thanks to the short-lived uranium boom and the wise foresight of early park mangers, the White Rim Road has become one of the premier recreational jeep and mountain biking roads in the United States. The Park Service has built nineteen primitive campsites along its 70-mile length (for which reservations are required), but no further development is contemplated.

Airport Camp (17.3 miles)

From Highway 313 the road proceeds south for 0.8 mile to the edge of Shafer Canyon. It then turns west onto a narrow bench just below the Navajo Sandstone, which it follows for the next 1.9 miles before beginning a series of dramatic switchbacks that lead down into the bottom of the gorge. This section of road, known as the Shafer Trail, was first developed as a horse trail around 1917 by a cattle rancher named Sog Shafer. Then in 1952 a group of local miners and other businessmen improved the road so it could be used to haul uranium ore from mines near Potash and the Colorado River to the top of the mesa.

After five large switchbacks the Shafer Trail straightens out and continues its descent down through the bottom of Shafer Canyon, finally arriving at the junction with the Potash Road 5.2 miles from the Highway. This junction marks the beginning of the White Rim Road, and you should bear to the right here. Continue east towards the Colorado River for another 1.3 miles until you see a small sign on the left marking the Gooseneck Trailhead.

The Gooseneck Trail offers the first opportunity along this road to get a good look at the Colorado River. It also serves as an introduction to the White Rim Sandstone, which first becomes visible in this area. The panorama of the Colorado River below the trail is very picturesque, but if you want to take pictures you should have a wide-angle lens. (See page 89 for a complete description of this trail.)

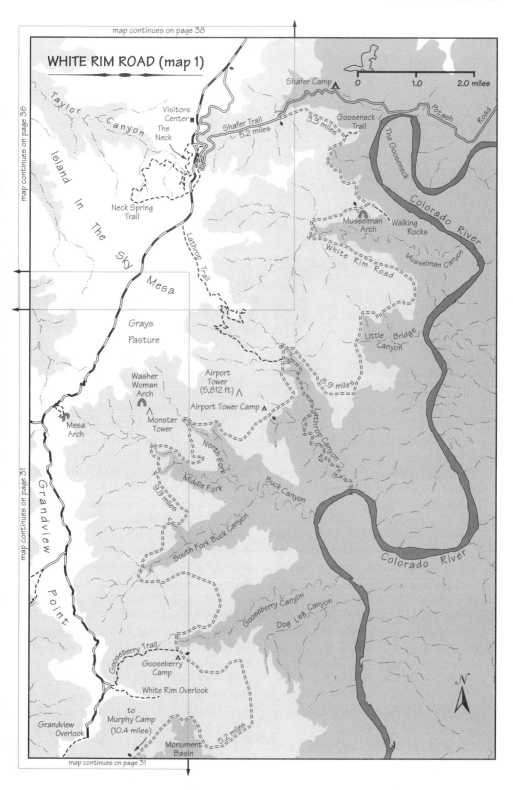

map continues on page 38

WHITE RIM ROAD (map 1)

map continues on page 38

Taylor Canyon

Shafer Camp

0   1.0   2.0 miles

Visitors Center
The Neck

Shafer Trail
~ 5.2 miles

3.3 miles

Gooseneck Trail

Potash Road

The Gooseneck

Colorado River

Island In The Sky Mesa

Neck Spring Trail

Lathrop Trail

Musselman Arch   Walking Rocks

White Rim Road

Musselman Canyon

Grays Pasture

Little Bridge Canyon

Washer Woman Arch

Airport Tower (5,812 ft)

Airport Tower Camp

2.9 mile

Mesa Arch

Monster Tower

North Fork

Lathrop Canyon

Middle Fork

Buck Canyon

9.9 miles

South Fork Buck Canyon

Colorado River

Gooseberry Canyon

Dog Leg Canyon

map continues on page 31

Grandview Point

Gooseberry Trail

Gooseberry Camp

White Rim Overlook

Grandview Overlook

to Murphy Camp (10.4 miles)

5.2 miles

Monument Basin

N

map continues on page 31

Walking Rocks

cracks occur where large blocks of the 20-foot-thick layer of sandstone have broken away from the main formation but are still supported by the underlying Organ Shale and have not yet fallen into the canyon below. Many of the cracks are only 6-18 inches wide; consequently it is possible to jump from one balanced rock to the next, like following a series of giant mushroom-shaped stepping stones that lead to nowhere. Crossing the narrow gaps between the blocks is not particularly dangerous, but gazing down at a hundred feet of empty space under your feet as you hop from rock to rock is very unnerving. It is not a good place for careless people, and I would definitely not recommend it for children. It is also not a place you would want to be during an earthquake. Indiana Jones would love the Walking Rocks

The next point of interest, the Musselman Arch, is only 0.2 mile beyond the Colorado River Overlook. The arch is located 150 yards from the main road at the end of another turnout on the left. Again, the arch was formed when a piece of the White Rim cracked away from the plateau, but this time the shale washed away from underneath its center forming a natural arch about 80 feet long. There is no easy way to get below the White Rim at Musselman Arch, but if you want to climb under the arch you can get there from the Walking Rocks. From there it is possible to climb to the bottom of the White Rim Formation and scramble back 0.5 mile to a point below Musselman Arch.

The road continues along the top of the White Rim Formation as it proceeds south from the Gooseneck Trailhead. Initially the sandstone layer is less than ten feet thick, but it gradually becomes much thicker. After another 1.8 miles you will come to another sign that says "Colorado River Overlook", and from there a short spur road leads to another overlook point just 300 yards from the main road. This view of the river is not as spectacular as the one from the end of the Gooseneck Trail, but no hiking is required to reach the Colorado River Overlook.

Although the Colorado River Overlook is not particularly impressive, there is an extremely interesting area a short distance east of the overlook point called the Walking Rocks. Walk along the rim from the car park for about 0.2 mile and you will begin to see a number of long narrow cracks near the edge of the White Rim Sandstone. These

The old timers in Moab tell an interesting story about how Musselman Arch got its name. Sometime in the early 1940s a man named Ross Musselman heard about the arch and persuaded a friend in Moab to show him where it was. He owned a dude ranch in the area and was looking for interesting places to take his guests. Word of the arch spread quickly after Musselman began showing it, and before long outsiders visiting the area started calling it the Musselman Arch. Needless to say this greatly irritated the local cowboys and ranchers who had known about the arch for decades before it was "discovered" by Ross Musselman. They grumbled for years about his ill-deserved fame. Now, as if to rub salt into the old timers' wounds, the USGS has also given Musselman's name to a nearby canyon and even to the 7.5 minute topographical map covering this section of Canyonlands.

For the next 7.5 miles after leaving Musselman Arch the White Rim Road continues southward over the flat sandy plateau, passing near the rim of Musselman Canyon, Little Bridge Canyon, and finally Lathrop Canyon. The Colorado River is no longer visible; nevertheless there are a number of impressive vistas along the way. On your right are the rouge-colored cliffs of the Wingate Formation plunging down from the top of the Island in the Sky, and on your left are the rugged canyons below the White Rim, deeply cut into the dark red shale of the Cutler Formation. The White Rim Road is usually good enough for almost any car to travel as far as Musselman Arch, but ordinary cars will run into trouble a few miles beyond the arch. Pickup trucks and other high-center vehicles can usually make it another 34 miles to the bottom of the Murphy Hogback.

Shortly after passing Lathrop Canyon you will come to a sign marking the Lathrop Trail, a 5-mile-long path leading from the White Rim Road to the top of the Island in the Sky. This trail was built sometime in the mid-1940s by a sheep rancher named Howard Lathrop who used the White Rim Plateau as a winter grazing range for his sheep. The trail was also used in the early 1950s by uranium miners who had claims

Lathrop Canyon Road and Airport Butte

just below the base of the Wingate cliffs. (See page 44 for a description of the Lathrop Trail.)

200 yards beyond the Lathrop Trail you will come to the Lathrop Canyon Road, a 3.7-mile side road that drops down from the top of the White Rim, through Lathrop Canyon, to the Colorado River. This road was built by the early uranium miners at about the same time the White Rim Road was built, but it is likely that Howard Lathrop also had a trail here ten years earlier for his sheep. Lathrop Canyon is the only place in Canyonlands National Park where the Colorado River can be accessed by car. The road is very rough and sandy, but it can be driven with a 4WD vehicle without too much difficulty. The Park Service has even established a picnic area at the bottom of the canyon and bulldozed a ramp to the river for pulling boats out of the water. This crude ramp represents the last chance for river

runners to get their boats out of the Colorado before reaching the notorious rapids of Cataract Canyon 27 miles further downriver (unless they choose to motor back up the Colorado or the Green River).

As you leave Lathrop Canyon on the White Rim Road you will see the Airport Tower Butte on the right side, and after 0.9 mile you will arrive at Airport Tower Campsites A and B, the first of the nineteen campsites along the White Rim Road. Sites C and D are 0.4 miles further.

Gooseberry Camp (10.6 miles)

Soon after leaving the Airport Tower Campsites C and D, another distinctive pinnacle of sandstone called the Monster Tower will come into view on the right side of the road. You can also see the Washerwoman Arch high on the sandstone cliffs of a smaller pinnacle on the north side of the Monster Tower. Look carefully at the smaller tower, and if you have a good imagination you should be able to identify the giant stone woman washing her clothes.

About a half-mile east of these landmarks the road crosses Buck Canyon, a heavily eroded canyon that was used by sheep rancher Howard Lathrop in the 1940s. Lathrop used the canyon to pen up his rams after the spring breeding season while the ewes were nursing their newborn lambs. Off-trail hikers might want to take note: It is a relatively easy walk of 5.2 miles from the road down Buck Canyon to the Colorado River. There are also several seasonal springs in the canyon.

From Buck Canyon the road continues to work its way southward along the base of Grandview Point, meandering around the heads of the Middle and South Forks of Buck Canyon, and then Gooseberry Canyon 8.5 miles later. The road passes very close to the rims of these canyons, but nowhere as close as at head of South Fork Buck

Monster Tower

Canyon. Be careful here, because at one point your left tires will be only three feet away from a 200-foot drop. Furthermore the White Rim is undercut by about 40 feet, leaving nothing but air under the road!

3.1 miles beyond South Fork Buck Canyon the road crosses the wash above Gooseberry Canyon, where you will see another sign marking the Gooseberry Trailhead. The Gooseberry Trail was built in the late 1930s by WPA workers, and many old timers in the area still call it the Government Trail. Like several other trails in the area, it was built to enable local sheep and cattle ranchers to take their livestock from the Island in the Sky Mesa to the White Rim Plateau for winter grazing. (See page 56 for a description of this trail.) Gooseberry Campsites A and B are located 0.3 and 0.4 miles past the trailhead.

White Crack Camp (9.5 miles)

4.1 miles after leaving Gooseberry Campsite B you will come to one of the most impressive sights on the White Rim Road: Monument Basin. This area is well known because so many people have seen it from above. It lies just below the heavily visited Grandview Overlook on the southern end of the Island in the Sky, and every day hundreds of tourists peer down at Monument Basin's fascinating collection of geologic sculpture 1,900 feet below the mesa top. The basin consists of a large rocky desert valley about a mile across and 500 feet below the White Rim Plateau that is filled with dozens of pillars of Organ Shale capped with blocks of White Rim Sandstone. The road first approaches the basin on its northeast

Monument Basin

side and then follows its perimeter for the next three miles, giving onlookers the opportunity to view the spectacle from many different angles. The vista is particularly impressive in the late afternoon when the shale turns a deep red color and the pinnacles cast long shadows across the canyon floor.

As you leave the last viewpoint on the west side of Monument Basin the road swings to the west and arrives shortly at a sign marking the spur to White Crack Camp. This campsite is located 1.3 miles from the main road at the extreme southern end of the White Rim Plateau. White Crack Camp, with its great views from the edge of the White Rim, is one of my favorites. Since it is located some distance from the main road it is quieter and more private, and there is room for only one group of campers.

The White Crack Camp was named after a crack in the White Rim Sandstone just south of the car parking area. This break in the White Rim was developed into a trail around 1918 so ranchers could get their animals to water in the lower canyons. Then in the early 1950s the trail was widened into a jeep road and extended to a mining camp above the Green River. Today the jeep road is no longer suitable for wheeled vehicles, but it is possible to hike along it to the old mining camp. The distance is 6.2 miles each way. There are no longer any standing buildings at the mining camp, but there are a few artifacts lying about and the trail also offers some great views of the Green River. The White Crack Trail is discussed in greater detail on page 92.

Murphy Camp (8.8 miles)

White Crack Camp lies at the extreme southern end of the Island in the Sky district. Upon leaving this area the road first goes west for about two miles in order to get around Junction Butte, and then makes a sharp right turn as it begins the long journey up the west side of Grandview Point. Soon it enters a region known as Murphy Basin, named after a family that ran cattle here just after World War One. There are several nice views along this section of road. If you look west across the Green River Gorge you can see many famous landmarks in the Maze District of Canyonlands off in the distance. The high needle-like formation seven miles to the southwest is Chimney Rock, and the flat-top mesa four miles west on the other side of the river is Ekker Butte.

Finally, 6.3 miles from White Crack Road, the White Rim Road crosses Murphy Wash, where a small sign marks the beginning of the Murphy Wash Trail. This is another livestock trail built by the Murphy brothers around 1917. The 3.7-mile-long trail ends near Murphy Point at the top of the Island in the Sky. (See page 52 for more

South side of Murphy Hogback

details about this hike.)

Shortly after leaving Murphy Wash, the road gets much steeper as it claws its way out of Murphy Basin up the southern side of the Murphy Hogback. You better shift into low gear before beginning this climb, and you had better have a 4WD vehicle. The elevation gain of the brief climb is only 250 feet, but it is very steep near the top.

The view from the top of the Hogback is a memorable panorama of the vast, heavily eroded canyons below. The scenery is especially interesting north of the narrow ridge where one can look down over the picturesque Soda Springs Basin. Murphy Campsite C is located just a few feet from the northern side of the Hogback, and the views into the basin below make it one of the most popular camps on the White Rim Road. Sites A and B are situated nearby, but closer to the middle of the crest.

There is also another trailhead at the top of the ridge near campsite C. A small sign marks the point where the Murphy Hogback Trail leaves the road for the top of the Island in the Sky. This trail joins the Murphy Wash Trail 2.8 miles from the White Rim Road, and an interesting loop hike is to walk as far as the junction and return to the road on the Murphy Wash Trail. The total distance of this loop, including the section of road between the two trailheads is 6.8 miles. (See page 52 for more details.)

Candlestick Camp (10.4 miles)

From Murphy Hogback the White Rim Road drops back down 600 feet to the White Rim Plateau and begins skirting around the northeastern side of Soda Springs Basin. After approaching the rim of the basin at several points the road departs from the west side of Soda Springs and heads across the desert just north of a big 180-degree loop in the Green River. You should stop the car at this point and walk to the edge of the rim

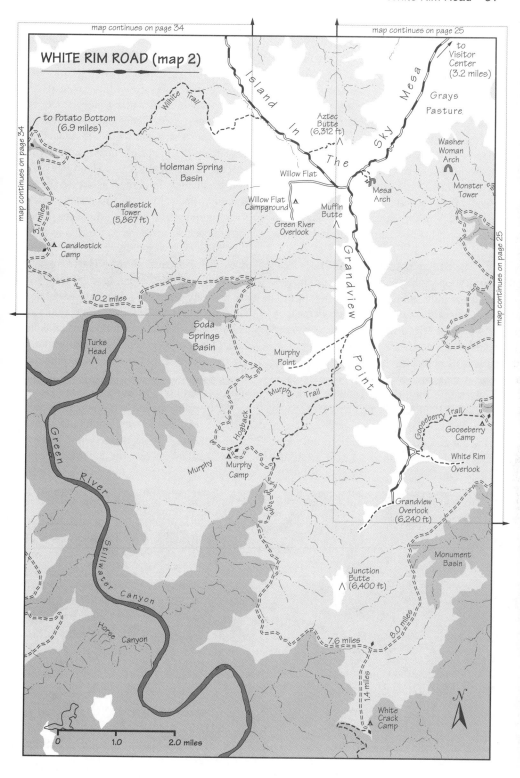

map continues on page 34
map continues on page 25

WHITE RIM ROAD (map 2)

map continues on page 34
map continues on page 25

Island In The Sky Mesa

Grays Pasture

to Visitor Center
(3.2 miles)

White Trail

to Potato Bottom
(6.9 miles)

3.1 miles

Holeman Spring Basin

Aztec Butte
(6,312 ft)

Washer Woman Arch

Monster Tower

Willow Flat

Mesa Arch

Candlestick Tower
(5,867 ft)

Willow Flat Campground

Muffin Butte

Candlestick Camp

Green River Overlook

Grandview Point

10.2 miles

Soda Springs Basin

Turks Head

Murphy Point

Murphy Trail

Hogback

Gooseberry Trail

Gooseberry Camp

Green River

Murphy

Murphy Camp

White Rim Overlook

Stillwater Canyon

Grandview Overlook
(6,240 ft)

Monument Basin

Junction Butte
(6,400 ft)

8.0 miles

Horse Canyon

7.6 miles

1.4 miles

White Crack Camp

N

0   1.0   2.0 miles

150 yards from the road for a terrific view of the water below. The river's gooseneck spreads across your field of view like the screen in an I-Max movie theater—even with a 24-mm lens I wasn't able to frame the entire loop in my camera. Below your vantage point the channel bends around an arc nearly a mile wide, and at the center of the half-circle lies a picturesque butte called the Turks Head. Although you can't see the river unless you get out of your car and walk to the edge of the rim, the huge flat top of the Turks Head is clearly visible from the road, so when you see it be sure to stop.

The bottom land below the Turks Head once supported a thriving community of Anasazi Indians, and the remnants of their occupancy are scattered throughout the area. If you study the cliffs above the lower terrace on the northeast side of the butte with a pair of binoculars you should be able to see at least three well preserved cliff dwellings where the ancient Indians lived and stored their corn. The area was extensively cultivated, and the presence of thousands of flint chips scattered about the ground shows that the Indians who lived here were also actively engaged in the production of spearheads or other stone tools.

From its confluence with the Colorado River to the Turks Head the Green River flows through Stillwater Canyon, a deep gorge in the Lower Cutler and Honaker Trail Formations that makes in almost inaccessible from the upper plateaus. But as you proceed north of the Turks Head you will notice a distinct difference in the river's personality. The canyon widens considerably, forming many flat areas, or bottoms along the water's edge, and the White Rim Formation dips down very close to the river, making it more accessible from above. Many of the river bottoms are very fertile areas for growing crops, and they have long been sites for human habitation. The Fremont and Anasazi Indians occupied this area for hundreds of years before their disappearance around 1300 A.D., and today many remnants of their presence can still be seen along the Green River north of Stillwater Canyon.

White men arrived in this area in the late 1800s, and they too were attracted to these river bottoms. Most of the white settlers raised cattle or sheep for a living or sup-

South of Soda Spring Basin

ported themselves by hauling supplies to the other settlers along the river. Some stayed on the bottomlands for only part of the year, and others brought their families with them and attempted to establish permanent homesteads. It has been about fifty years since anyone lived along the river, but the ruins of several of the old settlers' cabins are still visible.

From the Turks Head the road continues northwest, climbing over a low hill of shale, before arriving at Candlestick Camp 2.6 miles later. Note the pinnacle of Wingate Sandstone that rises abruptly from the desert floor two miles east of the camp; this is Candlestick Tower, the formation for which Candlestick Camp was named. Although you can't see the river from the campsite, Candlestick Camp is quite close to the edge of the White Rim. If you will drive 0.2 mile north of the camp, park your car, and walk to the rim you can see Valentine Bottom, a flat, green fertile piece of land on the south side of the channel. This was one of the first places in Canyonlands to be inhabited by white people. In 1892 the Valentines, a family of five adults and two children, attempted to settle the bottom, but they stayed for only one year. In 1893 they abandoned their homestead and moved upstream to the town of Green River.

Candlestick Tower

Potato Bottom Camp (10.2 miles)

Beyond Candlestick Camp the road veers north of the river in order to get around a small side canyon. At the head of the canyon, 2.2 miles from Candlestick Camp you will see a sign marking the Wilhite Trail, a five-mile-long trail leading to the top of the Island in the Sky. (See page 64.) The Wilhite Trail was built by local sheep ranchers in the late 1930s to facilitate moving sheep and supplies to their winter pasture below the top of the mesa.

As you cross the sandy wash below the

Wilhite Trailhead you will notice the slender opening of a gracefully sculpted sandstone narrows on the left side of the road where water occasionally rushes down a small side canyon on its way to the Green River. Numerous footprints in the bottom of the wash attest to the fact that many passers-by have yielded to an urge to stop and see what unexpected surprises might lie beyond the smooth, sensuous portal. Perhaps it is the curving femininity of the shape that draws them—the smooth, suggestive flow of the creamy white stone. The narrow channel continues deeper and deeper down into the White Rim Sandstone for a distance of about 300 yards before finally ending at a pouroff 50 feet above the canyon floor.

After the Wilhite Trailhead the road heads southwest towards the Bonita Bend, a sharp bend in the river named by John

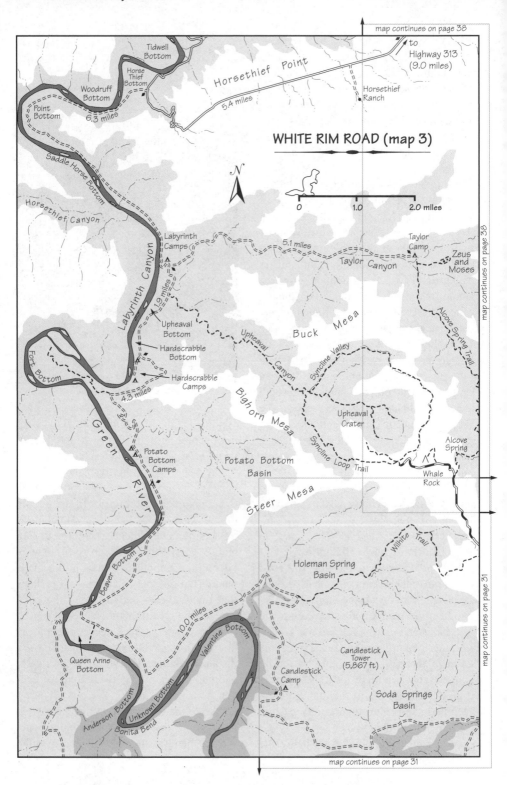

map continues on page 38

WHITE RIM ROAD (map 3)

to Highway 313 (9.0 miles)

Tidwell Bottom

Horsethief Point

Horse Thief Bottom

Horsethief Ranch

Woodruff Bottom

5.4 miles

Point Bottom

6.3 miles

Saddle Horse Bottom

Horsethief Canyon

N

0   1.0   2.0 miles

Labyrinth Camps

5.1 miles

Taylor Camp

Taylor Canyon

Zeus and Moses

Labyrinth Canyon

1.9 miles

Upheaval Bottom

Buck Mesa

map continues on page 38

Alcove Spring Trail

Hardscrabble Bottom

Upheaval Canyon

Fort Bottom

Hardscrabble Camps

4.3 miles

Syncline Valley

Bighorn Mesa

Green River

Upheaval Crater

Alcove Spring

Potato Bottom Camps

Potato Bottom Basin

Syncline Loop Trail

Whale Rock

Steer Mesa

Beaver Bottom

Holeman Spring Basin

Wilhite Trail

map continues on page 31

10.0 miles

Valentine Bottom

Queen Anne Bottom

Candlestick Tower (5,867 ft)

Candlestick Camp

Soda Springs Basin

Anderson Bottom

Unknown Bottom

Bonita Bend

map continues on page 31

White Rim Road, west of Wilhite Trail (Buttes of the Cross in the background)

Wesley Powell during his famous exploration of the Green River in 1869. If you stop your car at the point where the river first comes into view and the road makes a sharp turn to the north, 3.5 miles beyond the Wilhite Trailhead, and walk 200 yards to the edge of the rim you can look down river at the Bonita Bend with Anderson Bottom on its western shore.

Anderson Bottom figures prominently in the history of the Green River. It was named after Albert Isaac Anderson who attempted to establish a homestead there in 1909 but stayed for only three years. Anderson was followed by a succession of at least five more families who inhabited the bottom for varying lengths of time from 1912 until it became part of the national park in 1964.

see color photo, page 156

The first place where the Green River is easily accessible is Queen Anne Bottom, 1.5 miles upstream from Anderson Bottom. During the uranium boom in the 1950s a tram was built across the river on the northern end of the bottom. The tram is gone now, but some evidence of it can still be seen on the west side of the river. The bottom was named after a colorful lady named Anne who lived there alone for a few years around 1918. At one point she acquired a large flat-bottom boat and tried to start a business ferrying supplies to other settlers along the river. The business didn't do well, however, and before 1920 Anne had vacated her home and moved elsewhere. Watch for an old jeep road that leads from the White Rim Road to the river at Queen Anne Bottom. The Park Service has blocked the road off and it is now illegal to drive on it, but it is only a ten-minute walk down this road to the river. Unfortunately there isn't much to see at Queen Anne Bottom now except a jungle of tamarisk trees.

3.3 miles north of Queen Anne Bottom you will arrive at Potato Bottom Campsite A and, after another 0.7 mile, campsites B and C. All three sites are pleasantly located in the cottonwood trees on a bench just above the river. Notice that the White Rim Sandstone disappears beneath the surface at this point. The remainder of the White Rim

Road will be over the shale of the Moenkopi and Chinle Formations.

There is no evidence that Potato Bottom was ever homesteaded, but it was often used during the first half of the last century as a cowboy camp. One of the camps is located 0.3 miles south of Potato Bottom Campsite A, near where the White Rim Sandstone disappears underground. Drive back from the campsite to the last place where you can easily park off the road, then walk south along the bottom of the White Rim for another hundred yards to a small alcove behind the tamarisk. The small, nondescript alcove isn't much to look at now, but it was used for many decades by cowboys as a place to get out of the wind and rain. Sometime around 1930 a cowpoke named Art Murry placed a trunk in the alcove to store his groceries and belongings and, interestingly, the remains of the trunk are still there today.

Hardscrabble Camp (lower right)

Hardscrabble Camp B (4.3 miles)

Just beyond the last campsite in Potato Bottom the road encounters an obstacle that it must get around. This is where Bighorn Mesa, a long point of land on the west side of the Island in the Sky, ends, and the steep sloping sides of the mesa make it impossible for the White Rim Road to stay at the same elevation as the river. The road climbs 400 feet to get to the top of the ridge and then drops back down to the river on the other side. The section of road on the south side of the crest, known as the Walker Cut, is very steep and rocky, and as you start up you will be thankful you have a 4WD vehicle. The route follows an old cow trail that was built by a rancher named Mark Walker around 1890 and later widened to a jeep trail.

When you reach the top of the Walker Cut you will come to sign marking the Fort Bottom Trailhead. This 6.0-mile (round trip) trail is one of the more interesting trails in Canyonlands, and if you have the time you should definitely check it out. Looking west from the trailhead you will see a large bend in the river where the waterway turns almost full circle to get around the end of Bighorn Mesa. The ridge from the mesa ultimately ends at a small butte in the center of the gooseneck, and if you look carefully at the top of this butte you will soon see how Fort Bottom got its name. At the top of the butte there is a cylindrical stone tower that was built long ago by the Anasazi Indians. Its function is not known today, but it is easy to imagine the butte as a fort, with the stone tower serving as a lookout post over the houses and fields below. Turn to page 86 for more information on the trail to Fort Bottom and the Anasazi ruin.

As you start down the north side of the ridge you will see Hardscrabble Campsite B near the river directly below the road. Hardscrabble is, in my opinion, the most scenic and pleasant camp along the entire White Rim Road. It is well sheltered, not sandy, and has good river access. The short spur road to Hardscrabble Campsites A and B is at the bottom of the hill, 1.6 miles from the Fort Bottom Trailhead.

Labyrinth and Taylor Camps (7.1 miles)

From the spur to Hardscrabble Camp the road continues north at almost the same level as the river. After 1.4 miles you will come to an area where Taylor Canyon and Upheaval Canyon converge to form a large flat area on the east side of the river called Upheaval Bottom. As you cross the sandy wash in the center of the bottom you will see a small parking area next to a sign on the right marking the Upheaval Canyon Trail. This trail follows Upheaval Canyon to the bottom of Upheaval Crater. You can also get to the top of Island in the Sky on this trail by taking the Syncline Loop Trail from Upheaval Crater to the top of the mesa. (For more details on these trails turn to pages 72 and 82.)

There is also an old settler's cabin near the river on Upheaval Bottom that is worth seeing; it is located about 350 yards from the Upheaval Canyon Trailhead. To get there follow the wash towards the river for about 200 feet until you see a hiker-made

Art Murray's cabin, Upheaval Bottom

trail that climbs up the left side of the wash. Climb out of the wash at this point and continue following the trail west for another 250 yards. First you will see the remains of an old corral under a small grove of cottonwood trees. Then, after another 150 feet you should see the cabin hidden in the tamarisk trees. This cabin was built by a Art Murry in the early 1930s as a line cabin for cowboys working in the area. Though filled with a deep layer of sand now, the cabin is still in fair shape. It even has the remains of an old stove inside that, according to one old timer, the cowboys used to cook sourdough bread.

The Park Service used to maintain a campsite in Upheaval Bottom, but the site was closed in the early 1990s and a new one, the Labyrinth Camp, was established further upstream. Drive north along the river for another 0.7 mile to reach the Labyrinth Camp.

Just before arriving at Labyrinth Camp the road comes to a junction where the Taylor Canyon road departs on the right. This road winds through the flat, sandy bottom of Taylor Canyon for 5.1 miles, finally ending at the Taylor Camp. Although Taylor Camp is far from the river it does have a nice view of several interesting rock formations. Near the camp is a trail leading to the Moses and Zeus formations 0.6 mile further east in the canyon. This interesting trail climbs up to the vertical base of the formations and then circles around them in a loop (see page 79). The Alcove Spring Trail also begins at Taylor Camp. This 6.4-mile-long trail follows Trail Canyon for 4.4 miles, then climbs up to the Alcove Spring and ends shortly afterward at the Upheaval Dome Road. (See page 76 for more information on the Alcove Spring Trail.)

Highway 313 (27.8 miles)

From Labyrinth Camp the road follows

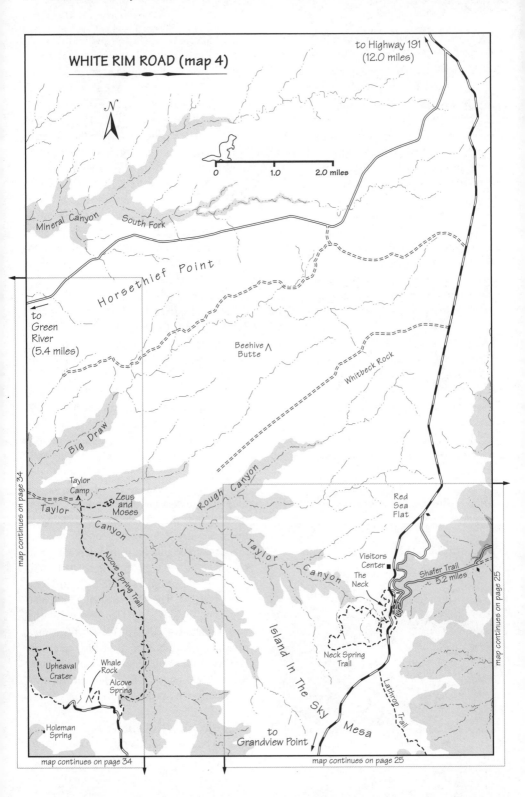

WHITE RIM ROAD (map 4)

N

0   1.0   2.0 miles

to Highway 191
(12.0 miles)

Mineral Canyon   South Fork

Horsethief Point

to
Green
River
(5.4 miles)

Beehive Λ
Butte

Whitbeck Rock

Big Draw

map continues on page 34

Taylor
Camp

Zeus
and
Moses

Taylor

Canyon

Rough Canyon

Taylor   Canyon

Red
Sea
Flat

Visitors
Center

The
Neck

Shafer Trail
5.2 miles

Alcove Spring Trail

map continues on page 25

Upheaval
Crater

Whale
Rock

Alcove
Spring

N

Neck Spring
Trail

Island In The Sky   Mesa

Lathrop Trail

Holeman
Spring

to
Grandview Point

map continues on page 34

map continues on page 25

closely along the river for the next 2.4 miles to the park boundary, then continues for another 3.9 miles to Horsethief Bottom and the junction with Horsethief Road. Here you must turn right for the climb up the switchbacks to the top of Horsethief Point and on to Highway 313.

Horsethief Road was so named because it follows a portion of the same route used by a group of horse rustlers who were operating in eastern Utah around 1890. After stealing horses from farmers and ranchers in the La Sal Mountains near the Colorado border the outlaws would drive them west across the Colorado River. They would then go up one of the canyons west of Moab and out onto Horsethief Point. At the end of the point they herded the animals down the talus slopes to the Green River, across the river, and up an old trail through Horsethief Canyon. Eventually the trail led them to a hideout about 20 miles east of Hanksville in an area now known as the Robbers Roost. The total distance of the journey, from the La Sals to the Robbers Roost would have

been about 100 miles, depending on exactly where the horses were stolen and what route they took to Horsethief Point. Much of this land was unexplored at that time, and a great deal of reconnoitering would have been necessary to determine a feasible route through the canyons and across the rivers. Some trail building was also necessary, particularly where the horses made the descent off Horsethief Point. Needless to say, the raids must have been carefully planned.

Later, in the early 1900s, the Horsethief Trail was improved by local ranchers running cattle in the area, particularly the Tidwells, who lived occasionally at Tidwell Bottom and ran cattle there until 1945. The present road was built in 1943 by the BLM for the purpose of servicing mining claims in Labyrinth Canyon. In the first 1.5 miles after leaving the river the road climbs 850 feet to the top of Horsethief Point, and then continues east over relatively flat terrain for the next 13.0 miles until it reaches Highway 131. The drive ends 8.5 miles north of the entrance gate to Canyonlands National Park.

Green River, south of Fort Bottom

Neck Spring Trail

☆ ☆ ☆   **day hike**

Distance:	6.1 miles (loop)
Walking time:	3¼ hours
Elevations:	260 ft. loss/gain Neck Spring Trailhead (start): 5,800 ft. lowest point: 5,580 ft.
Trail:	Well marked, easy to follow
Vicinity:	Near visitor center
USGS Maps:	Musselman Arch

The trailhead and parking area are located on the left side of the road 0.5 miles south of the Island in the Sky Visitor Center.

The most important natural resource in any desert environment is water, and this is certainly true in Canyonlands National Park. Canyonlands receives only about nine inches of rain annually, and without springs and seeps the park's mule deer, coyotes, bobcats, and other large animals could not survive. The water sources are well known to the animals, and most of them frequent the springs on a daily basis. They come not only for the water itself but also because of the greater abundance of food nearby.

Indians who inhabited Canyonlands as long ago as 8,000 years also depended on springs for their survival. Most of their permanent settlements were near the Green and Colorado Rivers or in canyons such as Lavender, Horse, or Salt, where there are many

reliable springs. But they also spent considerable time in places like the Island in the Sky, where game is plentiful but water is much harder to find.

This hike passes two important springs at the base of the Navajo Sandstone below the rim of the Island in the Sky Mesa. Don't expect to find large amounts of water, though. Cabin Spring, the second one you will see, usually has more water than Neck Spring, but neither of them normally produces more than a slow trickle of water. The two springs are particularly interesting because they were used extensively by ranchers who worked the area from about 1880 until 1964, and there are still many artifacts in the area that were left behind by the cowboys. The trail also passes through a small

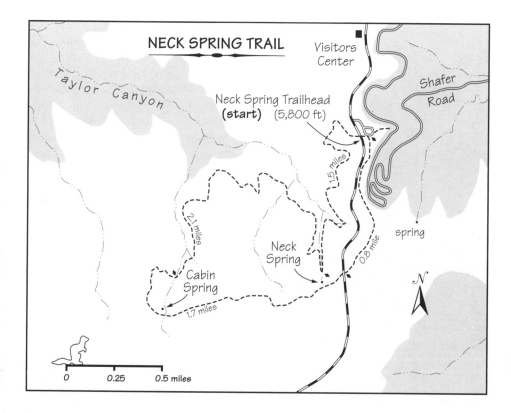

NECK SPRING TRAIL

Visitors Center

Taylor Canyon

Neck Spring Trailhead (start) (5,800 ft)

Shafer Road

1.5 miles

2.1 miles

Neck Spring

spring

0.8 mile

Cabin Spring

1.7 miles

N

0   0.25   0.5 miles

field of flint chips near Neck Spring—evidence that the area was occupied by prehistoric Indians long before the arrival of the cowboys.

From the parking area the trail turns west across the road and proceeds for a short distance along the upper rim of Taylor Canyon. Then, 0.1 mile from the trailhead, the path bends south and drops 120 feet below the upper rim of the canyon. After its descent into Taylor Canyon it meanders along the base of the Navajo Sandstone in a southerly direction for the next 1.2 miles.

Notice the many water stains along the bottom of the sandstone cliffs as you walk. Depending on how wet the year has been, there are many intermittent seeps at the bottom of this geologic layer. The Navajo Sandstone is not as dense as the of Kayenta

Sandstone directly below it; hence water tends to percolate straight down through the upper layer and reemerge only when it reaches the Kayenta Formation. Many of the springs in Canyonlands, including both Neck and Cabin Springs, are located at the boundary between the Navajo and Kayenta Formations.

About 40 minutes after leaving the trailhead you will pass a large alcove in the cliff that contains an unnamed spring. This spring is one of many that were developed by local ranchers, and near the trail you can see a long wooden fence-like structure that once held a watering trough for livestock. This is the first of at least four watering troughs that were built at the springs along the Neck Spring Trail. The mesa above the trail was once a coveted grazing area called Grays Pasture, and these springs were de-

Old watering trough near Neck Spring

desert of blackbrush and yucca. As you walk you may see occasional flakes of shiny white or reddish-brown flint lying in the sand. The flakes do not occur naturally; they were left behind by ancient craftsmen who struck the chips from larger pieces of chert to form knives, spear points, and other stone tools. The ancient peoples occupied Canyonlands for at least 8,000 years, and many of their chipping sites have been identified throughout the park.

Over the next 2.1 miles the trail makes a wide, irregular turn from north to south, finally reaching the Cabin Spring drainage about an hour after leaving Neck Spring. As you approach Cabin Spring you will begin to see many signs of early ranching activity; however much of the evidence is faint and easily missed. A broken fence across the trail, a pile of evenly cut logs that may have belonged to a cabin, a small iron tank 100 feet below the point where the trail

veloped so that cattle grazing there could have access to water.

After another 0.5 mile the trail passes below a much larger alcove that contains Neck Spring. This alcove is 200 feet wide, and the lush green vegetation at the base of the opening attests to the amount of water that is seeping out of it. Again, look for an old watering trough nearby. About 30 feet beyond the point where the trail crosses the bottom of the Neck Spring drainage you will see a faint hiker-made trail departing on the left. Turn here and within 10 feet you should see the old structure. There are probably other remnants of ranching activity in the area as well, but the thick undergrowth would make them difficult to find.

After leaving Neck Spring the trail turns north and begins veering away from the drainage, leaving behind the cool thickets of Gambel oak and entering into a sandy

Neck Spring Trail

crosses the Cabin Spring drainage, another dilapidated watering trough 250 feet upstream from the iron tank. The remnants are still there to see, but the hard work of the early cowboys is slowly succumbing to the forces of nature.

After crossing the Cabin Spring drainage the trail makes an abrupt right turn and begins climbing up the Navajo Sandstone slickrock to the top of the Island in the Sky. Then, after 250 feet of lung-busting elevation gain, the trail levels out again and turns south across the flat terrain of Grays Pasture. As you work your way around the head of Cabin Spring Canyon you will be treated to a series of spectacular views back into the canyons. Most of the first half of this hike is visible from the rim. The trail also passes by another watering trough near the edge of the rim. This one is in excellent shape—it was probably built less than 50 years ago. My guess is that the ranchers intended to pump water up from Cabin Spring to fill the trough, although there is now no sign of a pipeline.

From the head of Cabin Spring Canyon the trail proceeds in an easterly direction, across the sand and slickrock for 1.2 miles to the paved road. It crosses the road near the head of Neck Spring Canyon, and then turns north for another 0.5 mile to the Shafer Trail Viewpoint. From there it parallels the east side of the road for the last 0.3 mile to the trailhead.

Looking into Taylor Canyon from Neck Spring Trail

Lathrop Trail

☆ ☆ ☆   **day hike**

Distance: 11.0 miles (round trip), or
                     5.5 miles (one way to White Rim Road)

Walking time: 7 hours (round trip)
                     3 hours (one way)

Elevations: 1,600 ft. loss (one way)
                     Lathrop Trailhead (start): 6,000 ft.
                     White Rim Road: 4,400 ft.

Trail: Well marked and easy to follow, but very steep and rocky in one
                     area. There is no water so carry plenty.

Vicinity: Starts near the Island in the Sky Visitor Center

USGS Maps: Musselman Arch

The starting trailhead is located 2.0 miles south of the visitor center along the road to Grandview Point. The trail ends at the White Rim Road, 16.2 miles from the beginning of the Shafer Road or 1.1 miles north of the Airport Camp. (See page 23 for more information on the White Rim Road)

Most of the trails from the Island in the Sky Mesa to the White Rim Plateau were built during the first part of the last century by ranchers who used the White Rim Plateau as a winter pasture for their livestock. In the case of the Lathrop Trail the rancher's name was Howard Lathrop, a sheep man who moved from Colorado to Utah sometime in the early 1940s. Lathrop's trail was used by him and other sheep ranchers until the 1960s when Canyonlands became a national park. It was also used by uranium prospectors in the 1950s, and several of their mines can still be

see color photo, page 140

seen along the trail in upper Lathrop Canyon.

Originally the trail extended all the way down Lathrop Canyon to the Colorado River, but the lower part was made into a jeep road around 1953, shortly after the construction of the White Rim Road. The uranium prospectors used the road to obtain water from the Colorado for their mining operations.

For the first 1.6 miles the Lathrop Trail passes over a wide, flat prairie of lush grassland. This area must have been coveted as prime grazing land in the days before it became a national park; it is much more fertile

44

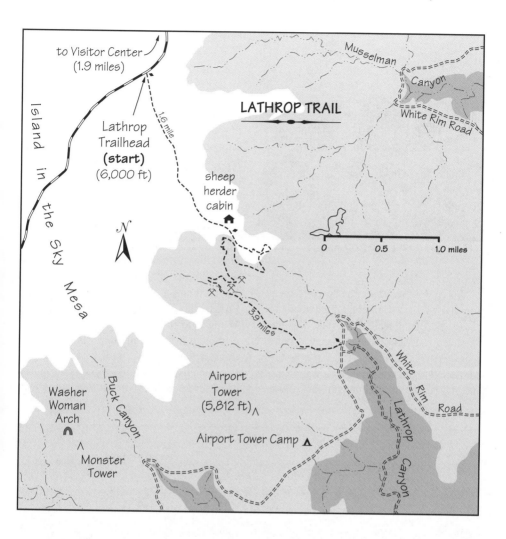

than the land below the rim where Mr. Lathrop grazed his sheep. But most of the grass that grows on the mesa now is cheat grass, a course, dry species that most grazing animals will eat only as a last resort. Cheat grass was brought to America from Europe around 1900, and it has now spread throughout the west.

The mesa top is still heavily grazed, although not by domestic animals. Today there is a large population of mule deer living on the mesa. Look carefully at the lush growth and you will see that in between the tall tufts of cheat grass there are smaller clumps of a much greener grass that have generally been chewed down almost to the roots. Where are the deer? Unlike mad dogs and humans, deer are generally smart enough to postpone their activity in this hot desert environment until the evening and early morning hours. During the heat of the day they are asleep under juniper trees and other hiding places. If you really want to see how many deer there are in the area try driving south of the visitor center just after sundown. It is not unusual to see 15-20 deer grazing along the side of

Sheepherders' cabin on Lathrop Trail

the road.

Just before reaching the rim of the canyon you will see a small tin shed about 150 yards east of the trail. This shed was used by sheep ranchers to store supplies before packing them down the trail. It was once connected to the main road by a wagon trail, and if you are observant you can still see

parts of the old track near the footpath.

Soon after leaving the sheepherders' cabin the trail crosses from the grassland into a slickrock environment and then begins meandering towards the canyon rim. Part of what makes this hike an interesting one is the variety of terrain you will encounter, and hiking over the slickrock is indeed very different from walking across the grassland. A series of cairns leads past several sandstone domes and potholes (which often contain rainwater), and then down a shallow, sandy arroyo filled with pinion and juniper trees.

Finally, 0.6 mile after leaving the grassland, the trail drops below the canyon rim where a fine view of the heavily eroded inner canyons awaits you. Lower Lathrop Canyon lies far below, with the thread of the White Rim Road snaking past its head. A portion of the Colorado River is also visible three miles further south where Lathrop Canyon ends. The trail descends through a small break in the Navajo Sandstone to a

Lathrop Canyon, viewed from the Island in the Sky Mesa

narrow bench above the Wingate Formation and then turns south and west to follow the bench along the top of the sheer cliffs.

The Wingate Sandstone is the most distinctive geologic formation in Canyonlands. Wherever it is exposed it tends to fracture into high vertical cliffs that form the greatest single obstacle to people trying to get in or out of the canyons below. Feasible routes through the Wingate are rare, and this trail must wind westward along the top of the 600-foot cliffs for a distance of 0.8 mile in order to reach an ancient landslide that offers a feasible descent route. In my opinion the walk along the narrow bench with Lathrop Canyon and the Colorado River far below is one of the most enjoyable parts of the hike.

Upon reaching the slide area the trail turns to the left and enters a long series of short switchbacks as it makes its way down. This portion of the trail is very steep and rocky; it must have been a challenge for the sheepherders' packhorses fifty years ago. But it doesn't last long. After an elevation loss of 900 feet the path begins to level out near the bottom of upper Lathrop Canyon. Also about this time the route begins to follow an old mining road, and walking becomes much easier. The road is heavily eroded, but it still makes a good foot trail. It has been closed to vehicles for many years.

The old jeep trail offers an interesting window onto the uranium boom that took place in Canyonlands during the 1950s. Look around as you walk and you will see several old mine shafts on both sides of the canyon. The road passes within a few hundred feet of at least six of them. The deserted mines in Lathrop Canyon are an in-triguing aspect of this hike, but they are also very dangerous places. The Park Service has gated the entrances to all of the mines and posted bright yellow signs warning people of the presence of radioactive material in the mines and their tailings. The springs in the area should also be avoided, since some of them have been contaminated by runoff from the mines.

After following the jeep road for 1.1 miles the trail branches off to the left and follows a shale ridge down to the sandy bottom of Lathrop Canyon. After following the wash for 15 minutes you will emerge at the White Rim Road near the head of lower Lathrop Canyon.

Upper Lathrop Canyon, Airport Tower

Mesa Arch

☆

Distance:	0.5 miles (loop)
Walking time:	20 minutes
Elevations:	60 ft. loss/gain Mesa Arch Trailhead (start): 6,120 ft.
Trail:	Well marked, easy to follow
Vicinity:	Near visitor center
USGS Maps:	Musselman Arch

The trailhead and parking area is located on the left side of the road 6.3 miles south of the Island in the Sky Visitor Center.

Mesa Arch (note Washerwomen Arch on left)

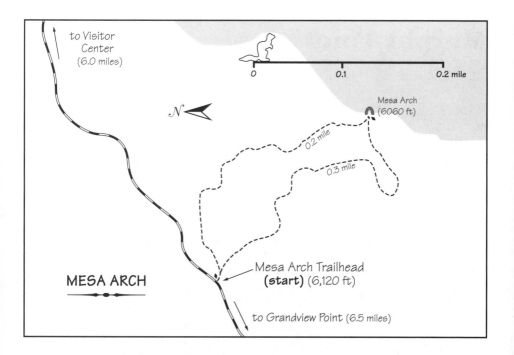

to Visitor Center (6.0 miles)

Mesa Arch (6060 ft)

0.2 mile

0.3 mile

MESA ARCH

Mesa Arch Trailhead
(start) (6,120 ft)

to Grandview Point (6.5 miles)

Mesa Arch lies right on the edge of the Island in the Sky Mesa, at the top of a 600-foot drop-off into Buck Canyon. The arch is small by Utah standards—roughly 50 feet long and 15 feet high. Nevertheless it presents some nice views of the canyons below. The La Sal Mountains are nicely framed by the opening, with the Monster Tower and Airport Tower rising from the White Rim Plateau in the foreground. If you look carefully you can also see the Washerwoman Arch through the opening of Mesa Arch. The Washerwoman is situated near the top of another sandstone pinnacle that stands just north of the Monster Tower, 1.4 miles from the rim.

The trail from the road to Mesa Arch is only 0.3 mile long over fairly level ground, so you can easily cover the distance in ten minutes. However part of the fun of this hike is learning something about the desert plants in the area, so don't be in a rush. A Park Service brochure that describes the flora is available at the trailhead, and there are several signs along the way pointing out various species.

The Navajo Sandstone, from which Mesa Arch was carved, was once a vast bed of sand dunes that eventually became covered by another layer of debris and hardened into stone. Mesa Arch was formed because the thin layer of stone at the surface is harder than the underlying rock in this area, and consequently the underlying layer eroded away first.

The arch receives many visitors early in the morning when the rising sun sometimes shines directly through the opening, but it is difficult to photograph without a flash at that time. The easiest time to get good photos of Mesa Arch is in the late afternoon when the sun is low in the west.

Murphy Point

☆   **short day hike**

Distance: 2.6 miles (round trip)

Walking time: 1¼ hours

Elevations: 90 ft. loss/gain
                     Murphy Trailhead (start):   6,190 ft.
                     Murphy Point: 6,100 ft.

Trail: Well marked and easy to follow

Vicinity: On the southern end of the Island in the Sky Mesa

USGS Maps: Monument Basin, Turks Head

Drive south from the visitor center following the signs to Grandview Point. 8.9 miles from the visitor center, or 3.6 miles before you reach Grandview Point you will see a well marked dirt road on the right leading to the Murphy Trailhead. Turn here and continue for another 0.5 mile to the parking area.

Murphy Point is the name given to a mile-long promontory of land that extends westward from the southern end of the Island in the Sky Mesa. It was named after the Murphy Brothers, who grazed cattle and sheep below the point from about 1916 until 1920. For many years the Park Service maintained a road to the end of Murphy Point, but in 1996 the last mile of the road was closed and made into a footpath.

Since the road was closed Murphy Point now receives far fewer visitors that any of the other named viewpoints on the mesa, but in my opinion there is no finer place in the park to watch the sunset. If you can arrange to be there at the end of the day your time and energy will be well rewarded. Not

see map, page 53

only is the view unmatched but you can also enjoy a touch of wilderness, with no road noise and, more often that not, no other people. If you have never experienced a desert sunset from a high canyon rim, alone with only the sounds and smells of nature to distract you, then you really should take advantage of this trail. Just be sure to take a flashlight with you for the walk back. Alternatively, you may want to obtain a backcountry permit at the visitor center and spend a night on the point.

From the parking area the trail heads out in a southwesterly direction along one side of what used to be the Murphy Point Road. The sandy two-track runs for about a mile before reaching the slickrock, and from there a well cairned footpath continues for the last 0.3 mile to the edge of the mesa. When you reach the end of the point a 270-degree panorama of canyons and buttes suddenly opens up below—ample reward for your half-hour hike across the desert.

The most prominent feature in the canyon below is the Murphy Hogback, a long tongue of Moenkopi Shale that rises some 200 feet above the White Rim Plateau. The hogback seems so close you could almost hit it with a

see color photo, page 141

rock, although it is 900 feet below the rim. Notice the foot trail that goes westward along the top of the Murphy Hogback. This is the Murphy Trail, which also begins at the end of the Murphy Point Road (see page 52). The White Rim Road is visible in several places on either side of the Murphy Hogback, and two miles away you can see where the jeep road climbs up the notoriously steep southern side of the obstacle.

The tall sandstone butte north of Murphy Point is Candlestick Tower, and to the left of the Candlestick, in the center of a large loop of the Green River, is one of my favorite landmarks: the Turks Head. Hundreds of years before Europeans entered this area the river bottom below Turks Head was farmed by Anasazi Indians, and today many of their artifacts can still be seen in the remote area. The view south of Murphy Point is also an interesting one. Grandview Point, the southernmost point on the Island in the Sky Mesa can be clearly seen, and just to the right of Grandview Point is Junction Butte. If you look beyond these two landmarks you can see the rugged country of the Needles District of Canyonlands some 12 miles away.

Grandview Point and Junction Butte, seen from Murphy Point

Murphy Trail

☆ ☆ ☆   **day hike**

Distance:	9.0 miles (loop)
Walking time:	6 hours
Elevations:	1,390 ft. loss/gain
	Murphy Trailhead (start): 6,190 ft.
	Murphy Hogback: 5,200 ft.
	Murphy Wash: 4,800 ft.
Trail:	Good trail most of the way, but very steep and rocky for a half- mile at the beginning and end. There is no water along the trail.
Vicinity:	On the southern end of the Island in the Sky Mesa
USGS Maps:	Monument Basin, Turks Head

Drive south of the visitor center following the signs to Grandview Point. 8.9 miles from the visitor center, or 3.6 miles before you reach Grandview Point you will see a well marked dirt road on the right leading to the Murphy Trailhead. Turn here and continue for another 0.5 mile to the parking area.

Hiking the Murphy Trail is an excellent way to gain an appreciation for the wild beauty and expanse of Canyonlands National Park. It is also a good way to sample some of the history of Canyonlands. The trail was built during World War One by the Murphy brothers, who grazed cattle in the area from 1917 until about 1920. The area on and below the Island in the Sky Mesa was used extensively for winter grazing by local cattle ranchers during the first half of the last century, and many remnants of their occupation can still be seen.

The Island in the Sky district was also an active exploration area for uranium prospectors during the 1950s. Uranium ore is often found in the Chinle geologic forma-

tion above the White Rim Plateau, and during the nuclear energy craze of the 1950s prospectors came from all over the country to try their luck in Canyonlands. There are no active mines in the area now, but if you stand just about anywhere on the rim of Island in the Sky and gaze down into the canyon you can see parts of the old roads and trails built by the miners.

When the area became a national park in 1964 prospecting was no longer allowed, but 4-wheeling and bicycling on some of the old roads have become very popular. In particular, the 100-mile-long 4-wheel-drive White Rim Road that circles the Island in the Sky has become one of the parks best known attractions. The middle 1.4 miles of

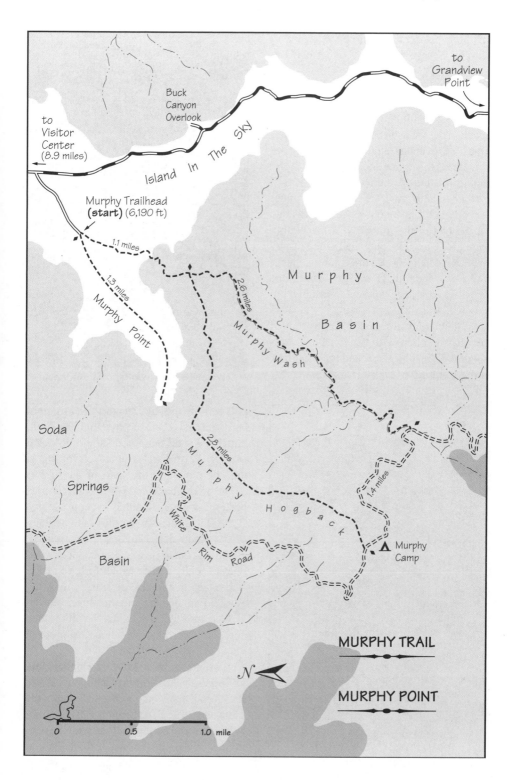

to
Grandview
Point

Buck
Canyon
Overlook

Island In The Sky

to
Visitor
Center
(8.9 miles)

Murphy Trailhead
(start) (6,190 ft)

1.1 miles

1.3 miles

Murphy Point

Murphy

Basin

2.6 miles

Murphy Wash

Soda

Springs

2.8 miles

Murphy

Hogback

1.4 miles

Basin

White

Rim Road

Murphy
Camp

MURPHY TRAIL

MURPHY POINT

N

0   0.5   1.0 mile

this hike, connecting Murphy Hogback to Murphy Wash, is along the White Rim Road.

From the parking area on Murphy Point the trail proceeds for 0.6 mile to the edge of the rim before plunging downward through a fault in the Wingate Sandstone. When you first look over the edge you may wonder how on earth anyone could get down there. But, miraculously, there is a way. The trail switchbacks down a series of ledges near the top, then finds a debris-scattered slope for the rest of the route. Near the bottom there is one exciting part where the Murphy brothers built a wooden bridge across a ten-foot gap in the trail. The logs in the bridge are close to a hundred years old now, but they still seem sturdy enough.

When the trail reaches the bottom of the cliff it splits, with the left fork heading down Murphy Wash and the right fork going out onto Murphy Hogback. If it is

White Rim Road on Murphy Hogback

Looking west from Murphy Trail

still early in the day I suggest you turn right here and take the Murphy Hogback Trail, but if it is near noon you should go down Murphy Wash first. The reason for this is that the most beautiful part of the hike is along the Hogback, and you should save this portion for when the sun is lower in the sky. If the sun is directly overhead the geology of the shadowless canyons is not as interesting. From a practical point of view it doesn't really matter which fork you take. The trails are joined at the other end by the White Rim Road, and the loop can be walked in either direction. I will assume here, however, that you choose to proceed via the Hogback trail.

The views from Murphy Hogback are so impressive that, upon reaching the White Rim Road, many hikers choose to return the same way. The Soda Springs Basin lies below you on the northwest side, with the photogenic towers of the Organ Rock Formation reaching up along the shores of the Green River. The river makes a huge meander into the basin, circling around another famous formation known as the Turks Head. Farther to the south, across the hidden recesses of the Colorado River, are the pinnacles of the Canyonlands Needles District. It is an immense 360 degree panorama. Many of the same features can more easily be seen from the viewpoints above the rim, but it is not quite the same up there. Down on the Hogback you get the feeling that you are more than just an observer. You are somehow a part of it all.

Once you reach the White Rim Road

see color photos, pages 137, 140

turn left and walk southeast along the road for 1.4 miles until you see a sign marking the beginning of the Murphy Wash Trail. Murphy Wash is interesting in a less dramatic way. The sandy wash is more protected and receives more water that the exposed Hogback; hence the plant life is quite different there. Soon after leaving the road you will pass by a small spring which, as the animal tracks attest, attracts a good deal of canyon wildlife. As you near the top of the wash you will pass by an old corral, one of many left by the ranchers who worked the area. Finally, 2.6 miles after leaving White Rim Road, the trail climbs out of Murphy Wash and rejoins the original trail for the climb back to the rim.

Looking south from the Murphy Trail

Gooseberry Trail

day hike

Distance:	10.4 miles (round trip), or 5.2 miles (one way to White Rim Road)
Walking time:	7 hours (round trip) 2³/₄ hours (one way)
Elevations:	1,510 ft. loss (one way) Gooseberry Trailhead (start): 6,260 ft. White Rim Road: 4,750 ft.
Trail:	Well marked and easy to follow, but very steep and rocky in one area. There is no water, so carry plenty.
Vicinity:	On the southern end of the Island in the Sky Mesa
USGS Maps:	Monument Basin

The starting trailhead is located in the picnic area near Grandview Overlook 12 miles south of the Visitor Center. The trail ends at the White Rim Road 0.3 mile north of Goosberry Campsite A. (See page 23 for more information on the White Rim Road.)

The Gooseberry Trail is the shortest of six established trails in Canyonlands that descend from the Island in the Sky Mesa to the White Rim Road. It is also probably the newest of the six. It was built just before World War II by WPA workers to access a spring below the rim and also to give the local ranchers better

see map, page 59

access to the pastures on the White Rim Plateau. It is doubtful in my mind, however, that the trail was ever used by livestock. It is extremely steep in places, and I can't imagine driving sheep or cattle down the trail. Most old timers know this trail as the Government Trail; it was renamed Gooseberry

Gooseberry Canyon

56

Viewpoint on Gooseberry Trail

mation is generally characterized by steer vertical walls, but for some reason in this area it has eroded into a much more reasonable slope. The route is certainly steep, but it is not unmanageable.

Back and forth, the narrow, rocky trail zigzags down a long series of short switchbacks until it finally reaches the bottom of the 400-foot cliffs. It then proceeds down across the slopes of sand, shale, and broken rock at the bottom of the Wingate for another 0.5 mile before finally dropping into a sandy arroyo on the White Rim Plateau which it follows the rest of the way to the White Rim Road. This final segment of the hike is the longest and hottest part, with somewhat less interesting scenery to catch your attention. But at least the terrain is reasonably level. You should arrive at the White Rim Road about 45 minutes after reaching the top of the plateau.

Trail by the Park Service in the 1960s.

From the parking area the trail proceeds for only two hundred yards along the top of the mesa before turning north to begin its descent down the cliffs beneath the White Rim Overlook Point. After the first hundred yards you will see a sign marking the junction where the Gooseberry Trail departs from the White Rim Overlook Trail. Turn left here, following the cairns across the slickrock, and soon you will come to the point where the route begins its descent. First the path descends through the Navajo Sandstone to a steep bench on the Kayenta Formation. It then levels out briefly before tackling the Wingate cliffs below.

As you go down you will probably wonder how the trail will ever get past the sheer vertical walls of sandstone that lie beneath the bench, but after a brief distance you will come to a break in the Wingate where a descent becomes feasible. The Wingate For-

Gooseberry Canyon

White Rim Overlook

☆ ☆   **short day hike**

Distance: 1.8 miles (round trip)

Walking time: 1 hour

Elevations: 140 ft. loss/gain
                     White Rim Overlook Trailhead (start): 6,260 ft.
                     White Rim Overlook: 6,120 ft.

Trail: Very easy trail

Vicinity: Near Grandview Overlook

USGS Maps: Monument Basin

The trailhead is located 12 miles south of the Visitor Center in the picnic area near Grandview Overlook.

Gooseberry Canyon from the White Rim Overlook

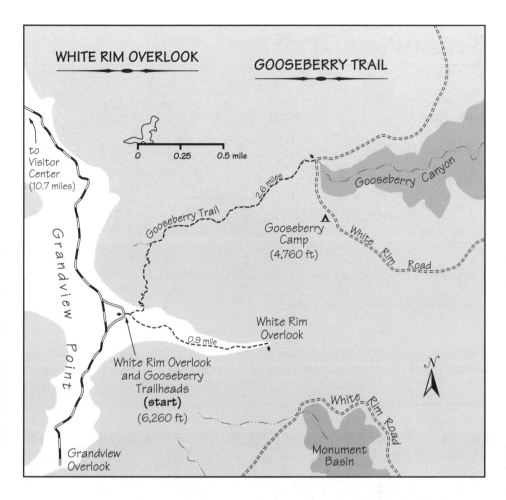

WHITE RIM OVERLOOK   GOOSEBERRY TRAIL

to Visitor Center (10.7 miles)

0   0.25   0.5 mile

Grandview Point

Gooseberry Trail

2.6 miles

Gooseberry Canyon

Gooseberry Camp (4,760 ft)

White Rim Road

White Rim Overlook

0.9 mile

White Rim Overlook and Gooseberry Trailheads **(start)** (6,260 ft)

White Rim Road

N

Grandview Overlook

Monument Basin

Trying to decide which is the best viewpoint in Canyonlands National Park is an impossible task, but the White Rim Overlook definitely ranks among the top two or three. The overlook point lies on the eastern end of a long, slender finger of land that extends outward for nearly a mile from the southern end of the Island in the Sky. From the end of the promontory it seems as if the whole world is below you. If you like sunrise vistas the White Rim Overlook presents a great vantage point for watching the morning's first rays of light make their way into the deep recesses of the vast desert below the rim.

The trail begins at the picnic area beside the road and immediately heads out with no change in elevation in an easterly direction. About half way along you will begin to notice the plateau becoming increasingly narrower, and ultimately the trail ends simply because there is no more room on the point for it. The canyon on the north side of the point is Gooseberry Canyon, and the White Rim Road can be seen for miles as it makes its way from Gooseberry around the east side of the viewpoint to Monument Basin in the south. The road follows the flat tableland of the White Rim Plateau, a thousand feet below the White Rim Overlook.

see color photo, page 138

Grandview Trail

☆☆☆   **short day hike**

Distance: 2.0 miles (round trip)

Walking time: 1 hour

Elevations: 20 ft. loss/gain
Grandview Trailhead (start): 6,260 ft.
end of Grandview Point: 6,265 ft.

Trail: Very easy trail

Vicinity: Southern end of the Island in the Sky Mesa

USGS Maps: Monument Basin

The trailhead is located at the Grandview Overlook, 13 miles south of the Visitor Center.

Monument Basin, from Grandview Trail

60

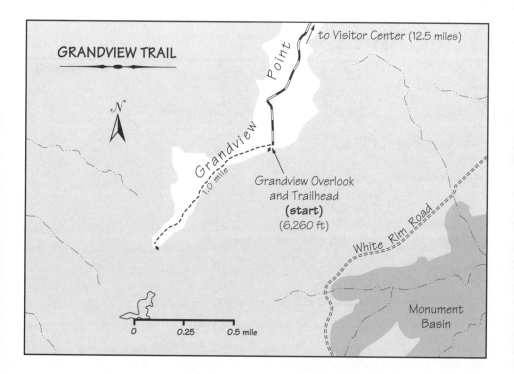

GRANDVIEW TRAIL

N

Grandview Point

to Visitor Center (12.5 miles)

Grandview

1.0 mile

Grandview Overlook
and Trailhead
(start)
(6,260 ft)

White Rim Road

Monument
Basin

0   0.25   0.5 mile

Grandview Point is situated high above the north side of a complex system of canyons known as Monument Basin, and it is the extraordinary panoply of views from the Grandview Trail into the basin that makes this hike so appealing. The trail skirts along the southeastern edge of the point for nearly a mile, finally ending at the southernmost end of the point where the impressive panorama is suddenly extended another ninety degrees to the north.

If at all possible you should save this hike for the late afternoon, when the dozens of dark red shale monoliths that dot the floor of Monument Basin begin to cast long shadows across the valley floor. As the sun moves lower and lower the monoliths, or monuments, turn deep maroon, while the white sandstone above them develops a pink translucent glow.

The well-marked trail leaves from the west side of the overlook point near the parking lot and proceeds westward along the rim. It is an easy walk with very little change in elevation, and you will probably see many photographers, young and old, along the way. If you didn't bring your camera you will wish you had.

There are several big round boulders at the end of the point where the trail ends, and almost every evening you can find a collection of camera enthusiasts that have climbed to the top of the rocks with their tripods to wait for the sunset. Initially their lenses are generally turned southeast for the view into Monument Basin. Then when the sun reaches the horizon most will swing their cameras around to the southwest to capture the reddish hues of *see color photo, page 141* Junction Butte, 0.5 mile southwest of the point. Don't worry too much about the walk back to the parking lot in the dark. The trail is on white sandstone and is not too difficult to follow at night.

Aztec Butte

☆ ☆

Distance:	2.2 miles (round trip, to all points of interest)
Walking time:	1¼ hour
Elevations:	300 ft. gain/loss Aztec Butte Trailhead (start): 6,080 ft. Aztec Butte: 6,312 ft.
Trail:	Easy trail with some climbing
Vicinity:	near Willow Flat Campground
USGS Maps:	Upheaval Dome, Musselman Arch

Drive south of the visitor center for 6.4 miles to the junction with the Upheaval Dome Road. Turn right here and continue for another 1.0 mile where you will see a sign marking the trailhead and parking area on your right.

Before 1300 A.D. there were many Anasazi Indians living within the boundaries of Canyonlands National Park. They generally lived in the canyons below the mesas where water was more abundant—particularly along the Green River. But they also made frequent trips to the mesa tops for the purpose of gathering food, and there is still a great deal of evidence of their habitation on the Island in the Sky Mesa. The best place to see the remnants of these prehistoric people is on Aztec Butte, where the Anasazis built a number of granaries for storing the food they collected.

see color photos, pages 141, 142

From the car parking area the trail goes east across the sandy desert for 0.6 mile to the base of the butte. It then heads up the west side of the hill, climbing steeply over the slickrock in a few places, and finally reaches the flat top of Aztek Butte after an elevation gain of 200 feet. Once on the top you will see several trails, and it may be confusing trying to decide which one to follow. Just remember that there is one ruin on the top southeastern side of the hill and several more just under the rim on the northern side. I suggest that you first make your way to the southeastern side of the butte to see the top ruin. Then find a primitive trail near that ruin that drops about 15 feet below the rim and follows a narrow bench around to the other ruins on the north side.

The ruin on the top of the mesa looks big enough to have served as a dwelling for a good-sized family. It has been heavily reconstructed, however, and it is hard to tell

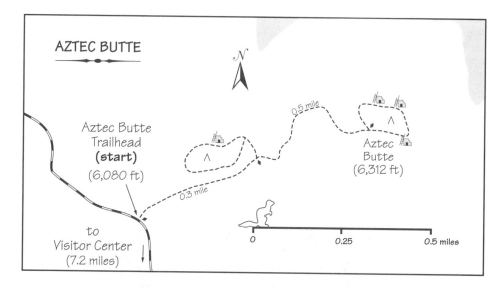

exactly what the original structure looked like. The most interesting ruins are located along the ledge on the north side of the butte, where there are a number of small alcoves. These well-protected alcoves would have been ideal locations for granaries, and at least a half-dozen of them contain Anasazi artifacts. Some of the structures are so crudely made, however, that I wonder if they were not built by other hikers rather than the Anasazis.

The high point of the hike is the last granary you will come to on the northwest side of Aztec Butte. This granary is in excellent condition, and it is also situated in a very picturesque setting. The alcove has two pillars of sandstone that rise from the floor to the ceiling, forming three small arches. There is also a magnificent view into Trail Canyon from the site. This location would have been a very pleasant place to rest after a hunting trip across the mesa below.

About halfway from Aztec Butte back to the trailhead you will see a secondary spur trail on the right leading to a small hill west of the larger butte. Be sure to explore this trail before returning to your car. It will lengthen your hike by only 20 minutes, but

your reward will be two more finely preserved granaries. After an elevation gain of about 100 feet the trail comes to the top of the low hill, and then drops into another alcove on the north side where the granaries are located. These granaries are each about 8 feet in diameter and 3 feet high.

Anasazi granary, Aztec Butte Trail

Wilhite Trail

☆

Distance: 11.4 miles (round trip), or
5.7 miles (one way to White Rim Road)

Walking time: 7½ hours (round trip)
3 hours (one way)

Elevations: 1,580 ft. loss (one way)
Wilhite Trailhead (start): 5,820 ft.
White Rim Road: 4,240 ft.

Trail: Generally well marked with cairns. There is no water on this trail, so be sure to carry plenty.

Vicinity: Begins on the Island in the Sky Mesa near Upheaval Dome

USGS Maps: Upheaval Dome

Drive south of the visitor center for 6.4 miles to the Upheaval Dome Road. Turn right here and continue on the paved road for another 2.2 miles where you will see a sign marking the trailhead and parking area. The trail ends at the White Rim Road, 2.2 miles north of Candlestick Camp. (See page 23 for more information on the White Rim Road.)

Wilhite Trail, on the top of the Island in the Sky Mesa

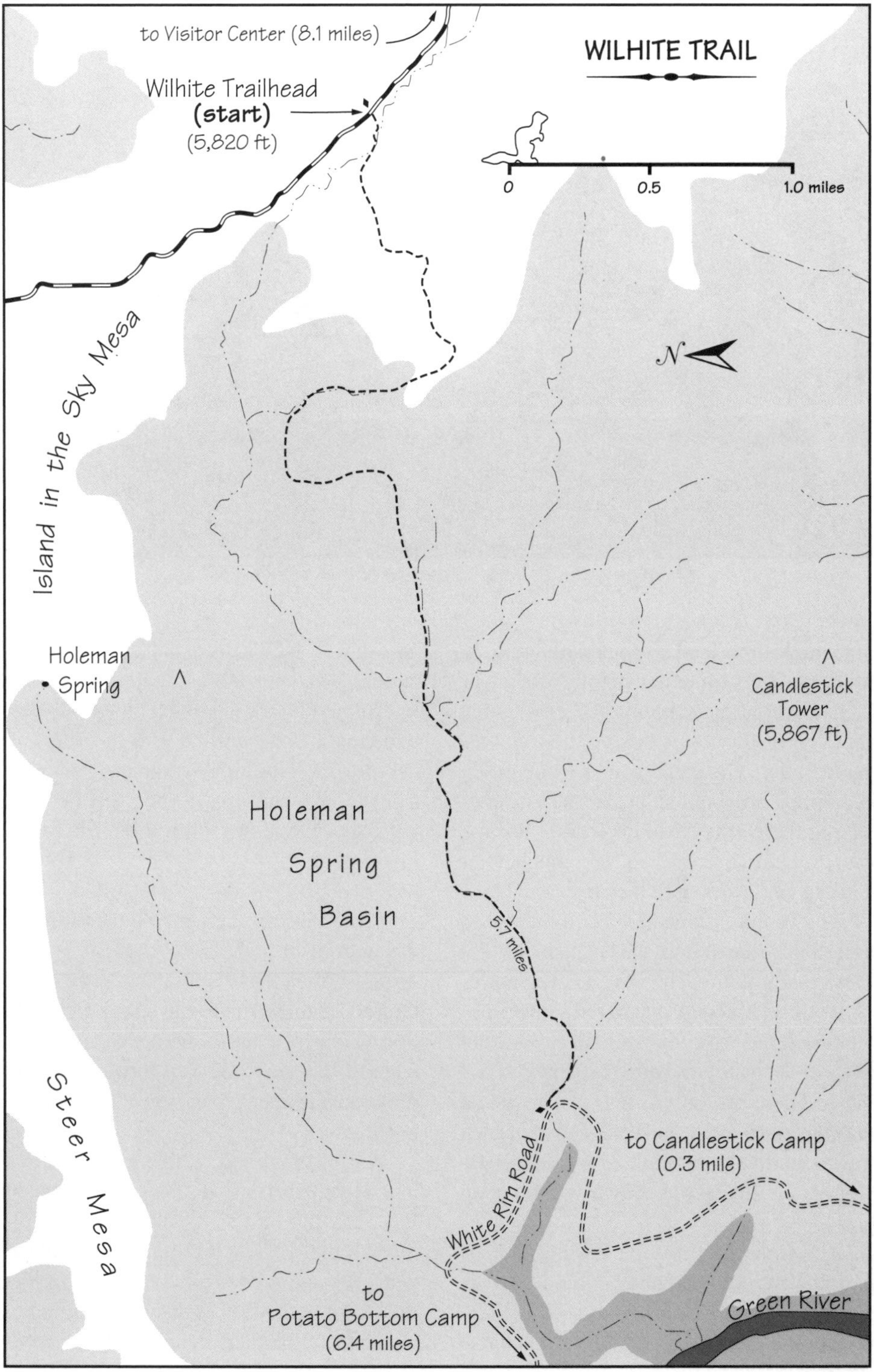

to Visitor Center (8.1 miles)

Wilhite Trailhead
(start)
(5,820 ft)

WILHITE TRAIL

0   0.5   1.0 miles

Island in the Sky Mesa

N

Holeman
Spring

Candlestick
Tower
(5,867 ft)

Holeman

Spring

Basin

5.7 miles

Steer Mesa

White Rim Road

to Candlestick Camp
(0.3 mile)

to
Potato Bottom Camp
(6.4 miles)

Green River

Wingate Sandstone Formation above Wilhite Trail

The Wilhite Trail was probably built by sheep ranchers sometime before World War II, but no one now seems to know much about its history or even who the trail was named after. The name comes from an old inscription on a boulder beside the trail containing the words "Wilhite Trail". Wilhite was probably one of the sheep ranchers or herders who worked in the area.

The Wilhite is one of six currently used trails that descend from the Island in the Sky Mesa to the White Rim Plateau. The builders of these trails all shared the same problem: finding a way down the sheer 400-foot cliffs of Wingate Sandstone that encircle the mesa. There are only a few places where feasible routes exist, and the location of each trail is uniquely determined by the necessity of finding a way down the Wingate cliffs.

The route used by the Wilhite Trail is particularly obvious, and I would be very surprised if the Indians who lived in Canyonlands a thousand years ago did not also have a well established trail at the same location. The Wingate Cliffs in this area are interrupted by a deep notch about 200 feet wide that has been filled in with rocks and debris from above. This natural chute is now a gift of nature to anyone who might be looking for a way down from the mesa to the plateau below.

From the parking area the trail follows the bottom of a shallow wash for a short distance, then heads south across the mesa top for 1.2 miles to the rim above Holeman Spring Basin. Shortly before reaching the edge of the mesa the trail turns north and drops down slightly to the top of the Wingate Formation.

At this point you will be looking down into Holeman Canyon, the centerpiece of Holeman Spring Basin, which the trail follows to the White Rim Road. The vertical walls of sandstone seem to close in on the trail from both sides in this area, but in between the cliffs there is an enormous accu-

Wilhite Trail

the White Rim Plateau before reaching the White Rim Road.

Just after crossing the White Rim Road the Holeman Canyon drainage enters an interesting slot canyon that you might want to explore while you are there. The narrow canyon extends into the White Rim Sandstone for about 300 yards before finally ending above a 40-foot pouroff only 0.5 mile from the Green River. It's a pity it isn't possible to walk all the way to the river through the crack. The short canyon joins the river on the shore opposite an interesting area known as Valentine Bottom, which was homesteaded by the Valentine family in the late 1800s. The bottom was also the center of an Anasazi Indian settlement in the late 1200s.

mulation of rubble that provides a feasible route to the bottom. Look to the right as the trail begins its descent and you will see a boulder on the right side of the trail with the words "Wilhite Trail" inscribed on it. This is the inscription that gave the trail its name.

The path down is rocky and steep, but not as steep as most of the other trails to the White Rim Plateau. Also, because the trail faces north, this part of the hike is in shade for all but 2-3 hours of the day. It will take you about 15 minutes to reach the bottom of the Wingate and another 15 minutes to reach level ground near the bottom of the Chinle Formation. From there the trail skirts along a bench for another 0.8 mile before finally dropping down the last 200 feet to the White Rim Plateau. For the last 2.6 miles the trail follows a series of dry washes across

Holeman Canyon, below White Rim Road

Whale Rock

☆   **short day hike**

Distance: 1.0 mile (round trip)

Walking time: $^1/_2$ hour

Elevations: 170 ft. gain/loss
Whale Rock Trailhead (start): 5,690 ft.
Whale Rock: 5,960 ft.

Trail: Easy trail

Vicinity: Near Upheaval Dome

USGS Maps: Upheaval Dome

Drive south from the visitor center for 6.4 miles to the Upheaval Dome Road. Turn right here and continue on the paved road for another 4.1 miles. You will see the trailhead and parking area on your right 0.8 mile before the end of the road.

Whale Rock

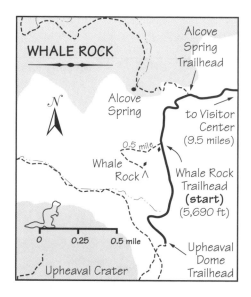

Whale Rock is a huge rounded dome of smooth, white Navajo Sandstone that lies half-buried in the sand about 600 yards west of Upheaval Crater. The rock is well named. Seeing it from the road it is easy to visualize Moby Dick breaking the surface of a calm sea, and it begs to be climbed by almost anyone who drives past. The hike to the top is a fun and easy way to spend an hour. Morning is the best time because then the eastern sun makes for a great view across the top of Upheaval Crater.

From the parking area the trail crosses the sand and slickrock for 0.4 mile before starting the 0.1-mile climb up the northeast side of Whale Rock. The Park Service has installed handrails on the steeper parts of the climb, but they aren't really necessary. The route is only moderately steep, and the elevation gain is only 170 feet. The best view from the top of the landmark is to the west, where you can peer across Upheaval Crater and beyond to Upheaval Canyon on the opposite side of the depression. There are also interesting views of Trail Canyon, 0.5 mile

to the northeast, and Holeman Spring Basin, 0.7 mile to the southwest. But for me the most engaging panorama is to the north.

Looking north from this vantage point it is clear that Whale Rock is but a small segment of a large concentric ring of uplifted sandstone that almost completely encircles the crater. The ring of rock looks strikingly similar to the outwardly radiating ripples of water that are always formed when a stone is thrown into a calm lake, and it isn't hard to imagine a similar event that once occurred here.

Geologists theorize that Upheaval Crater was formed about 60 million years ago when a large meteorite, perhaps one-third of a mile in diameter, impacted the earth in Canyonlands National Park. Immediately after the collision a stupendous wave of kinetic energy propagated outward from the point of impact, and it was this energy as well as the collapse of the crater that formed the concentric ring of exposed sandstone we now see. The Whale Rock Trail offers an opportunity to climb to the top of the circle of stone and ponder the forces that formed it.

Looking north from Whale Rock

Upheaval Dome

☆

Distance:	1.4 mile (round trip)
Walking time:	¾ hour
Elevations:	120 ft. gain/loss
	Upheaval Dome Trailhead (start): 5,680 ft.
	Upheaval Dome Viewpoint: 5,800 ft.
Trail:	Easy, generally well marked trail.
Vicinity:	On the western side of the Island in the Sky Mesa.
USGS Maps:	Upheaval Dome

Drive south from the visitor center for 6.4 miles to the Upheaval Dome Road. Turn right here and continue on the paved road for another 4.9 miles to the Upheaval Dome Picnic Area and Trailhead at the end of the road.

Upheaval Crater

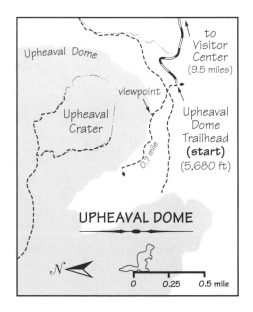

Upheaval Dome is one of the most interesting geologic formations in Utah. At first glance the unusual circular structure appears to be a large crater, but geologically it more closely resembles an ancient dome. The strange formation consists of a huge circular pit, about a mile in diameter and 1,100 feet deep, surrounded by concentric rings of uplifted rock that were originally deep under the surface.

What kind of natural force could account for such a structure? Volcanic forces often cause both uplifting and cratering, but it is highly unlikely that Upheaval Dome was created by a volcano. There is no evidence of volcanism anywhere in the area, and none of the rock in or around the dome is volcanic. A meteorite could have produced the crater, but it is difficult to explain how a meteorite could have caused the extensive uplifting. A third theory is that Upheaval

Dome is the remanent of an ancient salt dome that was pushed up by subterranean forces millions of years ago and then eroded to its present form. But this theory doesn't adequately account for the crater at the top of the dome.

In the past the salt dome theory had the widest following among geologists. However new research, including a microscopic study of the sand grains at the bottom of the crater, suggests that Upheaval Dome may indeed have been formed by a meteorite. Scientists now hypothesize that the meteorite that struck Upheaval Dome was about one-third of a mile in diameter, and fell about 60 million years ago—long before the formation of the Green River or the Colorado Plateau.

From the parking area an easy trail proceeds eastward across the rocky desert landscape, climbing about 100 feet to the top of the Upheaval Dome. After 0.3 mile you will arrive at the rim of the crater, where the Park Service has placed an interpretive plaque at the first viewpoint. From there a more primitive trail continues in an easterly direction across the slickrock for another 0.4 mile before finally fading away.

The best place to photograph Upheaval Crater is at the first viewpoint, but in my opinion the most interesting part of this hike is along the lesser developed second half of the trail. For another 15 minutes you can follow a series of rock cairns along the rim. Eventually the cairns disappear and you will be left to find your own way, but even with no trail you may want to extend your hike a little further. The walking is not difficult, and the views into the enormous, thousand-foot-deep crater are very impressive.

Syncline Loop Trail

☆ ☆ ☆   **day hike**

Distance:	8.0 miles
Walking time:	6 hours

Elevations: 1,460 ft. loss/gain
Upheaval Dome Trailhead (start): 5,680 ft.
Upheaval Canyon: 4,220 ft.

Trail: The trail is steep and rocky in one or two places, but well marked and easy to follow. There is usually water in Syncline Valley, 3.4 miles from the trailhead, but it must be purified before drinking.

Vicinity: On the western side of the Island in the Sky Mesa

USGS Maps: Upheaval Dome

Drive south from the visitor center for 6.4 miles to the Upheaval Dome Road. Turn right here and continue on the paved road for another 4.9 miles to the Upheaval Dome Picnic Area and Trailhead at the end of the road.

This interesting trail traces out a loop around Upheaval Crater, an ancient crater on the edge of the Island in the Sky Mesa. The crater lies at the top of what appears to be a huge salt dome, and for many years geologists thought the depression was the result of a collapse in the center of the dome. The structure was called Upheaval Dome. New geologic evidence, however, has almost completely ruled out this theory, and now most scientists believe the pit to be an impact crater. Currently accepted theory claims that the crater was formed by a large meteorite or comet that collided with the earth some 60 million years ago.

Midway through the hike the path inter-sects the Upheaval Canyon Trail which leads into the center of the crater, and if you wish to extend your hike by one or two hours this trail makes an interesting side trip (see page 82). But even if you choose not to walk into the crater, you should at least plan a lunch break near the trail junction. The two trails meet in a very pretty area called Syncline Valley. There is usually water in the bottom of the valley, and the Park Service has also established a primitive campsite nearby for overnight hikers with backcountry permits.

Walk north from the parking area on the Upheaval Dome Trail for about 150 feet un-

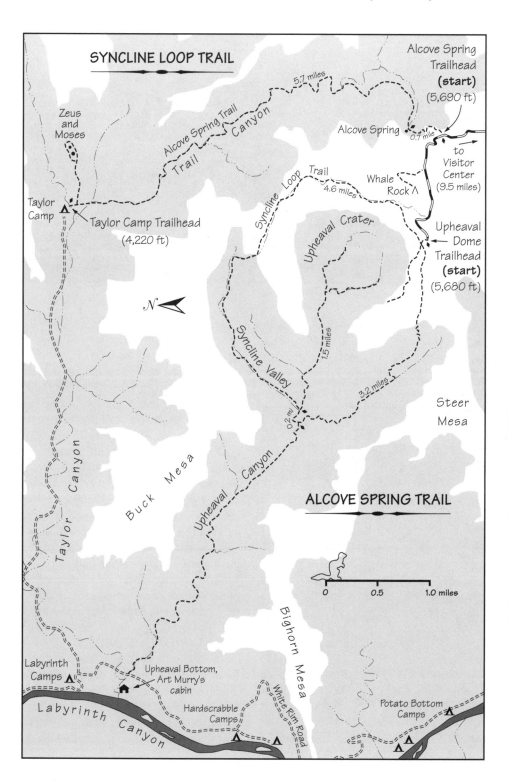

SYNCLINE LOOP TRAIL

Alcove Spring
Trailhead
(start)
(5,690 ft)

5.7 miles

Zeus
and
Moses

Alcove Spring Trail

Alcove Spring

Canyon

0.7 mile

Trail

to
Visitor
Center
(9.5 miles)

Syncline Loop

Trail

4.6 miles

Whale
Rock ⋀

Taylor
Camp

Taylor Camp Trailhead
(4,220 ft)

Upheaval Crater

Upheaval
Dome
Trailhead
(start)
(5,680 ft)

N

1.5 miles

Syncline Valley

3.2 miles

Steer
Mesa

0.2 mi

Buck   Mesa

Upheaval   Canyon

ALCOVE SPRING TRAIL

Taylor   Canyon

0   0.5   1.0 miles

Bighorn   Mesa

Labyrinth
Camps

Upheaval Bottom,
Art Murry's
cabin

Labyrinth   Canyon

Hardscrabble
Camps

White Rim Road

Potato Bottom
Camps

Upheaval Canyon, seen from Syncline Loop Trail

til you see a sign marking the junction with the Syncline Loop Trail. You can turn either way here, but I suggest you turn left and walk around the loop in a clockwise direction. This will insure that most of the best scenery will generally be in front of you.

The trail stays on fairly level ground for about 0.8 mile as it skirts along the southern edge of the crater, but soon it begins a downward plunge that will eventually take you to the bottom of Upheaval Canyon. The trail is steep, but the scenic rewards are ample. Occasionally you can catch a glimpse of the Green River peering up through the twists and folds of the canyons below. Finally, after a descent of 1,000 feet, the trail reaches the bottom of a wash and then continues downward at a more gradual grade until it arrives at the bottom of Upheaval Canyon. When you reach the floor of the canyon you will find a sign marking the trail to Green River, three miles away. You should turn right at this junction to stay on the Syncline Loop Trail.

A short walk upcanyon from the Green River Trail junction will bring you to the mouth of Syncline Valley, where you can usually find water. The trail then climbs about 100 feet to the rim of the shallow canyon where you will see a sign marking the

Syncline Loop Trail in Upheaval Canyon

beginning of the spur trail that leads into the center of Upheaval Crater. Again, this is an interesting side trip if you have an hour or two to spare. Inside the crater you will find a massive jumble of debris, including great piles of gray pulverized sand that were once a part of the White Rim geologic formation. It is this debris that has provided the strongest evidence to support the theory that Upheaval Dome was formed by a meteorite impact.

see color photos, page 143

From the junction with the Upheaval Crater Trail the Syncline Loop Trail continues north into Syncline Valley. Again, there is usually water along this part of the hike, sometimes in large pools. After less than a mile the lower part of Syncline Valley ends in a box canyon, and the trail begins following a steep and rocky route up the valley's north side. Some scrambling may be necessary at this point, but once you reach the upper valley the trail again turns into a pleasant walk. There isn't as much water in the upper part of Syncline Valley as in the lower part, but it is still a green oasis in the desert canyon country. The path meanders for about a mile through the tamarisk and cottonwood trees, and then suddenly exits to the south through a large, unexpected break in the canyon wall. Hidden as it is from the outside world, Syncline Valley is the kind of place that would have made a perfect hideout for a band of outlaws at the turn of the century.

Once you have climbed out of Syncline Valley through the narrow slot in the canyon wall you are back on top of the Island in the Sky. From there it is a relatively easy walk of about two miles through the juniper forest back to the trailhead and parking area.

Upheaval Dome and Crater

Alcove Spring Trail

☆ ☆   **day hike**

Distance:	12.8 miles (round trip), or 6.4 miles (one way to White Rim Road)
Walking time:	8 hours (round trip) 3½ hours (one way)
Elevations:	1,470 ft. loss (one way) Alcove Spring Trailhead (start): 5,690 ft. Alcove Spring: 5,250 ft. Taylor Camp: 4,220 ft.
Trail:	The trail through the bottom of Trail Canyon is not well marked, but the route is easy to follow. There is no water after the first 0.7 mile.
Vicinity:	Begins on the Island in the Sky Mesa near Upheaval Dome
USGS Maps:	Upheaval Dome

Drive south from the visitor center for 6.4 miles to the Upheaval Dome Road. Turn right here and continue on the paved road for another 3.6 miles. You will see the trailhead and parking area on your right 1.3 miles before the end of the road. The trail ends at Taylor Camp, 36 miles from the visitor center via the White Rim Road. (See page 23 for more information on the White Rim Road.)

Alcove Spring undoubtedly played an important roll in the lives of the prehistoric peoples of Canyonlands. The Anasazi Indians who lived in the canyons made frequent trips to the Island in the Sky Mesa for hunting and gathering purposes, but water is scarce on the mesa top because most of the springs are located far below the rim. Alcove Spring is unique because it is so easily accessible from the mesa. The Indians could always count on finding water there—even in late summer.

This spring was also well known to the sheep and cattle ranchers who grazed their animals in the area from the late 1800s. The present trail was probably built during the early 1900s by cattlemen in order to provide water for the livestock, but the details of its construction have been lost to history.

Many people walk this trail only as far as the spring before returning to the trailhead, and if you choose to do that the hike is relatively easy. Alcove Spring is only 0.7 mile from the parking area, with an elevation loss of 440 feet. If you cannot arrange a shuttle to

see map, page 73

Alcove Spring

The trail as far as the spring is very well constructed; the amount of effort put forth by the early ranchers to make the water accessible to their livestock was considerable. The route descends along the base of the Navajo Sandstone cliffs for about 0.3 mile, then switchbacks to the left and continues its descent for the rest of the way to the spring. The water is located at the bottom of a huge alcove about 200 feet in diameter near the base of the Navajo Sandstone formation.

Notice the green grass growing just below the alcove—a sure sign that there is water present. The main trail does not actually pass the spring, but if you are observant you will notice a hiker-made spur branching off to the left for the last 200 feet to the alcove. This primitive trail goes directly to the bright green patch of grass, under which you will find a tiny stream of water trickling down the slope.

pick you up in the canyon it is probably not worth walking all the way to the Taylor Camp Trailhead, but if a shuttle can be arranged there is a lot of interesting scenery to be seen along the route through Trail Canyon. You can also see the Moses and Zeus monoliths near the end of the hike.

It is interesting to note why the spring is located at this particular place. The Navajo Sandstone above the spring is well known for its water storage characteristics. This

Trail Canyon

Moses, Zeus, and Aphrodite Rocks, above Trail Canyon

geologic layer is composed of small grains of sand that were loosely deposited as sand dunes about 195 million years ago. The dunes were subsequently buried and then cemented together by lime and other minerals dissolved in the water that percolated down from above. The interstitial spaces between the grains of sand were not entirely filled in, however, and today these microscopic voids enable the sandstone to hold water as surely as if it were a storage tank.

Underneath the Navajo Sandstone there is another layer of clay and sand-based material called the Kayenta Formation that is relatively impervious to water. Water seeping down from the desert floor cannot go beyond this layer, so it has a tendency to move sideways and emerge in the form of springs wherever the boundary between the

Navajo and Kayenta Formations is exposed. It is also common to find alcoves in the sandstone above these springs, because the running water leaches out the minerals that bind the sandstone together.

As the trail leaves the Alcove Spring it begins to descend rapidly through a series of rocky switchbacks that take it down through the Kayenta and Wingate Formations to the sandy

see color photos, pages 142, 143

bottom of Trail Canyon. Once the path reaches the bottom of the canyon it becomes much more vague, but there are still frequent cairns to mark the way. The route simply winds down the dry desert wash for the last 4.4 miles to the Taylor Camp. There is no water along this part of the hike, so be sure to carrying plenty.

Moses and Zeus

☆

Distance: 1.8 miles (round trip)

Walking time: 1¼ hours

Elevations: 560 ft. loss/gain
Taylor Camp Trailhead (start): 4,220 ft.
base of Moses: 4,780 ft.

Trail: Steep and rocky, but mostly easy to follow.

Vicinity: near Taylor Camp, off the White Rim Road

USGS Maps: Upheaval Dome

The trailhead is located at Taylor Camp, 5.2 miles from Labyrinth Camp on the White Rim Road. (See page 23 for more information on the White Rim Road)

Note: This hike is usually done in conjunction with an overnight camp on the White Rim Road, but you must have a permit if you intend to spend a night in the area. See pages 15-16 for more information on how to obtain a permit.

Taylor Canyon, from the base of Moses and Zeus

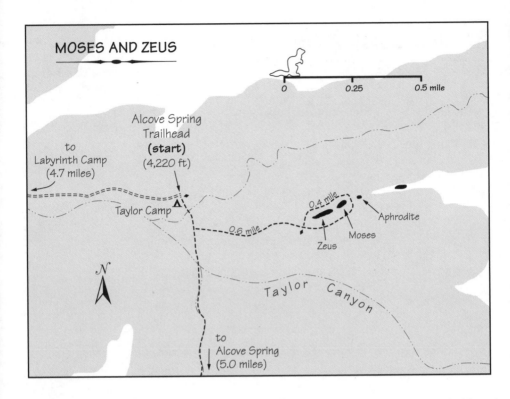

The landscape at the end of the Taylor Canyon Road is dominated by four slender spires of sandstone that beg to be investigated. The tallest pinnacle rises 410 feet from its base, or 930 above the end of the road, and with a little imagination it is easy to see why the spire was named Moses. It really does look like an old man wearing a long robe slightly hunched over as he gazes down upon the smaller figure, Zeus, in front of him. It is not clear why Moses would be talking to Zeus, but his posture is very solemn and reverent, as if he were about to utter something of great importance.

see color photo, page 143

Like most of the pinnacles in Canyonlands, these landmarks have been carved from the Wingate Formation, a hard, thick layer of dense ruddy sandstone that for some reason tends to fracture along vertical planes. They are the eroded remains of a long point of land that once protruded from the south side of Horsethief Mesa.

When I first saw this trail I wondered if the hike would really be worthwhile. From the road the Moses and Zeus formations looked impressive; however I couldn't see what would be gained by making the 500-foot climb up to the base of the rocks. But I was not disappointed. The hike turned out to be much more interesting than anticipated.

From the Alcove Springs Trailhead the path proceeds southward for 150 yards to a junction where a sign marks the beginning of the Moses trail. Then, soon after leaving the Alcove Springs Trail, the path starts its assent up the Moenkopi and Chinle Formations to the base of the Wingate Sandstone. The route meanders a great deal to get around the shale ledges and outcroppings in the Moenkopi, so there are occasional stretches of level ground and the climb is really not that tiring. There is one particularly interesting place where the trail crosses a 20-foot-long, windswept ridge of bentonite, just before the final climb to the base of Zeus.

After reaching the bottom of the monoliths the trail splits giving you the option of circling them in either direction. I recommend you turn right here and go first along the southern side. The trail becomes vague and sometimes confusing, but the route is clear. Just traverse along the base of the huge spires for a distance of about 0.2 mile until you reach the eastern side of Moses. Between Moses and the next chimney-shaped spire, called Aphrodite, the trail drops into a pass that allows you to access the north side of the formation so you can complete the loop.

Soon after you start west along the shady north side of the pinnacles you may spot a few cairns on your left. These cairns mark another spur trail that climbs 60 feet to a narrow bench higher up the side of Moses. The bench ends at the top of a cliff on the extreme eastern end of Moses, about 80 feet above the pass. What a spectacular place to eat your lunch and contemplate the scene. The view from the end of this flat sandstone bench includes a 360-degree panorama of the North and South Forks of Taylor Canyon, with Aphrodite (the Greek goddess of love and beauty) in front of you and Moses (looking the other way!) behind you.

The walk back to the western side of Zeus is quite straightforward, and from there you can retrace your footsteps back to the trailhead.

Moses and Zeus

Upheaval Canyon and Crater

★ ★   **4WD vehicle required**
                                                              day hike

Distance: 11.2 miles (round trip)

Walking time: 7 hours

Elevations: 660 ft. gain/loss
                         Upheaval Canyon Trailhead (start): 3,940 ft.
                         Upheaval Crater: 4,600 ft.

Trail: Much of the trail is not well marked, but the route is easy to follow.
                         There is usually water in Syncline Valley, 4.1 miles from the trail-
                         head, but it must be purified before drinking.

Vicinity: Trailhead is on the White Rim Road

USGS Maps: Upheaval Dome

---

*The trailhead is located at Upheaval Bottom, 0.7 mile south of Labyrinth Camp on
the White Rim Road. (See page 23 for more information on the White Rim Road).*

*Note: This hike is usually done in conjunction with an overnight camp on the
White Rim Road, but you must have a permit if you intend to spend a night in the
area. See pages 15-16 for more information on how to obtain a permit.*

Most of what we see in Canyonlands National Park today took millions of years to create, and on the scale of human experience it is often difficult to comprehend the geologic processes that produced it. The mesas, the canyons, and the dazzling rock formations were sculpted almost entirely by the slow but unrelenting erosive action of wind and water. The Island in the Sky district does, however, have one geologic artifact that was created by a rare force of nature powerful enough to do in minutes what would normally take eons to accomplish. That artifact is the Upheaval Crater.

Upheaval Crater was probably formed by a gigantic meteorite or comet that crashed into the earth some 60 million years ago. It is estimated that the object was about a third of a mile in diameter, and it was moving about 25,000 miles per hour when it struck the earth. The immediate result of the collision was the excavation of a huge bowl-shaped cavity over three miles across. The crater walls then collapsed to form concentric rings of terraces around a central pit with a "rebound peak" in its center.

Over time the crater has become so badly eroded that it is no longer obvious that it was formed by a meteorite. A vast, thick layer of subterranean salt lies deep under

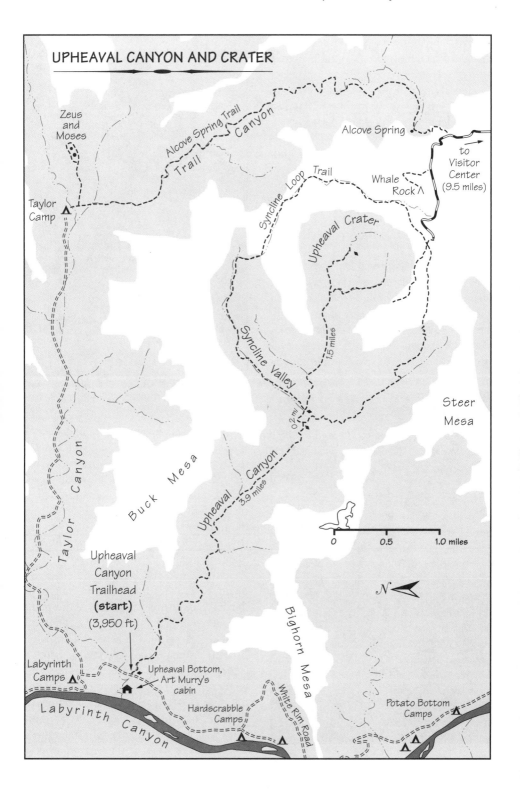

UPHEAVAL CANYON AND CRATER

Zeus and Moses

Alcove Spring Trail

Alcove Spring Trail Canyon

Alcove Spring

to Visitor Center (9.5 miles)

Syncline Loop Trail

Whale Rock ∧

Taylor Camp ∆

Upheaval Crater

Syncline Valley

1.5 miles

Steer Mesa

0.2 mi

Taylor Canyon

Buck Mesa

Upheaval Canyon

3.9 miles

0   0.5   1.0 miles

Upheaval Canyon Trailhead **(start)** (3,950 ft)

N

Bighorn Mesa

Labyrinth Camps ∆

Upheaval Bottom, Art Murry's cabin

White Rim Road

Hardscrabble Camps

Potato Bottom Camps ∆

Labyrinth Canyon

∆   ∆

∆ ∆

the park, and until recently most geologists thought the crater and its central peak had been formed by a swelling and shrinking of the underlying salt. However according to a recent seismic study the top of the salt layer under the crater is almost perfectly flat, and there is no evidence of any previous swelling or shrinking. That plus other studies of the rock in and around the crater make it much more likely that structure is an ancient meteor crater.

The Upheaval Canyon Trail begins near the Green River in an area known as Upheaval Bottom. Upheaval and Taylor Canyons both meet here to form a wide, flat sandy area nearly a mile across. The trail winds across this flat desert in an easterly direction, then the canyon quickly narrows to a width of about 0.3 mile. The route never strays far from the dry wash in the canyon

Trail into Upheaval Crater

Upheaval Canyon

floor.

As you walk you will see a rugged, convoluted wall of Navajo Sandstone about three miles ahead of you at the end of the canyon. These cliffs lie just above Upheaval Crater. You can also see a natural arch high on the north side of the canyon 0.5 mile from the trailhead. This canyon is exceedingly dry, and your view is unimpeded by any plants more than 18 inches high.

After the first 45 minutes the canyon begins to narrow further, and the bottom of the drainage becomes less flat. At this point you are walking through the Moenkopi Shale formation and the trail is not so sandy. 2.1 miles from the trailhead you may notice a seep on the right side of the trail where water seems to be leaking out of the base of the shale. Look for the cottonwood trees in the area; their presence nearly always indicates that water is nearby. But there isn't really enough water at the seep to drink—

just enough to make the plants a little greener.

3.8 miles from the trailhead you will come to a sign marking the junction where the southern half of the Syncline Loop Trail meets Upheaval Canyon. Bear left at the sign to continue towards the crater. After another fifteen minutes the canyon deadends at a pouroff, and the trail turns left up a crude stone staircase to a bench 100 feet above the canyon bottom. This is a very pretty area, with Syncline see color photos, page 143 Valley on the left and the trail into Upheaval Crater continuing straight ahead to the east. There is usually at least some water in the small creek that runs down Syncline Valley, and the Park Service allows camping nearby at a primitive campsite. However you must get a backcountry permit from the visitor center if you intend to stay overnight.

A hundred yards beyond the bottom of Syncline Valley you will come to the junction where the Syncline Loop Trail departs to the north and the trail into Upheaval Crater continues to the east. The trail into the crater follows the bottom of the dry wash that drains the crater. After 1.4 miles the wash reaches the west side of the peaks in the center of the crater and then splits, with one fork circling to the north and one going around to the south. Walking up either fork will allow you to get a close look at the jumbled rock that was pushed up after the meteorite impacted. The forks circle around and end about 350 yards from each other. With some off-trail scrambling it might be possible to climb out of one fork and down

to the other, but I have never tried this. On the map it looks like the scramble would involve only about 150 feet of elevation gain and loss.

The bottom of Upheaval Crater is an interesting place to spend some time looking around, especially if you are interested in geology. I have seen thin veins of something that looks and feels very much like charcoal imbedded in the rock. Could it be pieces of 60-million-year-old wood that was burned and covered with rubble after the meteor hit? I have also seen desert bighorn sheep on the sides of the crater.

Inside Upheaval Crater

Fort Bottom

☆ ☆ ☆ ☆

4WD vehicle required
day hike

Distance:	4.2 miles (round trip)
Walking time:	2¹/₂ hours
Elevations:	580 ft. loss/gain
	Fort Bottom Trailhead (start): 4,380 ft.
	Fort Ruin: 4,260 ft.
	Mark Walker's cabin: 3,960 ft.
Trail:	Well marked, easy to follow
Vicinity:	Near Hardscrabble Camp on the White Rim Road
USGS Maps:	Horsethief Canyon

The trailhead is located 1.7 miles south of Hardscrabble Campsite A, or 1.4 miles north of Potato Bottom Campsite C, on the White Rim Road. (See page 23 for more information on the White Rim Road)

Note: This hike is usually done in conjunction with an overnight camp on the White Rim Road, but you must have a permit if you intend to spend a night in the area. See pages 15-16 for more information on how to obtain a permit.

Fort Bottom was named after a tower-like structure that was built above the river bottom by the Anasazi Indians some 750 years ago. It isn't clear what the tower was used for, but many such towers have been found throughout the Southwest. Often they are located on mesa tops with lines of sight between them, which suggests that they may have been used for signaling between Anasazi settlements. If you have sharp eyes the Fort Bottom tower can be seen from the trailhead: it is located on the top of a butte in the center of the bend in the river at about the same elevation as the road.

The fertile bottom was also used by cattle ranchers before it became part of Canyonlands National Park in 1964, and a relic of the cowboy era can still be seen in the form

Anasazi Ruin above Fort Bottom

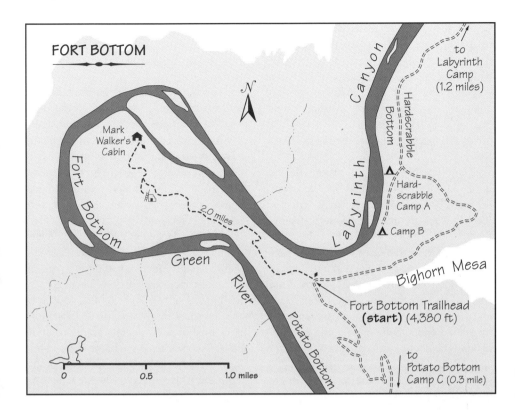

FORT BOTTOM

N

Mark Walker's Cabin

Fort Bottom

Green River

2.0 miles

Labyrinth Canyon

Hardscrabble Bottom

to Labyrinth Camp (1.2 miles)

Hard-scrabble Camp A

Camp B

Bighorn Mesa

Fort Bottom Trailhead **(start)** (4,380 ft)

Potato Bottom

to Potato Bottom Camp C (0.3 mile)

0   0.5   1.0 miles

of an old line cabin that was built near the river by one of the ranchers. The cabin was probably built in the late 1890s by a carpenter/cowboy named Mark Walker who moved to Moab in 1884. The cabin is in remarkably good condition after all these years, although its willow and mud roof has long since washed away.

Perhaps the greatest attraction of this hike

Mark Walker's cabin, Fort Bottom

is the terrific views of the Green River that can be seen from the trail. The trail follows a long ridge from the road to the center of a huge bend, where the river makes a 230-degree turn to get around the western end of Bighorn Mesa. At its narrowest point the ridge is only 300 yards wide, but the water flowing under the north side of the trail must travel over three

see color photo, page 144

miles around the perimeter of Fort Bottom before it comes back along the south side of the trail.

The trail is almost level for the first 0.5 mile, then it doubles back along the north side of the ridge for a short distance, turns west again, and begins the long gradual descent to Fort Bottom. Be careful of your belongings along this section of trail. The last time I was there a sudden gust of wind came up over the ridge, and the next thing I knew my favorite hat had been transformed into a flying saucer. My first impulse was to make a lunge for the hat, but the crest of the ridge was only four feet wide at that point and common sense overrode my instinct. I simply stared with fascination as the hat drifted down 300 feet to a wet landing in the Green River.

After 1.5 miles the trail arrives on the north side of Fort Butte and then descends the last 200 feet to Fort Bottom. Once it reaches level ground it heads north for the final 0.2 mile to Mark Walker's cabin. The cabin is about twelve feet square, with a fireplace and chimney on one end and a small bench along one wall. The logs have all been squared and notched by hand with an axe, and there are a few initials and dates carved by the old-timers who once found comfort inside. The shelter is located in a peaceful spot just a few feet from a channel of the river, with a veranda on the north side where many a cowboy has probably leaned back to

rest his weary bones. The timelessness of the setting suggests a lifestyle much different from the hustle and bustle of our modern world.

On your way back to the trailhead you will see a trail junction on the north side of Fort Butte where another path continues climbing upward to the rim of the small mesa. After some minor scrambling near the top of the butte the short spur trail reaches level ground just 200 feet from the ancient Anasazi ruins. The structure that can be seen from the road is actually the remnants of two towers, joined together with a door between them. The larger tower is about 10 feet in diameter and 10 feet high, though it was undoubtedly once much higher. There are also the remains of at least two other low stone structures nearby. In addition to these ruins there are also a few ancient granaries in the ledges just below the top of the butte. Their presence indicates that a significant number of Anasazis once lived in the area, and that they farmed the land near the river.

Green River from Fort Butte (note Anasazi ruin in lower left corner)

Gooseneck Trail

short day hike

Distance:	0.8 miles (round trip)
Walking time:	20 minutes
Elevations:	100 ft. gain/loss
	Gooseneck Trailhead (start): 4,744 ft.
	Gooseneck Overlook: 4,840 ft.
Trail:	Well marked, easy to follow
Vicinity:	Off the White Rim Road
USGS Maps:	Musselman Arch

Gooseneck Trailhead is located on the White Rim Road 6.5 miles from Highway 313, or 1.3 miles east of the junction where the White Rim Road departs from Shafer Trail and the Potash Road. (See page 23 for more information about the White Rim Road.) The road is very rough and rocky in a few places, but with care most ordinary cars can get as far as the trailhead.

The Colorado River, as seen from the Gooseneck Overlook

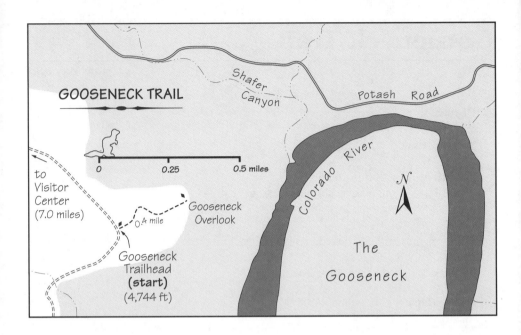

The Gooseneck Trail leads to an overlook point high above a huge meander of the Colorado River. The Colorado turns abruptly north below the overlook and then bends around to the south again, tracing out a 180-degree arc that is four miles long. Dead Horse Point State Park is situated just one mile north of the Gooseneck, and many visitors stop to gaze 1,900 feet down at the river from that vantage point. But in some ways the view from the Gooseneck Trail is better. The river is only 940 feet below Gooseneck Overlook and it is not possible to see the entire meander from there, but standing nearly a thousand feet above the river at a point that is also a thousand feet below the canyon rim provides its own special sensation. From there you aren't just looking into the canyon, you surrounded by it.

The trail heads east across the slickrock from the trailhead, winding its way between the cactus plants and stunted juniper trees to the rim of the Colorado gorge just 0.4 mile from the road. From there you can look almost straight down at the tranquil, muddy water below. Dead Horse Point is 1.8 miles northeast of the trail, and the Potash Road is clearly visible as it snakes across a bench above the north side of the river. Potash Road is a popular jeep road that goes from the White Rim Road down Shafer Canyon to the Colorado and eventually ends near Moab.

While looking down at the Gooseneck people often wonder what could have caused the Colorado River to suddenly turn north and flow four miles out of its way before continuing its journey south. To answer that question you must understand that the Colorado is a very old river. It began some 30 million years ago as a slow-moving stream that meandered lazily across a flat, featureless landscape with few obstacles to block its way. At that time Canyonlands National Park was in the middle of a relatively level plain of sedimentary rock that had been formed earlier at the bottom of a shallow inland sea. Lacking a well-defined gradient to guide its descent, the primordial river turned this way and that in its random search for the ocean. The resulting twists and turns of its streambed are typical of all plains rivers.

Then some 25-30 million years ago the Colorado Plateau began to rise and tilt, causing the river to hasten its flow rate and cut deeper into its bed. The changes came very gradually so the river had ample time to maintain its course, and as its channel deepened the ancient meanders were slowly locked into place. The casual twists and turns of the ancestral steam now lie thousands of feet below their original location and have become a permanent part of the landscape.

The Gooseneck, as seen from Dead Horse Point

White Crack Trail

☆ ☆

4WD vehicle required
day or overnight hike

Distance:	12.4 miles (round trip)
Walking time:	7 hours
Elevations:	540 ft. loss/gain White Crack Camp (start): 5,200 ft. abandoned mining camp: 4,660 ft.
Trail:	Generally well marked and easy to follow. There is no easily obtainable water on this trail, so be sure to carry plenty.
Vicinity:	Off the White Rim Road
USGS Maps:	Monument Basin, The Loop, Spanish Bottom

The trailhead is located 38 miles from the visitor center at White Crack Camp, the southernmost camp on the White Rim Road. See page 23 for more information on the White Rim Road.

Note: You must have a permit if you intend to camp at White Crack Camp or any other campsite along the White Rim Road. You must also have a backcountry permit if you intend to make this an overnight hike. See pages 15-16 for more information on how to obtain permits.

The White Crack Trail was named after a natural fissure in the White Rim Formation that was once used by cowboys and mining prospectors seeking access to the lower benches of Canyonlands. The first recorded use of the crack was by a group of cattle ranchers who developed it into a trail around 1918 so they could use the lower plateaus for grazing. Then in the early 1950s the crack was widened by uranium miners while they were constructing a jeep road to a point near the Green River. Today the jeep trail no longer appears on Park Service maps, and it has so deteriorated that it would now be impossible to drive a jeep over it. Nevertheless, the old road makes an interesting hiking trail. It ends at an abandoned mining camp on the edge of a plateau 760 feet above the river.

The hike to the mining camp and back can be done in one day, but there are several interesting side trips in the area if you wish to spend a night above the river. Unfortunately there is no easily accessible water nearby. If you are lucky enough to be doing this hike right after a storm you can

see color photo, page 144

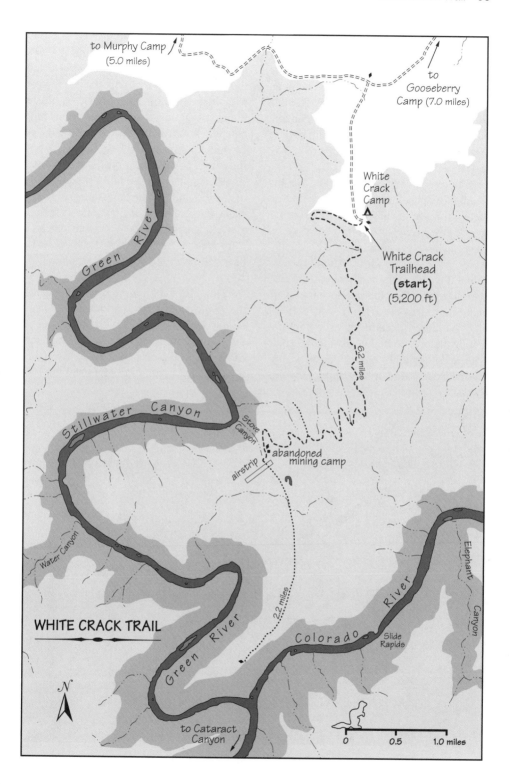

to Murphy Camp
(5.0 miles)

to
Gooseberry
Camp (7.0 miles)

White
Crack
Camp

White Crack
Trailhead
(start)
(5,200 ft)

Green River

Stillwater Canyon

Stove Canyon

6.2 miles

abandoned
mining camp

airstrip

Water Canyon

2.2 miles

WHITE CRACK TRAIL

Green River

Colorado River

Slide
Rapids

Elephant Canyon

N

to Cataract
Canyon

0   0.5   1.0 miles

find water in numerous sandstone potholes along the trail, but these potholes usually dry up within a few days. The only other alternative is to get water from the Green River. The river is a 45 minute scramble from the mining camp down Stove Canyon, but then you have a 760-foot climb back to the camp—a lot of work for a drink of muddy water!

The most interesting side trip from the mining camp is the cross-country hike to the confluence of the Green and Colorado rivers. Few people make this relatively easy hike, and largely for that reason it is a memorable one. Aside from the stunning view above the rivers, the walk across the flat, open desert on the plateau above the rivers is an interesting experience. Your field of view is uninterrupted for miles in every direction, there is no trail of any kind to guide you, and the landscape is complete unmarred by any sign of humanity. I did this hike alone in the early hours of a spring morning, and I found it to be almost a religious experience. At first the emptiness and the silence of the morning seemed almost overwhelming. But then I began to notice things that at first I hadn't seen. A lone bird chirping to attract others of its kind. A ground squirrel standing motionless, hoping I wouldn't see it. A brilliant red cactus flower challenging the more subdued colors of the sand and shale. Nature is rarely silent, but here in the desert she rarely speaks above a whisper. And we must listen carefully with all of our senses if we expect to hear her message.

The trail starts on the southern side of the White Crack Camp parking area. There are no signs marking the trailhead, but if you look carefully you will see the remnants of an old jeep road departing to the south towards the canyon rim. After walking 150

White Crack Trail, just below the White Rim

yards along this road you will come to the edge of the White Rim Formation where, on your left, you can see the White Crack. Before the 1950s the White Crack was just a cleft in the White Rim Sandstone, but now it is a 12-foot-wide roadbed that has been blasted out with dynamite.

From the rim you can clearly see the first mile of trail winding across the plateau below. After its descent through the crack it heads west for another 0.4 mile to the base of a large stone pinnacle. It then turns and switchbacks down the rest of the way to the top of the bench 400 feet below the White Rim. After this initial descent the trail stays at an almost constant elevation for the next 5.8 miles to the abandoned mining camp. It winds along the benches, first in a westerly direction, then south, and finally east, always twisting and turning to get around side canyons and other obstacles. For a long while the route never strays far from the 4800-foot contour line, then in the last two miles it slowly descends the last 150 feet to the mining camp

The first good views of the Green River will come about a mile before you reach the mining camp. At one point, 5.4 miles from the trailhead, the path crosses the end of a long, narrow finger of land that juts out for 0.3 mile above the east side of the river. If you take the time to drop your pack and walk out on the promontory you will rewarded with a superb view of the river and its canyons.

The trail finally reaches Stove Canyon on its east side, and then follows a narrow shelf of sandstone for another 200 yards to the remains of the old mining camp. The cabin that was once here burned down about 15 years ago, but two iron beds still stand incongruously on the slickrock facing the river below. With a spring bed to sleep on and a view like that at your front door, maybe life for those old prospectors wasn't

so bad after all. It's too bad the old beds are no longer usable. What a place to stretch out on a clear night and gaze up at the stars!

If the mining camp is your final destination this round-trip hike can easily be completed on one day. However, if time and especially water are not a problem there are a couple of interesting ways to spend another day in this area.

Stove Canyon

Before the White Crack Road was built the uranium prospectors accessed this area by way of the Green River. There is some evidence that they had a crude tram for hauling supplies and equipment up from the bottom of Stove Canyon, and a nearby pile of iron pipes indicates that they probably intended to build a water line down to the river. There is a crude hiker-made trail through Stove Canyon to the Green River, and an

Old mining camp above Stove Canyon

Stove Canyon

interesting side trip is to retrace the miners' steps down to the water. It will take you about 45 minutes to reach the river and, depending on what kind of shape you are in, an hour and a half to get back up. There is just enough scrambling to make the hike interesting

The beginning of the trail can be seen near the top of the canyon on the opposite side from the mining camp. The trail works its way down several narrow benches along the west side of the ravine before finally reaching the streambed 150 feet below the camp. It then heads straight down the drainage, loosing another 200 feet of elevation, until the canyon opens up above the river. For the last 400 feet the trail descends down an old slide area above the river. There are some great campsites near the Green River if you want to haul your pack down Stove Canyon.

Green and Colorado River Confluence

The hike from the mining camp to the confluence is 2.2 miles each way, and will take you about 2½ hours to complete. The route is very easy walking with little elevation gain, but there are no trail markers of any kind to follow. You should have a compass for this walk.

From the mining camp the road continues for a short distance beyond the end of Stove Canyon and then soon disappears on the sandy plateau above. The miners once had an airstrip here. From the lay of the land it must have been oriented in an east-west direction, but I was not able to pinpoint its exact location. Fifty years of wind and rain have pretty much erased its mark from the land.

Before starting out across the plateau you should make a mental note of what the area above the mining camp looks like so

Colorado and Green River Confluence

you will know how to get back. The confluence is almost due magnetic south of the mining camp, but it is better if you start initially in a southeasterly direction. Otherwise your route will take you too close to the top of the Green River gorge, where the land is not as flat. Start out on a compass heading of about 145 degrees, or 35 degrees east of south, and after you have walked about 15 minutes you can start turning south. By now you will see the top of the Green River gorge on your right. Keep walking south until you see the Colorado River gorge on your left and then turn a little to the west, staying approximately in the center of the two gorges.

As you approach the confluence there will be many little side drainages veering off both on the right and the left. Be careful not to drop into any of these arroyos—just stay on the slickrock at the top of the watershed. Near the end there will be two prominent outcroppings of sandstone on either side of the route. Go between them, staying closer to the outcropping on the left, and soon you will arrive at the northern rim of the Colorado River gorge just a short distance upstream from the confluence. The dramatic view of the two mighty rivers coming together is awesome, and there is no better place in the national park to see it.

When returning to the mining camp you can use Junction Butte as a landmark to keep you headed in the right direction. The prominent landmark rises almost due magnetic north of the confluence, about four miles north of the mining camp. But, again, you will have to veer initially to the east on the way back to get around the uneven terrain near the Green River gorge.

There is another item of interest above the mining camp that you might want to check out on your way back from the confluence. Pay attention to the low cliffs on your right as you approach the old airstrip, and you should see a large alcove two hundred yards off the trail with two small holes in its roof. This alcove makes an interesting stop. There is also evidence that the area around the alcove was once inhabited by the Anasazis. I wasn't able to find any ruins, but there are hundreds of flint flakes scattered across the wash in front of the alcove. These flakes do not occur naturally; they were the tools of a stone-age culture. The flakes were chipped from larger chunks of chert, a hard igneous rock that was mined by prehistoric people throughout Canyonlands.

Alcove near Stove Canyon

Needles District

The Needles District, separated from the rest of Canyonlands by the mighty Colorado River, offers a lesson in geology very different from that presented by the Island in the Sky. Missing are the impressive red cliffs of Wingate Sandstone, and gone is the wide, flat plateau of White Rim Sandstone. These geologic strata have been largely eroded away from the land immediately east of the Colorado, leaving exposed large patches of the much older Cedar Mesa Sandstone.

The process of erosion is very uneven, but it is also unrelenting. Perhaps in another million years the Cedar Mesa Formation will also have been washed away by the Colorado, but for now the task is only half finished. The once solid layer of Cedar Mesa Sandstone has been only partially etched away, and what is left is an astonishing array of pinnacles and towers, that protrude from the landscape like hundreds of stone needles poking out of a giant's pincushion.

Why does this stone erode in such an odd fashion? The Wingate tends to form vertical cliffs, while the Navajo Sandstone erodes into round domes. The Entrada forms arches, and the Cedar Mesa Sandstone forms needles. It is an fascinating puzzle. But whatever the reasons, the Needles District of Canyonlands National Park is an incredible place for hikers. A wide selection of trails meander through the canyons and spires, sometimes entering surprisingly flat meadows where the sandstone has been completely removed.

The parks and meadows of the Needles District were a great attraction for local ranchers before Canyonlands became a national park, and cattle were grazed there throughout the first half of the last century. Most of the jeep roads in the Needles were built by the early ranchers, including the famous Elephant Hill Road that will be described later. The ranchers even maintained landing strips for small airplanes in a few of the meadows. The largest and best know of the ranches was the Dugout Ranch. Although cattle are no longer grazed within the boundaries of the national park, the Dugout Ranch is still in operation just east of the park boundary.

Before 1300 AD there were a large number of Indians living on the east side of the Colorado River, and many of their artifacts can still be seen in the Needles District. The ruins are especially numerous in Lavender, Davis, Horse, and Salt Creek Canyons near the park's southern boundary. The prehistoric Indian dwellers were primarily Anasazis, although there are a number of fine pictograph panels in the area that were made by the Fremont Indians. The two cultures seem to have peacefully cohabited the area for several centuries, but archeologists are still not sure what their relationship was. Before the mid-1990s it was possible to drive a jeep into all four canyons, but now Davis and Salt Creek Canyon are open to hikers only.

Colorado Overlook Road

4WD vehicle required
1-day jeep ride

Distance:	14.3 miles (round trip)
Road conditions:	With care the first 3.0 miles of the road can be driven by most ordinary cars, but the last 2.6 miles definitely requires a vehicle with high clearance. This is also an excellent road for mountain bikes. No permits are required.
Vicinity:	Near the Needles Visitor Center
USGS Maps:	The Loop

The road starts at the Needles Visitors Center.

Colorado Overlook Road

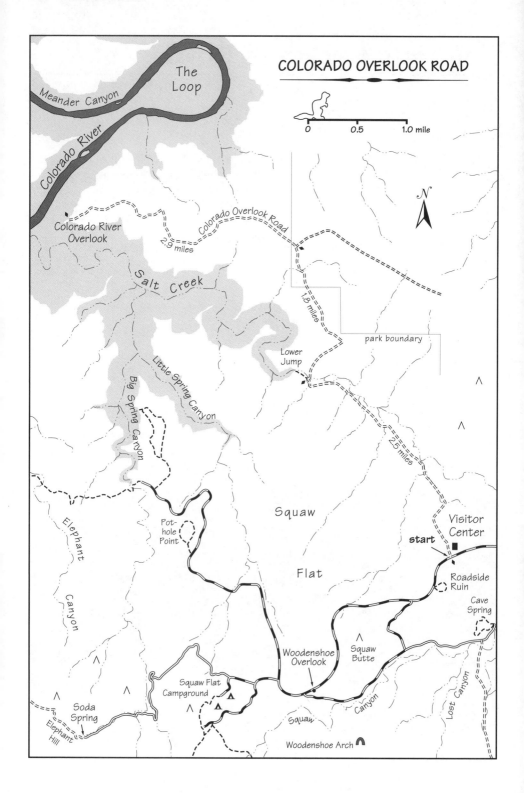

COLORADO OVERLOOK ROAD

The Loop

Meander Canyon

Colorado River

Colorado River Overlook

Colorado Overlook Road

2.9 miles

N

0   0.5   1.0 mile

Salt Creek

Little Spring Canyon

Big Spring Canyon

1.8 miles

park boundary

Lower Jump

2.5 miles

Squaw Flat

Pot-hole Point

Elephant Canyon

Visitor Center

start

Roadside Ruin

Cave Spring

Woodenshoe Overlook

Squaw Butte

Lost Canyon

Squaw Flat Campground

Soda Spring

Elephant Hill

Squaw Canyon

Woodenshoe Arch

This short but interesting jeep trail is a favorite among mountain bikers. The beginning of the road is conveniently located at the visitor center parking lot and, although there is no water along the way, the round-trip ride can easily be completed in a few hours. There are a few sandy spots, but most of the route is over relatively well packed dirt and slickrock.

The first 3.0 miles of this road can be driven by almost any car, but beyond that the road gets more and more rocky. High-clearance 2WD vehicles can usually make it all the way to the end; however if you are driving an ordinary passenger car you will probably have to walk the last 2.6 miles.

The first two miles of this jeep ride are across a relatively featureless landscape of sand and sagebrush, but then you will begin to notice a line of tamarisk bushes on your right as the road approaches Salt Creek Wash. At 2.5 miles the road dips down to cross the wide, sandy bottom of the wash, then it immediately climbs out the opposite side.

Although it is nothing more than a dry, shallow arroyo at this point, Salt Creek is an important feature of Canyonlands National Park. It begins 15 miles to the south, on the northern slopes of the Abajo Mountains and intersects the Colorado River near the end of the Overlook Road. Although in this area the streambed is almost always dry, water is generally available in other parts of Salt Creek and its character can change drastically from one mile to the next.

Just 200 yards west of the road Salt Creek Wash suddenly plunges downward through the rugged, fractured layers of sandstone, mudstone, and limestone that make up the Elephant Canyon geologic formation. This drop-off, called the Lower Jump, is one of the major features of Salt Creek, and a short trail leads to it from the road. Park your car

Salt Creek Canyon, from Colorado Overlook

in the wash and look for a sign on the west side of the road marking the trailhead.

It is possible to stand on the rim of the Lower Jump and gaze straight down for 250 feet to the bottom of lower Salt Creek Canyon. But be careful—there are no guardrails! There is usually some water in the gorge, and if you are lucky enough to be there after a rain, you may see a waterfall. The lower gorge of Salt Creek Canyon is also an ideal habitat for the park's bighorn sheep, and they can occasionally be seen grazing lazily below the Lower Jump. If you have a pair of binoculars be sure to look for them.

Evaporation from the springs and seeps around the Lower Jump has left behind large patches of white alkali, and in some respects the area looks like it has been dusted with fresh snow. It is this salty crust that probably gave Salt Creek its name.

At 3.1 miles you will come to a rocky

section of road that presents the first challenge for 2WD cars. The difficult part is only 150 yards long, however, and if you can get around it you will be able to continue for another mile before the road gets bad again. At 3.6 miles the road again approaches the rim of Salt Creek Canyon. This time it is only a 100-foot walk to the edge of the canyon, but the view is not nearly as impressive as it is at the Lower Jump.

At 4.3 miles you will see another road leaving to the right. This road leads to an outcropping of rocks a short distance away where there are some excellent campsites just outside the park. If you were unable to get a site in the national park campground, or if you just want to spend a night in the backcountry you might consider camping there. The area is managed by the BLM, and no permits are required.

The scenery starts to get much more interesting about two miles before the end of the road as the Colorado River gorge becomes visible in the north. The top of the gorge is decorated with a rugged array of sandstone needles, and the Island in the Sky Mesa stands out clearly on the horizon. Grandview Point and Junction Butte are directly across the river at this point. The road also starts to get much more challenging about this time, and if you don't have a 4WD vehicle you will probably be stopped before you enter the last mile. There is a stair-step at 6.1 miles that, in my opinion, is the most serious obstacle on this road.

When you reach the end of the road, park your car and walk in a westerly direction for another 100 yards for a marvelous view of Salt Creek Canyon and the Colorado River gorge. At this point you are 1040 feet above the confluence of the two canyons. The Colorado flows in from the northeast, and Salt Creek comes in from the southeast. For the best photographs try to be there around 10:00 in the morning, when the light is high in the east.

Colorado River, from Colorado Overlook

Elephant Hill

☆ ☆ ☆ ☆ ☆   **4WD vehicle required**
overnight jeep ride

Distance:	32.4 miles (round trip, to all points of interest)
Road conditions:	Extremely challenging in a few places
Campsites:	The Park Service maintains eight campsites along this route, but camping elsewhere is not permitted. None of the campsites have water. See pages 15-16 for more information on how reserve the sites and obtain camping permits.
Vicinity:	6.0 miles west of the Needles Visitor Center
USGS Maps:	Cross Canyon, Spanish Bottom, Druid Arch, The Loop

Follow the signs for 6.0 miles from the Visitor Center to Elephant Hill, where there is a small parking area and picnic ground at the beginning of the 4WD road.

Note: This is a very popular jeep ride. There are only eight vehicle campsites in this area and they are usually full, so if you intend to camp in one of them you should make reservations as far in advance as possible.

The road over Elephant Hill is, in my opinion, the most challenging jeep road in Canyonlands National Park. It presents drivers with a series of obstacles ranging from loose rock and stairstep drops to steep grades with hairpin turns. One of the turns is so tight that most vehicles must back down the succeeding switchback. With skill, however, the road can be negotiated with an ordinary 4WD vehicle—I have driven my Jeep Cherokee over Elephant Hill many times. The park service has even poured concrete in a few critical places to make the road passable for stock vehicles, but it is still a difficult road.

The road over Elephant Hill Road was originally built in the early 1940s by a man named Puge Stocks, a bulldozer operator who was working at the time for the Dugout Ranch. Cattle had been grazed in the Needles area since the 1800s, but the road greatly facilitated the enterprise. Several small airstrips were also built in the area after the road was finished, so light airplanes could service

see color photo, page 145

the ranching operations. Although it is not visible today, one of the runways was near the road on the top of Elephant Hill!

The basic loop described below is only 9.4 miles long and will take most drivers less than three hours to complete. However there is a great deal to see beyond Elephant Hill, and, for the most part, once you are past the first 3.5 miles the roads are much better. It would be a shame not to enjoy the fruits of your efforts (and your car's!) for a day or

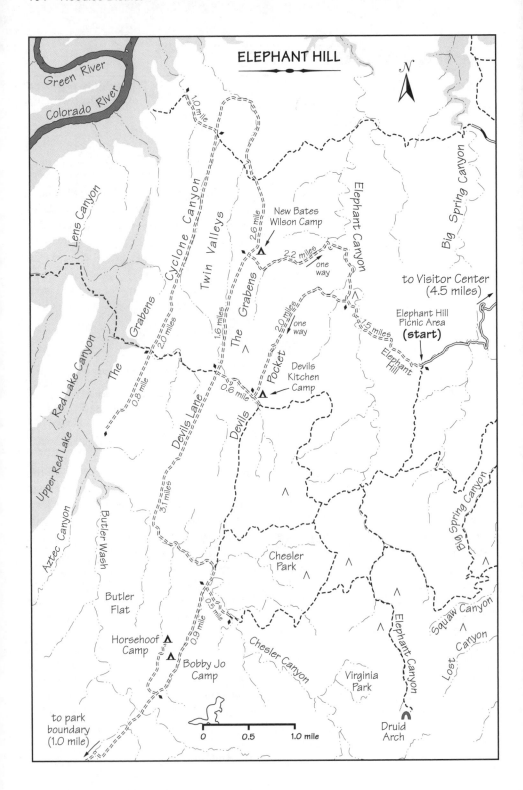

ELEPHANT HILL

Green River

Colorado River

Lens Canyon

Cyclone Canyon

Twin Valleys

1.0 mile

2.6 mile

New Bates
Wilson Camp

2.2 miles
one way

Elephant Canyon

Big Spring Canyon

to Visitor Center
(4.5 miles)

Elephant Hill
Picnic Area
(start)

Elephant
Hill

1.5 miles

The Grabens

2.0 miles

The Grabens

1.6 miles

2.0 miles
one way

Devils
Kitchen
Camp

Red Lake Canyon

2.0 miles

0.8 mile

0.6 mile

Devils
Pocket

Devils Lane

Devils

3.1 miles

Upper Red Lake

Aztec Canyon

Butler Wash

Butler
Flat

Chesler
Park

Big Spring Canyon

0.5 mile

Horsehoof
Camp

0.9 mile

Bobby Jo
Camp

Chesler Canyon

Virginia
Park

Elephant Canyon

Squaw Canyon

Lost Canyon

to park
boundary
(1.0 mile)

Druid
Arch

0   0.5   1.0 mile

two before returning to the pavement. If you want to check out the remaining 21 miles of jeep roads east of Elephant Hill or perhaps go on one of the hiking trails I suggest you spend a night in one of the Park Service's campgrounds. The best 4 campsites are at Devils Kitchen, but there are also 4 other sites to choose from.

The road begins a steep climb immediately upon leaving the Elephant Hill parking area. For anyone with lingering doubts, it quickly becomes apparent that this road is for 4WD vehicles *only*. After an intense 150-yard lesson on the finer points of hill-climbing, the jeep trail briefly levels out on a small turn-around pad about 150 feet above the parking area. This small, strategically placed flat area serves two vital purposes: it allows the vehicle to make a 180-degree turn before heading into the next switchback, and it provides an opportunity for anyone who might have overestimated himself or his vehicle to turn around and make a hasty retreat back to 2WD country.

The road climbs the last 100 feet to the top of Elephant Hill over the next 300 yards, and then enters a relatively flat area at the top of the hill that lasts for about 0.3 mile. The next order of business is to drop down the east side of Elephant Hill. Again, the route is very steep, but not unreasonable, and the Park Service has used concrete in a few vital places to allow passage by conventional 4WD vehicles. The route drops about 150 feet to a bench that marks the end of the most difficult part of the jeep trail.

After leaving Elephant Hill the road descends into Elephant Canyon and turns north to arrive at the junction where the one-way section of the loop begins. Over the next 1.5 miles the road makes a long, sweeping turn to the south, gradually climbing out of Elephant Canyon through a small side canyon on its east side. Then, just before reach-

Elephant Hill Road

ing Devils Pocket and the Devils Kitchen Camp, the route passes through an exceedingly narrow slot between two rock formations (which I am reminded of every time I look at the scratch on my jeep's left side mirror). If you are driving an overly wide vehicle you will probably be stopped at this point, but if you get through you will arrive at the Devils Kitchen Camp 0.3 mile later.

Devils Kitchen's 4 campsites, situated in the midst of a field of huge, picturesque sandstone boulders, are among the nicest campsites you will find anywhere in Canyonlands. They are also conveniently located, with several other points of interest nearby. If it can be arranged, you should try to spend one or two nights at the Devils Kitchen Camp and make it a base for your exploration of the area.

Upon leaving Devils Kitchen the road makes an abrupt right turn and continues in a westward direction for 0.6 mile to another interesting canyon called Devils Lane. Here

Driving down the east side of Elephant Hill

you must turn right in order to complete the loop, and drive up Devils Lane for 1.6 miles to a junction where another one-way section of road begins that leads back to Elephant Hill. Just before reaching the junction the road drops down a short section of challenging road that has been affectionately named the Silver Stairs. This is one of the many places along this drive where you should stop your car and study the route down before you proceed. If you bear too far to the left at one point your front wheels will fall off a 2-foot ledge.

If you are looking for the New Bates Wilson Camp you should bear left at the junction below the Silver Stairs; the camp is located 100 yards north of the junction. But you must turn right at this point in order to return to Elephant Hill and complete this loop. Soon after leaving the junction the road to Elephant Hill begins following a sandy wash that, after a distance of 1.4 miles, drops back into the bottom of Elephant Canyon. The road then turns south and follows the bottom

of the canyon for another 0.8 miles before joining the 2-way road over Elephant Hill. From there you must retrace your tracks for the last 1.5 miles over the hill to the Elephant Hill Picnic Area where the jeep road ends.

Side Trips from New Bates Wilson Camp

The most popular side trip from the New Bates Wilson Camp is the drive/hike to the overlook point above the confluence of the Green and Colorado Rivers. To get there you must continue driving north through Devils Lane Canyon for a distance of 2.6 miles from the camp. At the end of Devils Lane the road makes a long, sweeping turn into the north end of Cyclone Canyon where it meets the spur road to the confluence trailhead. Turn right here and follow the spur for another 1.0 mile to the trailhead. From there a short trail leads to a high vantage point above the rivers. (See page 129 for

The Silver Stairs

Elephant Hill Road

more information on this hike.)

The road through Cyclone Canyon continues south for a distance of 2.8 miles before finally reaching the southern end of the strange, flat-bottomed canyon. After 2.0 miles you will see a small sign on the right marking the beginning of the Red Lake Canyon Trail, a 4.0-mile-long footpath that ends at the Colorado River. This trail makes an interesting day hike if you have the time. It ends 3.6 miles below the confluence with the Green River, and it is not difficult to walk along the Colorado to the confluence if you are so inclined. (See page 178 for more information on the Red Lake Canyon hike.)

By now you may have noticed a similarity between Cyclone Canyon, Devils Lane, and Devils Pocket—all three canyons have unusually flat bottoms bordered by vertical walls of sandstone, and all run in roughly the same direction. If you have any interest in geology you are probably wondering how these odd canyons could have been formed. They certainly aren't the result of erosion or glaciation.

Actually there are many more nearby canyons in this part of Canyonlands with characteristics similar to Cyclone Canyon. Together they form an area known as The Grabens. If you look at a map of the area you will soon notice Cyclone Canyon is located only two miles east of Cataract Canyon, a 1,000-foot-deep gorge in the Colorado River bed. Cyclone, as well as Devils Lane and the rest, also run in the same direction as the Colorado, and that bit of information provides a strong hint as to how they were formed.

The fact is that the entire plateau, back as far as four miles from the Colorado, is slowly slipping down into Cataract Canyon. This movement is facilitated by the presence the Paradox Formation, a huge deposit of salt that lies far below the surface in this area. The deep deposit of salt provides a relatively low friction surface on which the overburden can slide. Shifting activity within the unstable, fluid-like layer of salt has also put great stress on the overlying layers of sedimentary rock, causing the land to fault and collapse into long, parallel valleys, or grabens, as it slides westward.   The land is moving very rapidly, geologically speaking, and the grabens are widening measurably, year by year, as they slide towards the river.

Side Trips from Devils Kitchen Camp

There is an excellent 5.1-mile loop hike that begins at the Devils Kitchen Camp: the Devils Pocket Loop Trail. The trail first heads south through an area known as the Devils Pocket, then skirts around the northern edge of Chesler Park and returns along the eastern rim of Elephant Canyon. (For more information see page 175).

To explore the area south of Devils Kitchen you must drive west for 0.6 mile to

Devils Lane Canyon and turn left. Drive south down Devils Lane for 1.0 mile and you will see a turnout to the right where a small panel of well preserved prehistoric pictographs attests to the fact that this area was occupied by Indians long before the arrival of Europeans. It is impossible to tell how old these pictographs are, but we know that Indians were living in the canyons at least 8,000 years ago.

Immediately after leaving the pictograph panel the road comes to another obstacle that requires some careful driving. The graben that forms the upper portion of Devils Lane ends here, and in order to continue southward the jeep trail must turn west and drop down into another nearby graben. The difference in elevation between the two canyons is only about 60 feet, but the rocky road down is very narrow and has a difficult 90-degree turn at the halfway point. Local drivers call this slope SOB Hill.

After leaving SOB Hill the road contin-

ues south for 1.0 mile to Chesler Canyon, and then turns west for another mile to a junction where a short spur departs to Chesler Park and the Joint Trailhead. The Joint Trail is one of the most interesting trails in the Needles District. A few hundred yards from the trailhead the route leads into a series of cracks, or joints, in the sandstone. It follows the bottoms of the joints, sometimes only 2-3 feet wide, for nearly 300 yards before finally climbing up a flight of primitive stone steps to the southern end of Chesler Park. This trail is actually part of a loop that extends all the way around Chesler Park, a total distance of 5.2 miles. (See page 168 for more information on this hike.)

Bobby Jo and Horsehoof Camps are 0.9 and 1.5 miles south of the turnout Chesler Park. There was once a natural arch at the Horsehoof Camp, but unfortunately it collapsed sometime in 1999. Now all that is left is a massive pile of freshly broken sandstone 100 yards west of the camp.

Cyclone Canyon

Horse and Salt Creek Canyons

☆ ☆ ☆ ☆   **4WD vehicle required**
                                                     1-day jeep ride

Distance: 20.2 miles (round trip, to all points of interest)

Road conditions: The road is generally very sandy. With a 4WD vehicle, however, it is an easy drive.

Campsites: The only established campsite in this area is the Peekaboo Camp, but camping elsewhere is not permitted. See pages 15-16 for more information about camping regulations and reservations.

Vicinity: Near the Needles Visitor Center

USGS Maps: The Loop, Druid Arch, North Six-shooter Peak, South Six-shooter Peak

Drive south of the Visitor Center for 0.9 mile, then turn left, following the signs to Cave Spring and Salt Creek. Just before the road ends at Cave Spring you will see the Salt Creek Road on your right. Turn here and drive the last 0.3 miles to the Salt Creek gate and parking area. The jeep ride begins here. The gate is normally locked, but when you obtain your permit from the visitor center you will be given the combination.

Only a limited number of vehicles are allowed into Horse and Salt Creek Canyons each day, and you must obtain a day-use permit from the Visitor Center prior to your trip. It is usually possible to obtain a permit with only a day or two of notice, but in order to avoid possible disappointment it is best to make reservations further in advance. See pages 15-16 for more information on reserving a permit.

Horse Canyon, a major tributary of Salt Creek Canyon, was probably named by the Milton family who ran horses in the canyon around 1930. There is no easy way out of the upper part of the canyon, and with a fence across the lower canyon it made a perfect enclosure. The Canyon was also important to the prehistoric Indians, and several archeological sites attest to their early habitation. Most of the ruins were built by the Anasazis, but there is also at least one panel of Fremont pictographs. Unlike Salt Creek Canyon there is now little water in Horse Canyon, but perhaps that was not the case 800 years ago when the Anasazis were growing their crops.

Before 1998 it was possible to drive 4WD vehicles up Salt Creek Canyon all the way to Angel Arch, but in an effort to better preserve the canyon ecology the road has now been closed. Hikers are still permitted

see color photos, pages 145, 147

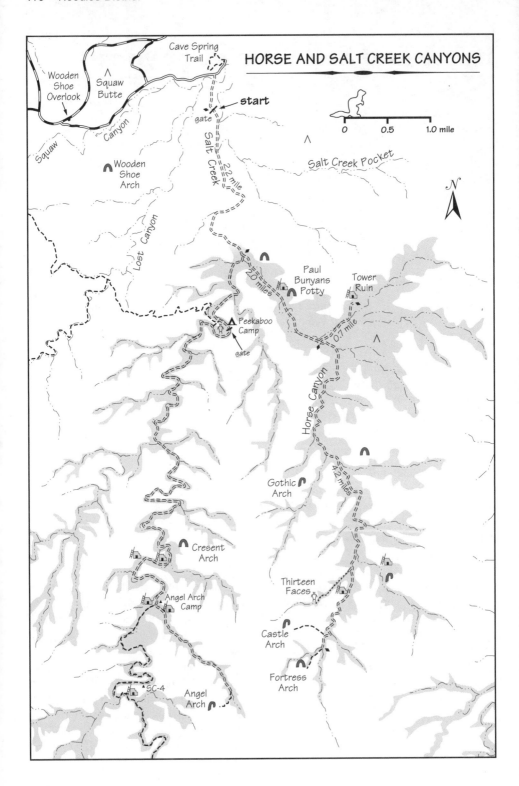

HORSE AND SALT CREEK CANYONS

Cave Spring Trail

Wooden Shoe Overlook

Squaw Butte

start

gate

Squaw Canyon

Salt Creek

Wooden Shoe Arch

Lost Canyon

Salt Creek Pocket

N

0   0.5   1.0 mile

2.2 mile

2.0 miles

Paul Bunyans Potty

Tower Ruin

Peekaboo Camp

gate

0.7 mile

Horse Canyon

4.2 miles

Gothic Arch

Cresent Arch

Thirteen Faces

Angel Arch Camp

Castle Arch

SC-4

Fortress Arch

Angel Arch

Salt Creek Road

to use upper Salt Creek Canyon, but vehicles are now allowed only as far as the Peekaboo Camp. (See page 189 for a description of the Salt Creek Trail above Peekaboo Camp.)

From the locked gate the road heads south along Salt Creek for 2.2 miles to the confluence between Salt Creek and Horse Canyons. There are generally a few pools of water along this part of the road, as well as dense groves of tamarisk. The road is also very sandy which, unfortunately, means that it is not a particularly good place for mountain bikers.

When you reach the confluence turn right and continue up Salt Creek for another 1.0 mile to the first item of interest. Just before the road ends at Peekaboo Camp there is a small parking lot and trailhead on the right, and if you walk up the trail 150 feet you can see an unusual panel of Indian pictographs. This art was probably painted sometime between 1000 and 1300 A.D. by

Fremont Indians who occasioned the area. The shield-like figures are interesting in their own right, but what makes this panel even more fascinating is the fact that the Fremont pictographs were painted over the top of another set of faint drawings that are at least one or two thousand years older. The older pictographs are a product of the Archaic People who inhabited Canyonlands from about 6000 B.C. until the time of Christ. It is easy to miss the older rock art, but if you look carefully you will immediately recognize the faint reddish-brown figures..

If you will return to the junction between Horse and Salt Creek Canyons and take the east fork you will soon come to the first of several natural arches in Horse Canyon. 0.5 mile east of the junction there is a large unnamed natural arch high on the east rim of the canyon. This arch is actually just a large hole in the top of an alcove just below the

Anasazi granary near Paul Bunyan's Potty

Tower Ruin

rim. Then another 0.5 mile will bring you to Paul Bunyan's Potty, the best known arch in the canyon. Again, Paul Bunyan's Potty consists of a large hole in the top of an alcove on the east side of the canyon. The alcove is about 150 feet in diameter, with the opening at the top about half that size. It is well named—it looks just like a giant toilet seat.

Even more interesting than Paul Bunyan's Potty is a picturesque Anasazi ruin on the same side of the canyon 100 yards northwest of the arch. The ruin is situated behind some bushes about 10 feet above the streambed. It is right beside the road but it is easy to miss while driving into the canyon; you must look back to the north to see it. Arches must have had a special significance for the ancient Indians because they often built dwellings near them.

1.0 mile after leaving Paul Bunyan's Potty you will come to a spur road on the left that leads to Tower Ruin, the canyon's best known archeological site. Turn left here

and drive 0.7 mile to a small parking area at the end of the road, then look up into the large alcove 200 feet above the canyon floor where the Anasazis resided. The site consists of at least three well preserved structures, including a square tower about 8 feet wide and 10 feet high. The tower is in excellent condition, with several 800-year-old juniper rafters still in place near the top of the walls.

If you return to the main road in Horse Canyon and continue south for 3.4 miles you will come to Trail Fork, a large side canyon that comes in on the east side of Horse Canyon. If you are in the mood for exploring, there is at least one ruin site and one natural arch in Trail Fork Canyon. The ruins are located in a small side drainage on the north side of the canyon about 0.5 mile from the road. Once in the side drainage you should be able to spot the large south-facing alcove in the cliffs where the structures are located. The arch is located on the north side of Trail Fork, about 0.3 mile southeast of the ruins.

Gothic Natural Arch

Arch Trailhead, located on the west side of the road 0.9 mile south of the Thirteen Faces Trailhead. Watch for a small sign beside the road. You can't see the arch from the road, but again, if you have an hour to spare this short hike is a fine way to stretch your legs. See page 185 for a detailed description of the hike.

By the time you reach the Castle Arch Trailhead you are almost at the end of Horse Canyon. The canyon is very narrow at this point and the streambed is cluttered with huge boulders that have rolled down from the rims. It is apparent that the road can't go much farther, and in fact is ends after only another 0.2 mile. One last item of interest awaits you at the end of the road: the short trail leading to Fortress Arch. Again, you can't see the arch from the road, but if you have the time and inclination to check out the trail you will be amply rewarded. See page 187 for more details.

There is also an old, little-used trail in the back of Trail Fork that offers access to top of the canyon rim. (This canyon was named by Michael Kelsey in 1992 after he discovered the trail. It is described more fully in his book, *Hiking, Biking and Exploring Canyonlands National Park*.)

Driving south from the mouth of Trail Fork the road passes through a large grove of cottonwood trees, and within 300 yards it reaches a fork where a short road departs on the right into a smaller canyon. You won't be able to get far into the smaller canyon; the Park Service has blocked the entrance to vehicles. Nevertheless, if you have an hour to spare it is worth parking your car for a short hike up the unnamed canyon. Your reward will be a fine panel of Fremont pictographs called the Thirteen Faces. This hike is described in more detail on page 182.

The next point of interest is the Castle

Horse Canyon Road

Lavender Canyon

☆ ☆ ☆

4WD vehicle required
1-day jeep ride

Distance:	36.6 miles (round trip)
Road conditions:	very sandy, but not technically difficult
Campsites:	The Park Service does not maintain any campsites along this route, but people occasionally camp in Lavender Canyon east of the national park boundary. After leaving Highway 211 the road crosses BLM land for 14.2 miles before reaching the park boundary.
Vicinity:	off Highway 211, in the southeast corner of the Needles District
USGS Maps:	North Six-shooter Peak, South Six-shooter Peak, Cathedral Butte, Harts Point South

Drive 7.6 miles east of the Needles entrance gate until you see an unpaved road near a sign that says "Davis Canyon". The Lavender Canyon Road begins here.

Note: Only a limited number of vehicles are allowed into Lavender Canyon each day, and you must obtain a day-use permit from the Visitor Center prior to your trip. It is usually possible to obtain a permit with only a day or two of notice, but in order to avoid possible disappointment it is best to make reservations further in advance. See pages 15-16 for more information on reserving a permit.

The eastern mountains stand in hard, sharp lines against the sunrise.... The world is awake – except the canyon, its bottom still lost in fathomless black. Slowly the sun climbs higher. Deep down the purple shadows stir and swirl. Light breaks through the blackness, tinting the walls.

David Lavender[2], 1943

Lavender Canyon was named after David Lavender, a rancher-turned-author who was an occasional guest of the nearby Dugout Ranch and knew the area well. When Canyonlands National Park was created in 1964 its boundaries were drawn to include the upper parts of Lavender Canyon, so now we can all experience a

> see color photo,
> page 144

small part of what inspired Lavender to write so eloquently about the American West.

Immediately after turning off Highway 211 you will come to an unlocked gate which

---

[2] David Lavender, *One Man's West*, University of Nebraska Press, 1977. (with permission)

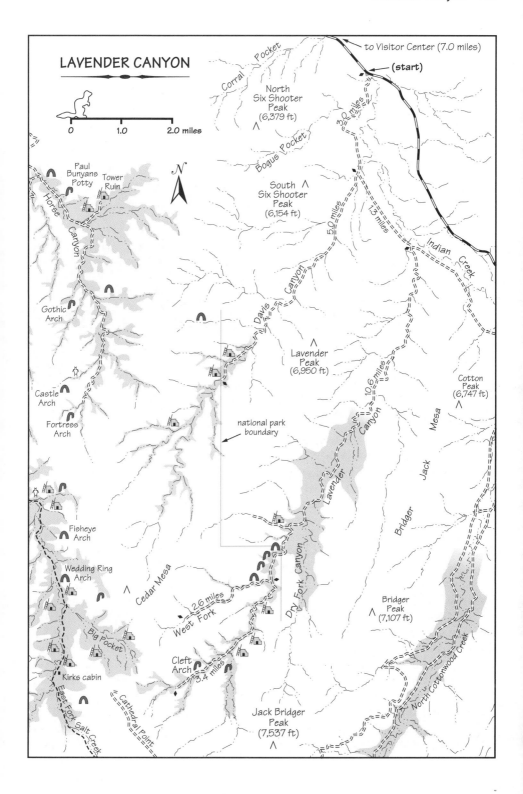

LAVENDER CANYON

0   1.0   2.0 miles

N

to Visitor Center (7.0 miles)

(start)

Corral Pocket

North Six Shooter Peak (6,379 ft)

Bogus Pocket

3.0 miles

South Six Shooter Peak (6,154 ft)

5.0 miles

1.3 miles

Indian Creek

Horse Canyon

Paul Bunyans Potty

Tower Ruin

Davis Canyon

Lavender Peak (6,950 ft)

Cotton Peak (6,747 ft)

Gothic Arch

national park boundary

10.6 miles

Lavender Canyon

Jack Mesa

Castle Arch

Fortress Arch

Fisheye Arch

Wedding Ring Arch

Cedar Mesa

Big Pocket

Kirks cabin

West Fork

2.6 miles

Cleft Arch

3.4 miles

Dry Fork Canyon

Bridger

Bridger Peak (7,107 ft)

North Cottonwood Creek

East Fork Salt Creek

Cathedral Point

Jack Bridger Peak (7,537 ft)

you must open in order to continue. Then after another 0.8 mile the road comes to an old corral where it passes through a second gate. Be sure to close both gates behind you. This section of road winds through a wide picturesque valley that is almost completely surrounded by distant cliffs of Wingate Sandstone. Indian Creek lies beneath the cottonwood trees just east of the road, and the eye-catching landmark two miles to the west is North Six-shooter Peak. From this angle the butte looks something like a giant anthill with a straw stuck in the top.

1.4 miles after leaving the corral the road drops into Davis Canyon, a shallow, sandy desert wash that at this point hardly deserves to be called a canyon. The wash is 100 feet wide, with sides that seldom exceed 5 feet in height, and the road proceeds right down the middle. If there has been a recent rain the sand is usually firm enough for easy driving, but after a few dry weeks the wash quickly turns into a sand trap that you can't get out of without a 4WD vehicle.

Unnamed natural arch in Lavender Canyon

The road continues down Davis Canyon for just 0.8 mile before coming to another fork where you must bear left to climb out the east side of the wash. From there it is another 1.3 miles across the flat desert country to Lavender Canyon. Just before reaching Lavender you will enter a grove of large cottonwood trees where there is another fork in the road. Bear right here, across a cattle guard, and continue in a southwesterly direction through the bottom of the sandy wash.

Like Davis Canyon, Lavender is initially not much of a canyon at all, but rather a shallow, featureless arroyo that meanders across the desert landscape toward the distant highlands. There is slightly more water in Lavender than Davis, however, and unless you are traveling in the middle of summer you will probably see an intermittent trickle of the life-giving liquid making its way down

canyon towards Indian Creek.

Finally, about 8.0 miles up Lavender Canyon the streambed starts to cut into the Cedar Mesa Sandstone, and the gulch begins to look more like a real canyon. Another 0.5 mile will bring you to a major confluence where Dry Fork Canyon enters Lavender from the south. The sandstone walls on either side of the confluence are about 30 feet high at this point, and the scenery is much more appealing. There is a short spur road turning into Dry Fork that passes several excellent campsites, but the ravine is too narrow for the road to go far.

Beyond Dry Fork the road soon enters the most engaging part of Lavender Canyon. The first item of interest is an Anasazi ruin just 1.0 mile beyond the Dry Fork junction. Turn right onto an obvious side road, and within 200 yards you will see a deep alcove in the sandstone cliff about 30 feet above

Cleft Arch

the canyon floor. The alcove contains the remains of at least five dwellings. The structures are well protected from the weather in the deep alcove, and must have provided a relatively comfortable shelter for a family of Indians when the Anasazis occupied this area. The road continues up a minor side canyon for another 0.9 mile beyond the ruin, but I was unable to spot any more Anasazi sites in the area.

The national park boundary is located 0.6 mile south of the alcove containing the five Anasazi dwellings, and you will not be able to continue beyond that point unless you have obtained a day-use permit from the visitor center. There is a locked gate at the boundary, and the combination to the lock is changed daily. Although camping inside the park boundary is not allowed there are many good campsites just outside the boundary, and many people choose to spend a night

outside the boundary before continuing into the park.

Watch the canyon wall on the west side of the road as you drive south from the park boundary, and within 0.5 mile you should spot at least two natural arches near the rim of the canyon. According to the USGS maps there are four arches in this area, but I was only able to find two. They are difficult to locate because from the road it is not possible to see sky through them; however if you park your car and walk 200 yards to the west you will be treated to a stunning panorama that includes two picturesque arches high on the edge of the canyon with daylight streaming through them.

After you have driven 0.6 mile from the park boundary you will come to another side road on the right that goes up the West Fork of Lavender Canyon. There is a natural arch on the right near the beginning of this road, but other than that there isn't much to see in the West Fork. The road ends after an uneventful 2.6 miles.

Continuing up Lavender Canyon from the junction with West Fork you should see at least three more Anasazi cliff dwellings. They are all situated on the left or east side of the canyon at 0.8, 1.8, and 2.0 miles from the junction, respectively. They all consist of single structures about 10 feet wide and 7 feet tall that were built in alcoves about 100 feet above the floor of the canyon. The first one is 200 yards from the road, but the others are closer and easier to see. All appear to be in excellent condition.

It is interesting to me that only one of the dwellings I have seen in Lavender Canyon is rectangular in shape; all of the others are cylindrical. I estimate that about 75 percent of the other Anasazi dwellings I have encountered in Southern Utah are rectangular; hence it would appear that some ancient architect in this area who liked round structures must have had a great deal of influence in the community!

There are also at least two natural arches south of the West Fork junction, located 2.3 and 2.9 miles from the junction respectively. The first arch is located high on the southeast rim of the canyon, and the second, called Cleft Arch, can be seen just above the north side of the road. Cleft Arch is particularly impressive. I estimate the opening to be about 120 feet wide and 80 feet tall, shaped roughly like a triangle with a 50-foot-thick bridge of sandstone above it. The road ends 0.6 miles beyond the bottom of Cleft Arch.

Davis Canyon

If you have the time and inclination to extend your trip beyond Lavender Canyon you might want to consider checking out Davis Canyon before you return to the highway. Together these two canyons make a very pleasant overnight jeep ride, and you won't have any trouble finding a good camp-

site in either canyon. The area east of the park boundary is managed by the BLM, and there are few camping restrictions.

After returning to the junction where the Lavender Canyon road leaves Davis Canyon turn left and proceed down Davis Canyon in a southerly direction. The first thing you will notice is how similar the two canyons are. Like Lavender, the lower part of Davis Canyon is little more than a sandy desert arroyo with little or no water. The road ends at the boundary of Canyonlands National Park, 5.0 miles from the junction, where a barrier has been erected to prevent cars from entering upper Davis Canyon.

Davis Canyon is also a fine area for day hiking. Like Lavender, it was once inhabited by the Anasazi Indians, and there are a number of ruin sites within the canyon as well as several natural arches. (See page 201 for more information on hiking in Davis Canyon.)

Anasazi ruin, Lavender Canyon

Roadside Ruin

☆

Distance: 0.3 miles (loop)

Walking time: ¼ hour

Elevations: 30 ft. loss/gain
Roadside Ruin Trailhead (start): 4,960 ft.
Roadside Ruin: 4,960 ft.

Trail: Well marked, easy to follow

Vicinity: Near visitor center

USGS Maps: The Loop

Drive south of the Needles Visitor Center for 0.4 mile until you see a sign marking the Roadside Ruin Trailhead and parking area on the left.

Roadside Ruin

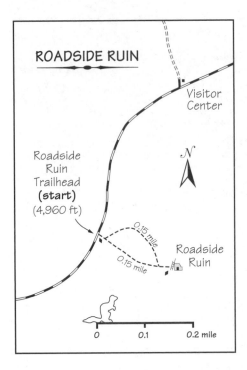

ROADSIDE RUIN

Visitor
Center

Roadside
Ruin
Trailhead
(start)
(4,960 ft)

𝒩

0.15 mile

0.15 mile

Roadside
Ruin

0   0.1   0.2 mile

high, and it was built in a small alcove where it is sheltered from the wind and the rain. Unlike most Anasazi granaries the Roadside Ruin granary's door is located on its roof, but the stone and mud construction of the walls is typical.

The Park Service maintains a developed loop trail from the road to Roadside Ruin, and even sells a trail guide near the trailhead to help you enjoy the walk. Signs posted along the way will help you to identify a few of the native plants that were used as food and medicine by the Anasazis. Each side of the loop is about 250 yards long across almost level ground.

Roadside Ruin Trail

Artifacts from the prehistoric Indians that once occupied Canyonlands are scattered throughout every district of the national park. Most of the relics are hidden away in remote canyons and alcoves, far from public sight, and hikers must often walk many miles for the opportunity to see them. But the Needles District is fortunate to have a very well-preserved prehistoric granary only a 5-minute walk from the road.

This granary was built by the Anasazi Indians who lived in the area before about 1300 A.D. They cultivated corn, squash, and beans and stored their crops in small masonary enclosures. Roadside Ruin is similar to most of the granaries they left behind. It is about 5 feet in diameter, 4 feet

Cave Spring Trail

☆ ☆ ☆ ☆

short day hike

Distance:	0.6 mile (loop)
Walking time:	¹/₄ hour
Elevations:	40 ft. gain/loss Cave Spring Trailhead (start): 4,950 ft.
Trail:	Well marked, easy to follow
Vicinity:	Near visitor center
USGS Maps:	The Loop

Drive west from the Needles Visitor Center for 0.7 miles and turn left, following the signs to Cave Spring and Salt Creek. Turn left again onto a gravel road after another 0.7 miles. The trailhead is at the end of this road, 1.0 mile from the pavement.

Cave Spring Cowboy Camp

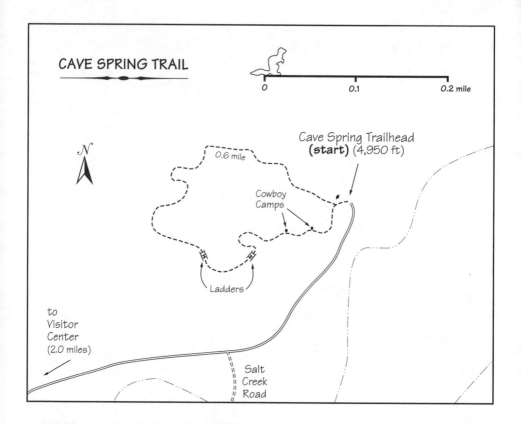

CAVE SPRING TRAIL

0   0.1   0.2 mile

Cave Spring Trailhead
(start) (4,950 ft)

0.6 mile

Cowboy
Camps

Ladders

to
Visitor
Center
(2.0 miles)

Salt
Creek
Road

A hundred years ago the cattle and sheep business was probably the most important industry in the West. That was also a time when there were virtually no laws governing where sheep and cattle could graze, and ranchers were constantly seeking new pastures for their animals. It was around 1890 when they first began bringing livestock into what is now Canyonlands National Park.

see color photo, page 146

Canyonlands was extremely remote at that time. Just to get to the pastures often required a 2-3 day ride, and cowboys frequently had to stay in the backcountry with the herd for months at a time. To make life a little more pleasant for the cowboys a series of camps were established throughout the area, and in the Needles District the Cave Spring Camp was one of the most impor-

tant.

Today the Cave Spring Camp is still largely intact, and it offers a fascinating insight into what a cowboy's life was like in the early 1900s. The camp was first established around the turn of the century, but after 1918 when the Indian Creek Cattle Company was formed it gained particular prominence. Within ten years the company had become the largest cattle operation in Utah, with its headquarters at the Dugout Ranch just 15 miles east of the national park.

Cave Spring Camp is almost the first thing you will see on this short trail. Bear left at the fork, proceeding around the loop in a clockwise direction, and you will come to the open-air cooking area just a few hundred feet from the trailhead. The kitchen consisted of a simple stove, a few wooden

Cave Spring

simple pictographs that were placed there by Indians long before the arrival of the cowboys. Water has always been a precious resource in this dry desert country, and springs like this one were used by Indian residents and hunting parties for centuries.

A few feet past the spring you will come to the first of two ladders where the trail climbs onto the low slickrock plateau above the alcoves. This portion of the hike is extraordinarily scenic as the trail winds across smooth, white sandstone for the next half-mile with views of North and South Sixshooter Peaks and the LaSal and Abajo Mountains. Finally, just before the end of the hike the route drops down from the slickrock plateau and rejoins the original trail near the trailhead.

tables, storage chests, and an odd assortment of frying pans, Dutch ovens, and other basic tools. The staple foods were rice, biscuits, canned food and, of course, coffee. Beans were appreciated, but they are hard to prepare without a good stove. Contrary to popular belief, cows were not often slaughtered because there was no way to keep the meat from spoiling. The area was fenced off to prevent horses from wandering into the camp.

Beyond the cooking area the trail passes several alcoves were the cowboys slept, and in the back of the last alcove you will see the spring that gave the camp its name. Look carefully at the soot-blackened walls of this alcove and you will see a few handprints and

Cave Spring Trail

Pothole Point

☆   **short day hike**

Distance: 0.6 mile (loop)

Walking time: ¹/₄ hour

Elevations: 30 ft. loss/gain
                     Pothole Point Trailhead (start): 5,060 ft.
                     Pothole Point: 5,060 ft.

Trail: Well marked, easy to follow

Vicinity: Near visitor center

USGS Maps: The Loop

Follow the signs from the Needles Visitor Center to Big Spring Canyon and the Confluence Overlook Trailhead. 1.5 miles from the end of the paved road, or 5.1 miles from the Visitor Center you will see a sign marking the Pothole Point Trailhead on the left side of the road.

Pothole Point

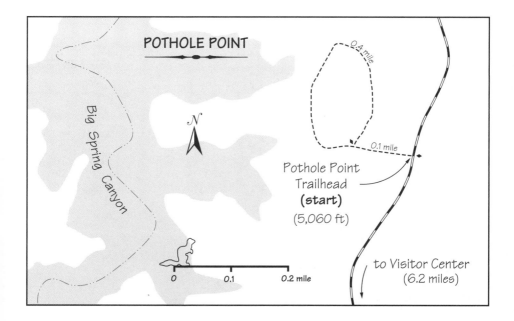

This trail is a disappointment to many because the trail guide that the Park Service distributes at the trailhead implies that the potholes are often full of water. In fact rain is so infrequent in the high desert environment, and the rainwater evaporates so quickly that the potholes rarely contain water. However, if you are lucky enough to be in the park right after a rain when the potholes are full of the precious liquid this short hike can be a memorable one.

From the parking area the trail proceeds in a westerly direction for 200 yards and then turns north to begin a 0.4-mile loop over a wide, barren expanse of sun-bleached slickrock. Near the northwestern side of the loop the trail crosses a particularly long stretch of flat, featureless sandstone that is heavily pitted with shallow depressions; hence the name Pothole Point. The potholes are the result of thousands of years of exposure to rainwater with tiny amounts of carbon dioxide dissolved in it. The solution forms a weak acid that, over time, dissolves the calcium compounds that bind the sand into stone, causing potholes to form on the flat surface.

Normally this sea of slickrock is dry, dusty and lifeless, but for perhaps 15-20 days out of the year, especially during the months of August and September, the desert calm is broken by thundershowers that fill the depressions with water. When this happens Canyonlands undergoes a series of rapid changes that are fascinating to watch. Flowers bloom, the grass turns green, and on the slickrock each water-filled pothole is suddenly transformed into a microcosm of life. Within days the pools become filled with tadpoles, mosquito larvae, snails, beetles, and other tiny organisms. Amazingly, some of these animals are able to hibernate in the sand at the bottom of the potholes for a year or more while they wait for rain. Others complete their life cycle in just a few days and then lay eggs that are programmed to hatch with the arrival of the next rain.

Slickrock Trail

☆ **short day hike**

Distance:	2.9 miles (loop)
Walking time:	1¹/₄ hours
Elevations:	80 ft. gain/loss
	Slickrock Trailhead (start): 4,980 ft.
	Viewpoint 4: 5,010 ft.
Trail:	Well marked, easy to follow
Vicinity:	Near visitor center
USGS Maps:	The Loop

Follow the signs from the Needles Visitor Center to Big Spring Canyon and the Confluence Overlook Trailhead. 0.2 mile from the end of the paved road, or 6.4 miles from the Visitor Center you will see a sign marking the Slickrock Trailhead on the right side of the road.

Needles from the Slickrock Trail

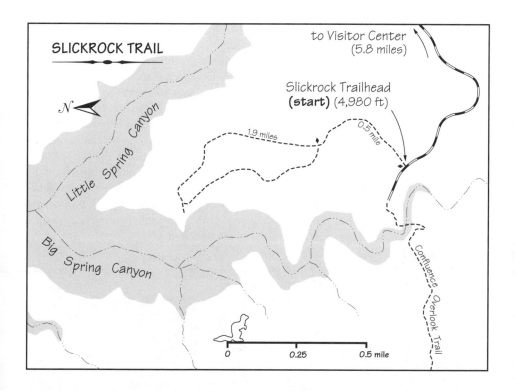

Slick rock is a Utah staple.
The eternal wind whisks the dirt
off whole hills and vales,
leaving nothing but the framework,
like a coyote with its hide peeled off.

David Lavender[3], 1943

This trail forms a big loop around the northern end of the mesa that separates Big Spring Canyon from Little Spring Canyon. It is a high, windswept tableland, very flat and very dry, with little topsoil to support any kind of vegetation. Any soil that might form from the erosion of the sandstone bedrock quickly blows away into the canyons below; consequently most of the hike is across a landscape of smooth, white slickrock with very few obstructions to impede the view.

The Park Service has designated four specific viewpoints along the way where hikers can pause to enjoy the scenery, but in fact there are many viewpoints along this trail. You don't really need the Park Service tell you where to stop; the high, open terrain presents a continuous 360-degree panorama of the surrounding countryside. The vistas are especially attractive at the end of the day when the long shadows reveal hidden patterns in the slickrock and the reddish hues of the Cedar Mesa Sandstone are accentuated.

see color photo, page 146

From the road the trail proceeds in a northeasterly direction for 0.3 mile to the first viewpoint where you will be treated to

---

[3] David Lavender, *One Man's West*, University of Nebraska Press, 1977. (with permission)

a gorgeous view of the La Sal Mountains. The mountains are 40 miles away, but the air is usually so clear in this remote part of the United States that they look much closer. After leaving the first viewpoint the trail turns north for another 0.2 miles, where you will see a primitive sign marking the beginning of the loop.

Bear right at the sign and soon you will see another sign directing you to the second viewpoint overlooking Little Spring Canyon. The trail becomes somewhat rockier in this area as it climbs toward the northern end of the mesa. Again, the dominant view is of the La Sal Mountains. Two other prominent mountain ranges can be seen from the Slickrock Trail, the Abajo Range to the south and the Henry Mountains to the west. But the picturesque La Sals are the peaks that seem best to catch the eye. They are the second highest range of mountains in Utah, after the Uintas in the north, and they are usually covered with snow well into the summer.

Next the third viewpoint will appear on your right, again overlooking Little Spring Canyon, then soon afterward the trail turns west to the other side of the mesa. You may want to do some off-trail hiking at this point to get nearer the confluence of Big and Little Spring Canyons. But if you follow the cairns you will soon come to the fourth and last viewpoint overlooking Big Spring Canyon. Big Spring Canyon is deeper and more rugged that Little spring Canyon, but in my opinion the views to the west are not as majestic as those to the east.

Viewpoint 4 is roughly at the halfway point on this hike. From there the trail starts southward again along the rim of Big Spring Canyon. This part of the hike is notable because the greatest concentration of needles in Canyonlands is south of the trail, and as you walk back to the trailhead the horizon will seem to be filled with needles. The view to the south is particularly beautiful at sunset, when the color of the needles turns to deep red.

After you have gone 0.7 miles from the last viewpoint the trail descends a small hill to the beginning of the loop, and from there you can retrace your steps the last 0.5 mile to the trailhead.

Slickrock Trail and the Abajo Mountains

Confluence Overlook

☆ **day hike**

Distance:	10.4 miles (round trip)
Walking time:	6 hours
Elevations:	220 ft. loss/gain
	Big Spring Canyon Trailhead (start): 4,940 ft.
	Big Spring Canyon: 4,820 ft.
	Overlook point: 4,920 ft.
Trail:	Easy well marked trail, but no water.
Vicinity:	6.5 miles west of Needles Visitor Center.
USGS Maps:	The Loop, Spanish Bottom

Follow the signs west from the visitor center to Big Spring Canyon and the Confluence Overlook Trailhead. The trailhead is located at the end of the road, 6.5 miles from the visitor center.

Alternatively, you can begin your hike from a trailhead located near the New Bates Wilson Camp on the Elephant Hill jeep road. The overlook point is only 0.5 mile from that trailhead, but to get there you will need a 4WD vehicle. See page 103 for more information on the Elephant Hill Road.

Canyonlands, the largest of Utah's five national parks, is neatly split into thirds by the intersection of the Green and the Colorado Rivers. Both rivers have carved thousand-foot-deep canyons through the high surrounding desert, and the view of their confluence at the center of the park is one of Canyonlands' most impressive sights.

Both of the famous rivers have now been largely tamed by a series of dams built over the last sixty years, but from this prospective one can still see the same wild scene that John Wesley Powell saw during his historical voyage down the Green and Colorado Rivers in 1869. In July of that year, while his party was camped on the north side of the confluence, Powell and one of his men climbed above the rivers to a point just south of the present day overlook trail. In the following passage, first printed in Scribner's Monthly in 1875, Powell describes what he saw:

From the north-west came the Green in a narrow, winding gorge. From the north-east came the Grand [Colorado] through a canyon that seemed, from where we stood, bottomless.... Wherever we looked there was a wilderness of rocks—deep gorges where the rivers

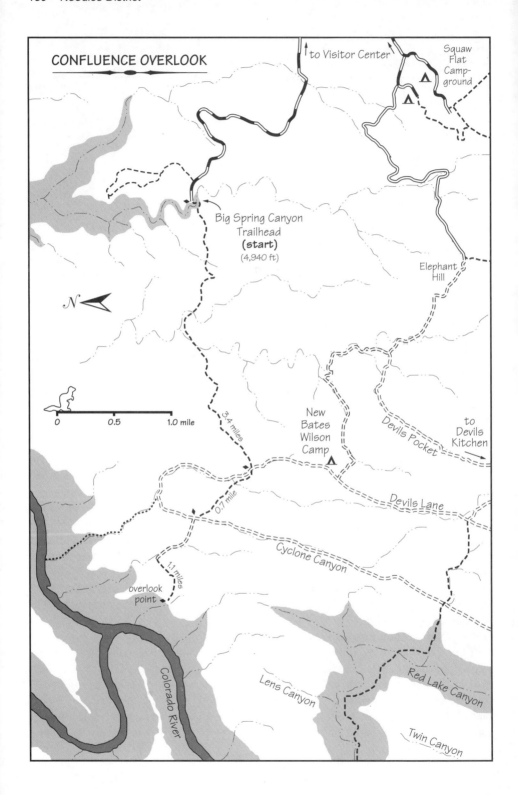

CONFLUENCE OVERLOOK

to Visitor Center

Squaw Flat Camp-ground

Big Spring Canyon Trailhead **(start)** (4,940 ft)

Elephant Hill

N

0   0.5   1.0 mile

3.4 miles

New Bates Wilson Camp

Devils Pocket

to Devils Kitchen

0.7 mile

Devils Lane

1.1 miles

Cyclone Canyon

overlook point

Colorado River

Lens Canyon

Red Lake Canyon

Twin Canyon

Elephant Canyon from the Confluence Overlook Trail

are lost below cliffs, and towers, and pinnacles, and ten thousand strangely carved forms in every direction, and beyond them mountains blending with the clouds.[4]

From the trailhead the path immediately drops into Big Spring Canyon and then climbs up the other side. This is really the only strenuous part of the route, but it doesn't last long. Big Spring Canyon is only 120 feet deep at this point. After leaving Big Spring Canyon the trail meanders pleasantly across the open desert for another 3.1 miles before crossing a jeep road at the northern end of another shallow canyon called Devils Lane. After another 0.7 mile the trail crosses the road again as the road doubles back into Cyclone Canyon. At the point where the trail meets the jeep road the

second time you will see another spur road branching off to the west. The trail continues down this road.

After walking west on the spur road for 0.6 miles you will come to a dead end, where there is a small outhouse and a parking area for jeeps. A Park Service sign points the way to the trail that will lead you the last 0.5 mile to the overlook point.

The Colorado River

After seeing the rivers from the overlook point, many hikers feel a great urge to descend into the canyon to the shore of the Colorado. There are at least two ways to do this. Three if you include Powell's route, but I would hardly recommend his way down. It is quite exposed and requires some rock climbing skills. (Amazingly, Powell did it with only one arm! He had lost his

---

[4] John Wesley Powell, *The Canyons of the Colorado*, reprinted by Outbooks, Golden, Colorado, 1981.

right arm 7 years earlier in the Civil War.)

The easiest way to get to the Colorado River is on the Lower Red Lake Canyon Trail. This trail begins 2.4 miles further south on the road into Cyclone Canyon and ends at the river 3.6 miles below the confluence. (See page 178 for more information on this trail.)

For the adventurous there is another route to the Colorado River that departs from the northern end of Cyclone Canyon. Return to the point where the Overlook Trail crosses the Cyclone Canyon jeep road and follow the road north for 0.5 mile. The road starts out heading almost due north, and then swings around to the east. Just after the turn to the east you will see the beginning of a drainage that heads off in a northwesterly direction towards the river. You can follow this drainage all the way to the Colorado River. The route involves about 1.5 miles of off-trail hiking, but many hikers have gone before you and the way is clearly marked by cairns. The route becomes very steep as you approach the water and some scrambling is necessary, but the danger is minimal if you are careful to follow the cairns. Once you reach the Colorado it is another 0.9 mile walk downstream to the confluence itself.

Confluence of the Green and Colorado Rivers

Peekaboo Trail

Distance: 10.4 miles (round trip), or
5.2 miles (one way to Peekaboo Camp)

Walking time: 6¹/₂ hours (round trip)
3 hours (one way)

Elevations: 560 ft. loss, 500 ft. gain (one way)
Squaw Flat Trailhead (start):   5,120 ft.
Lost Canyon: 5,100 ft.
Peekaboo Camp: 5,060 ft.

Trail: Well marked, easy to follow

Vicinity: Begins at Squaw Flat Campground

USGS Maps: The Loop, Druid Arch

---

*Follow the signs from the Visitor Center to Squaw Flat Campground, Section A.
Near the end of the road you will see a parking area on the left near a sign
marking the Squaw Flat Trailhead. This is where the hike begins.*

*The hike ends at Peekaboo Camp which is accessible via the Salt Creek jeep
road; hence if you don't want to do the round-trip hike it is possible to arrange a
shuttle from Peekaboo Camp back to the beginning trailhead. Traffic on the Salt Creek Road
is strictly regulated, however, so you will need a permit to drive a vehicle to Peekaboo Camp.
Furthermore the road is not suitable for 2WD cars. See pages 15-16 for more information
on obtaining a day-use permit for the Salt Creek Road or a camping permit for the Peekaboo
Camp. See page 109 for more information on the Salt Creek Road.*

This interesting trail connects Squaw Flat Campground with the road through lower Salt Creek Canyon. An ideal way to enjoy the hike is in combination with an overnight car camp at Peekaboo Camp on the Salt Creek Road followed by a jeep ride out the next day. Most people, however, do it as a round trip from the Squaw Flat Campground in a single day.

The route crosses two other canyons on the way to Salt Creek, and some minor scrambling is required in a few places to get in and out of the streambeds. The last half of the trail is the most interesting, as the trail navigates its way

see color photos, pages 146, 147

across the frozen sea of slickrock separating Lost Canyon from Salt Creek Canyon. The area is a labyrinth of sandstone canyons and side canyons, which the trail

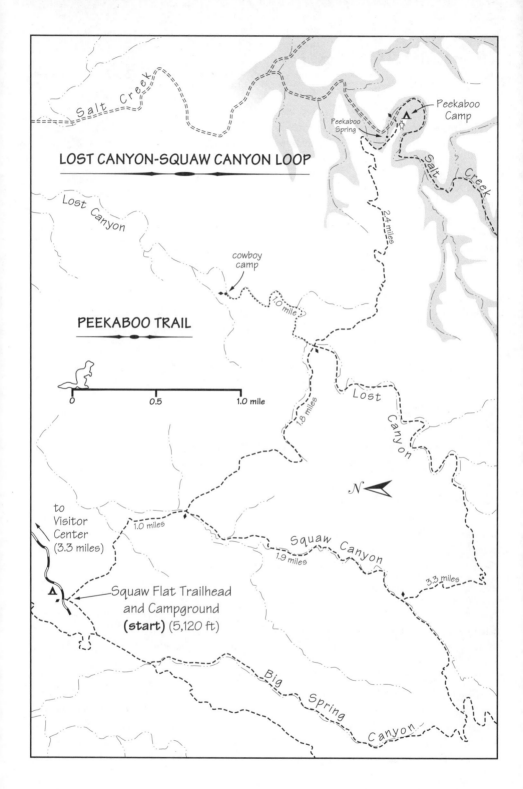

Salt Creek

Peekaboo Camp

Peekaboo Spring

LOST CANYON-SQUAW CANYON LOOP

Lost Canyon

Salt Creek

2.4 miles

cowboy camp

PEEKABOO TRAIL

1.0 mile

0   0.5   1.0 mile

Lost Canyon

1.8 miles

N

to Visitor Center (3.3 miles)

1.0 miles

Squaw Canyon

1.9 miles

3.3 miles

Squaw Flat Trailhead and Campground **(start)** (5,120 ft)

Big Spring Canyon

avoids by following a tortuous route across the ledges and benches above the canyon rims.

Bear left at the junction 150 feet from the trailhead and begin the hike by walking in a southeasterly direction across the broad expanse of Squaw Flat. The desert terrain is uncharacteristically gentle for the first 1.5 miles, with only an occasional outcropping of sandstone along the way, but that will change soon. After 0.7 mile the trail begins skirting along the west side of a dry wash, which it crosses ten minutes later. This is Squaw Canyon, although at this point it is not really much of a canyon.

Finally, 1.7 miles from the trailhead, the trail leaves Squaw Flat and begins to enter the rugged up-and-down country that surrounds Lost Canyon. The path first climbs a low sandstone ridge, then skirts around the north side of a small canyon, and finally,

Slickrock on Peekaboo Trail

Peekaboo Trail, near Lost Canyon

with the help of a short ladder, descends to the sandy streambed below. It then proceeds down the unnamed side canyon for the next 0.8 miles to the bottom of Lost Canyon.

Lost Canyon was an important location for the early ranchers who ran cattle in the Needles District during the first part of the last century. It was important because it is one of the few canyons in this area that contains a relatively reliable water source. The cowboys maintained a permanent camp in Lost Canyon which can still be seen today. See page 162 for more information about this camp and how to get there.

You will be in Lost Canyon only briefly before climbing out its east side, and from that point to the end of the hike your feet will touch almost nothing but stone. From there the trail stays high on the canyon rims, winding around the depressions and high spots in an attempt to gain and loose as little elevation as possible. From Lost Canyon to Salt Creek Canyon is only 1.2 miles by air, but the distance by trail is twice that. None of the intervening canyons are more than 200 feet deep, but climbing in and out of them would be very impractical. The route taken by the trail, while not the shortest way, is the path of least energy.

A few hundred yards before it reaches Salt Creek Canyon the trail enters a crack in the sandstone where the Park Service has placed another short ladder to facilitate the descent. From there the trail, once again on dirt, continues down a short distance to the flat sandy floor of the canyon. Peekaboo Camp is just 100 feet south of the end of the trail.

Just before reaching Salt Creek Road the trail passes below an interesting panel of Indian pictographs. If you look up to your right you can easily see them from the trail. This art was painted on the cliff face by members of the Fremont culture sometime before 1300 AD. The white, shield-like drawings are typical of Fremont art, although there is no evidence that the Fremonts ever established permanent dwellings in the canyon. Look carefully and you will see that the drawings were laid down over the top of another very faint collection of reddish-brown paintings that are obviously much older. In fact the underlying art was painted on the cliff face at least a thousand years before the Fremont artist deposited his work. It was placed there by the Archaic People who lived in these canyons between 2,000 and 8,000 years ago. Please be careful not to touch or otherwise damage the ancient paintings.

Peekaboo Trail, near Salt Creek Canyon

Top: *Soda Springs Basin, from the Murphy Hogback (pages 23, 55)*
Bottom Left: *Monster Tower and Washerwoman Arch above White Rim Road (page 23)*
Bottom Right: *Monument Basin below the White Rim Road (page 23)*

Top: *Green River at Beaver Bottom, from the White Rim Road (page 23)*
Bottom Left: *Colorado River Overlook, from the White Rim Road (page 23)*
Bottom Right: *Monument Basin, from the White Rim Overlook (pages 23, 59)*

Top: *Green River near Hardscrabble Camp (page 23)*
Bottom: *Soda Springs Basin, from the Green River Overlook (page 23)*

139

Top: *Water-filled potholes, from the Lathrop Trail (page 44)*
Bottom: *Junction Butte, from Murphy Wash Trail Junction (page 55)*

Top: *Monument Basin, from the Grandview Trail (page 61)*
Bottom Left: *Junction Butte, from Murphy Point (page 51)*
Bottom Right: *Aztek Butte Trail (page 62)*

Top: *Anasazi Granary on Aztec Butte (page 62)*
Bottom: *Trail Canyon below Alcove Spring (page 78)*

Top: *Jumbled debris in the center of Upheaval Crater (pages 75, 85)*
Bottom Left: *Moses and Zeus Rocks (pages 78, 80)*
Bottom Right: *Desert bighorn sheep in Upheaval Crater (pages 75, 85)*

Top: *Green River, from the Fort Bottom Trail (page 87)*
Bottom Left: *White Crack Trail (page 92)*
Bottom Right: *Anasazi Ruin in Lavender Canyon (page 114)*

Top: *Paul Bunyan's Potty, Horse Canyon (page 109)*
Bottom: *Chesler Canyon (pages 103, 169)*

Top: *Peekaboo Trail near Lost Canyon (pages 133, 162)*
Bottom Left: *Cave Spring Trail (page 122)*
Bottom Right: *Slickrock Trail (page 127)*

Top: *Salt Creek Canyon and Peekaboo Camp, from Peekaboo Trail (pages 109, 133, 200)*
Bottom: *Fremont pictographs near Peekaboo Camp (pages 109, 133, 200)*

147

Top: *Lost Canyon – Squaw Canyon Loop Trail (page 162)*
Bottom Left: *Big Spring Canyon – Elephant Canyon Loop Trail (page 164)*
Bottom Right: *Big Spring Canyon – Elephant Canyon Loop Trail (page 164)*

Top: *Chesler Park (page 171)*
Bottom: *Elephant Canyon, near Druid Arch (page 174)*

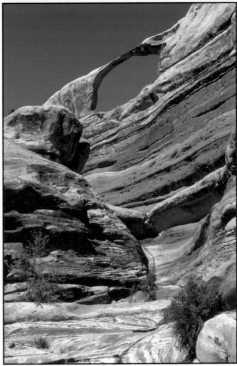

Top: *LaSal Mountains, from Chesler Park Trail (pages 171, 177)*
Bottom Left: *Elephant Canyon (pages 164, 174)*
Bottom Right: *Castle Arch, Horse Canyon (page 186)*

Top: *Angel Arch, Salt Creek Canyon (page 190)*
Bottom: *All American Man Pictograph Panel (page 190)*

151

Top: *Petroglyphs near confluence of Salt Creek and West Fork (page 190)*
Bottom Left: *Pottary shards below Big Ruins, Salt Creek Canyon (page 190)*
Bottom Right: *Anasazi Granary above Eightmile Spring in Davis Canyon (page 201)*

Top: *Panorama Point, from Millard Canyon Benches (page 211)*
Bottom: *Rainwater filled potholes near Ekker Butte (page 211)*

Top: *Green River at the mouth of Millard Canyon (page 211)*
Bottom: *Elaterite Butte and Elaterite Basin (page 211)*

Top: *Dollhouse Rock (page 233)*
Bottom: *North Trail Canyon (page 234)*

Top: *Maze Overlook Trail (page 244)*
Bottom: *Green River and Anderson Bottom, from the White Rim Road (pages 35, 247)*

Top: *The Chocolate Drops, from the bottom of Pictograph Fork (pages 244, 252, 253)*
Bottom: *The Land of Standing Rocks (pages 226, 252)*

Top: *Sunset behind Chimney Rock (pages 226, 253, 257)*
Bottom: *Trail between Shot and Water Canyons (page 257)*

Top: *Green and Colorado Rivers Overlook Trail (page 262)*
Bottom Left: *The Maze near Chimney Rock Trailhead (pages 253, 257)*
Bottom Right: *Water Canyon (page 257)*

Top: *Colorado River and Lower Red Lake Canyon, from Spanish Bottom (pages 181, 265)*
Bottom: *Pictograph panel in Horseshoe Canyon (page 279)*

Lost Canyon–Squaw Canyon Loop

☆ ☆   **day hike**

Distance:	9.0 miles (loop)
Walking time:	5¼ hours
Elevations:	360 ft. gain/loss
	Squaw Flat Trailhead (start): 5,120 ft.
	Lost Canyon: 5,100 ft.
	highest point: 5,460 ft.
Trail:	Easy, well marked trail. There is usually water in some sections of Lost Canyon, but Squaw Canyon is generally dry.
Vicinity:	Near Squaw Flat Campground
USGS Maps:	Druid Arch, The Loop

From the Needles Visitor Center just follow the signs to Squaw Flat Campground, Section A. Near the end of the road you will see a parking area and a sign marking the Squaw Flat Trailhead.

Although they are scarcely a mile apart Lost Canyon and Squaw Canyon are very different in character. Squaw Canyon is dry and generally uninteresting, while Lost Canyon is deeper and has a surprising amount of water and vegetation. Because of its water, Lost Canyon was well known to the cowboys who lived and worked in the Needles District during the first half of the last century. Even when other sources of water had given way to the dry summer heat, their animals could always depend on finding a pool or two of the life-sustaining liquid in the green recesses of Lost Canyon.

The route described here takes advantage of the Peekaboo Trail, which cuts across the lower parts of both canyons, to form an interesting loop hike. The path also passes within a mile of an old cowboy camp that was once used by local cattle ranchers. There is no trail leading to the cowboy camp, but it isn't too difficult to find. If you wish to include it in your hike it will add about an hour to the time specified above.

see map, page 134

After leaving Squaw Flat Campground the trail proceeds southward for about 150 feet, then splits. Turn left at the fork, following the signs to Lost and Squaw Canyons. The trail winds across the flat desert country for another 1.0 mile before reaching a junction in the bottom of the Squaw

Canyon drainage. This junction marks the beginning of the loop through the two canyons. It doesn't make much difference which direction you take around the loop, but I will describe a clockwise direction here with the initial part of the walk through Lost Canyon and the return through Squaw Canyon.

After crossing Squaw Canyon the trail continues for another mile before dropping down a slickrock slope into the head of a small, unnamed arroyo. It then winds along the sandy bottom of the ravine for another 0.8 mile before coming to a three-way junction in the middle of a large intersecting wash. A Park Service sign in the wash will tell you that you have reached Lost Canyon.

If you wish to take a detour to the historic Lost Canyon cowboy camp you will have to leave the trail at this point and begin walking down the canyon in a northerly direction. (This side trip is described below in more detail.) Otherwise, turn right here and continue south along the trail that heads up the bottom of Lost Canyon.

The trail continues up Lost Canyon for a distance of 2.0 miles before climbing out the northwest side to the top of a ridge that separates Lost Canyon from Squaw Canyon. From there the path immediately drops back down to the bottom of Squaw Canyon and proceeds north for 1.9 miles to the beginning of the loop. Finally, you must retrace your steps the last 1.0 mile back to the Squaw Flat Trailhead.

see color photos, pages 146, 148

The Lost Canyon Cowboy Camp

Cattle ranching was much different in the early 1900s than it is today. There were few motor vehicles and fewer roads to drive them on; consequently tending cattle often meant spending weeks or even months away from home. For many of the cowhands the range was home, and they often tried to establish semi-permanent camps where they could rest

Lost Canyon Trail

and cook their food nearer their work. Cave Spring, near the Visitor Center was one of these camps; the Lost Canyon Camp was another.

To get to the Lost Canyon cowboy camp you must turn north at the point where the Peekaboo Trail crosses the bottom of Lost Canyon and hike down the dry streambed for 1.0 mile. The going is difficult in a few places because of the thick underbrush that now grows in the canyon, but if you try to stay just above the streambed on the west side you will encounter less brush. Don't look for a trail; there is none.

After you have been walking for 25 minutes start watching the left bank for a large alcove. The alcove lies behind a row of cottonwood trees 50 feet northwest of the streambed and about 20 feet higher. Unfortunately the underbrush makes it impossible to see the floor of the alcove from the canyon bottom, but if you look carefully you can see some of the cowboy graffiti higher up in the back of the alcove. The alcove is about 150 feet long, 25 feet deep and 30 feet high. It is well protected from the rain, and must have once been a very comfortable home away from home.

It appears that little has changed in the Lost Canyon camp for many decades. The old grub box where the old-timers once stored their food is still there, and there is even a small table nearby as well as many old cans, bottles, boxes, and pieces of Dutch ovens and other cooking implements. There is an old steel drum still half filled with grain that the cowboys must have used to feed their horses, and in one corner a big pile of hay where someone must have made his bed.

But perhaps the most interesting part of the old cowboy camp is the cowboy graffiti on the walls. The rocks are adorned with several charcoal drawings of horses, numerous names and initials, and even what appears to be a wanted poster for Negro Bill, a black cattle rancher who lived in Moab dur-

ing the late 1800s. The oldest dated signature I could see on the walls was "Ellis Hatch, 1919".

What fascinating tales the walls of the sheltered camp would tell if they could talk. We can only image the long-forgotten men that must have gathered here in days past, and the yarns they must have exchanged to pass the lonely nights. Now all that remains is a small collection of artifacts, signatures, and drawings, but these simple treasures offer a priceless window through which visitors can imagine what life in the camp was like so long ago. Enjoy their presence, but please don't be tempted to remove anything. Here the relics are treasures, but in another context they would be of little value to anyone. Also, refrain from the urge to add your name to the signatures the old cowboys scratched onto the walls of the alcove. Leave the Lost Canyon cowboy camp as you find it, so that others too can enjoy this rare connection with Utah's past.

Lost Canyon Cowboy Camp

Big Spring Canyon–Elephant Canyon

☆ ☆ ☆ ☆ ☆   **day hike**

Distance:	10.9 miles (loop)
Walking time:	6¼ hours
Elevations:	490 ft. loss/gain
	Squaw Flat Trailhead (start): 5,120 ft.
	Elephant Canyon: 5,240 ft.
	highest point: 5,550 ft.
Trail:	Well marked, easy to follow
Vicinity:	Near Squaw Flat Campground
USGS Maps:	The Loop, Druid Arch

The trailhead and parking area are located on the south side of Squaw Flat Campground near the campground pay station.

There are at least three nice loop hikes beginning at the Squaw Flat Trailhead. Each has its own rewards, but if I had to choose a favorite I think I would name the one described here as the best of the three. The trail passes through three major canyons and several minor ones where a half-dozen springs make water [see color photos, pages 148, 150] available for most of the year. Numerous outcroppings of huge sandstone needles, banded with streaks of red and white, make the rugged terrain extremely attractive, and, as the map suggests, several interesting side trips are possible if you wish to extend the length of the hike.

There are numerous points of interest along this trail, but the two-mile section from Squaw Canyon to the top of Big Spring Canyon is particularly exciting. This area is a fantasyland of slickrock. Like a giant outdoor funhouse, it has steep wavelike slides, spiraling redrock slot canyons, and several ladders bolted into the rock to help you up ledges and down dropoffs. In short, this hike is not only incredibly scenic, it is also a lot of fun.

Begin by walking south from the Squaw Flat Trailhead, then bear right at the first junction 150 feet from the trailhead. After another ten minutes you will see another trail coming in on the right from Squaw Flat Campground "B". Bear left here following

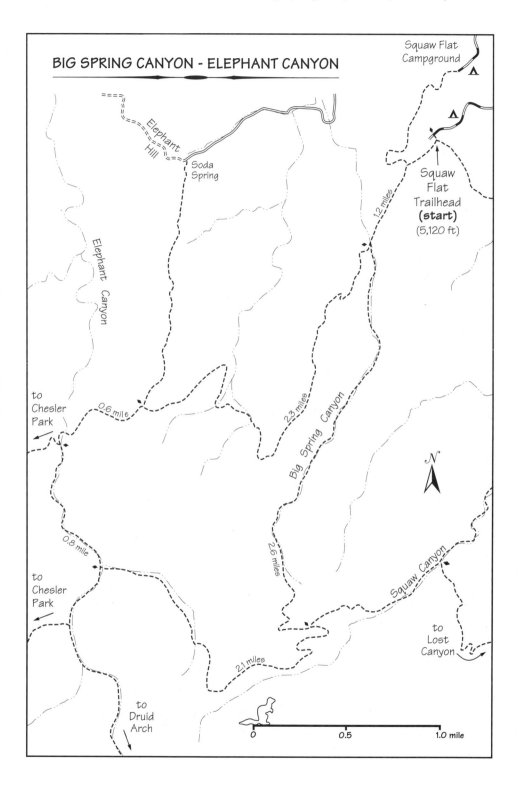

BIG SPRING CANYON - ELEPHANT CANYON

Squaw Flat
Campground

Elephant
Hill

Soda
Spring

Elephant Canyon

Squaw Flat
Trailhead
(start)
(5,120 ft)

1.2 miles

to
Chesler
Park

0.6 mile

2.3 miles

Big Spring Canyon

N

to
Chesler
Park

0.8 mile

2.6 miles

Squaw Canyon

to
Lost
Canyon

2.1 miles

to
Druid
Arch

0   0.5   1.0 mile

Looking down into Squaw Canyon

the signs to Big Spring Canyon. Finally, at a distance of 1.2 miles from the road, the trail dips down to cross Big Spring Canyon. The canyon is little more than a shallow desert ravine at this point, although there is a spring nearby and the streambed often contains water. You will also encounter another trail junction in the bottom of the ravine, where you must bear right. The trail on the left is the one you will use on the second half of this hike to complete the loop from Elephant Canyon back to the trailhead.

The first 3.5 miles of this hike are across relatively flat, open desert, but upon leaving Big Spring Canyon the terrain begins to acquire a more rugged character, dipping in and out of small arroyos and crossing frequent outcroppings of sandstone. About 40 minutes after leaving Big Spring Canyon you will come to a large pool of water in a shady spot beside the trail. Listen carefully and you can hear water gurgling into it from a hidden spring under the surrounding rocks. This is the largest spring you will see on the hike. Finally the route converges with the Chesler Park Trail coming in from the Elephant Hill Trailhead, and soon afterward it drops into the bottom of Elephant Canyon. You will be hiking through canyons now for most of the remainder of the hike.

After dropping into Elephant Canyon the trail turns left into the sandy streambed and continues in a southerly direction for the next 1.0 mile. Stay in the canyon bottom as you walk past the junction with the Chesler Park Trail, then, 20 minutes later you will come to another junction where you must turn left into a smaller side canyon. This unnamed canyon provides a route to the rim above Squaw Canyon where, in my opinion, the best part of the hike begins.

After 1.0 mile the trail climbs out the left side of the unnamed canyon and makes its way to the top of the ridge separating it from Squaw Canyon. The trail gets steeper and steeper as it approaches the ridge, ultimately reaching a point where a ladder be-

Big Spring Canyon Trail

comes necessary to get up the last 10 feet. The route then crosses the top of the slickrock ridge and, with the help of another steel ladder, drops down the other side to a bench above Squaw Canyon.

The cairned trail never actually enters Squaw Canyon, but continues along the bench above its west side for 0.6 mile to the Squaw Canyon/Big Spring Canyon trail junction. Here you must turn left and climb up over another long sloping ridge of slickrock to get into Big Spring Canyon. The climb is steep but not difficult, and once the trail reaches the top of the ridge it immediately plunges down the other side across another smooth, unfractured surface of weathered sandstone. There is a certain beauty in the gently curving surface of the white and pink stone. It contains no abrupt angles and no straight lines—only smooth curves. The scene reminds me of a three dimensional graph of some complex differential equation.

After a long tortuous route downward over the slickrock the trail finally reaches the bottom of Big Spring Canyon and then proceeds to work its way northward to the beginning of the loop. You will recognize the junction where the trail finally leaves the canyon. From there you can retrace your footsteps the last 1.2 miles back to the trailhead.

Big Spring Canyon Trail

Chesler Park

☆ ☆ ☆ ☆ ☆   **day hike**

Distance:	10.9 miles (loop)
Walking time:	6 hours
Elevations:	500 ft. gain/loss Elephant Hill Trailhead (start): 5,120 ft. Chesler Park: 5,600 ft.
Trail:	Well marked and well maintained. A short portion of this hike is over a jeep road east of Chesler Park.
Vicinity:	The trailhead is at the Elephant Hill picnic area.
USGS Maps:	Druid Arch, The Loop

Follow the signs from the Needles Visitor Center to Elephant Hill where you will see the trailhead and parking area at the end of the graded road. The distance is 6.0 miles, with the last 3.0 miles unpaved.

Deep inside the rugged Needles District of Canyonlands lies an unexpected refuge of gentle grassland called Chesler Park. The flat, circular-shaped park, or meadow, is about a mile in diameter and is almost completely surrounded by towering needles of pink sandstone. Before 1964 this area was used by the Dugout Ranch as a grazing pasture for cattle, and the remnants of an old cowboy camp can still be seen on the southern side of the park. The ranchers even flew small airplanes into the park on occasion, but any signs of the old landing strip have long since disappeared. It has been more than a quarter century since cattle were grazed in Chesler Park, and the sandy meadow has once again been reclaimed by a thick growth of grasses and desert shrubs.

The trail described here begins at the Elephant Hill Trailhead and heads south to the northeast side of Chesler Park. It then circles the perimeter of the park before returning to Elephant Hill. As the map suggests, however, there are several other possible routes to Chesler Park. One particularly nice overnight hike combines a visit to Chesler Park with the Big Spring Canyon—Elephant Canyon loop (page 164). Another possibility is to do the Druid Arch hike (page 173) as an overnighter with a camp in Chesler Park. There are five backcountry campsites in Chesler Park and spending a night in one of them can be a memorable experience. Sites CP-4 and CP-5 are particularly interesting; they are located near the old cowboy camp on the southern side of the park. See pages 15-16 for more information on obtaining backcountry permits and reserving campsites.

If you have a 4WD vehicle you can begin your hike from the Chesler Park Trailhead in Chesler Canyon. The hike from the jeep road around the perimeter of Chesler Park is only 5.3 miles long, and many people walk the loop in conjunction with the Elephant Hill jeep ride (page 103).

see color photo, page 145

After leaving Elephant Hill the trail follows the ridge above Elephant Canyon for a distance of 1.3 miles before turning west. The ridge is a fantasyland of needles and pinnacles, and the trail follows a tortuous route through the confused landscape as it works its way south. After 40 minutes the path intersects the trail from Squaw Flat where you must turn right. Then a short

distance later you will come to a steep, rocky section of trail that ends on the sandy bottom of Elephant Canyon. You should see a sign nearby marking backcountry campsite EC-1.

Elephant Canyon contains a number of springs, and water can usually be found in intermittent pools along the canyon bottom. This is a useful thing to know if you plan to camp in the area; there is no water in Chesler Park. The Elephant Canyon trail stays in the bottom of the canyon all the way to Druid Arch, but almost immediately after entering the canyon you will see a sign marking the turnoff to Chesler Park. You must turn right at the sign and climb out through a minor side canyon to the slickrock plateau above the west side of Elephant Canyon.

Soon after leaving Elephant Canyon the path intersects the Devils Kitchen trail, where you must turn left. This is a particularly pretty area, with a dense outcropping

Chesler Park

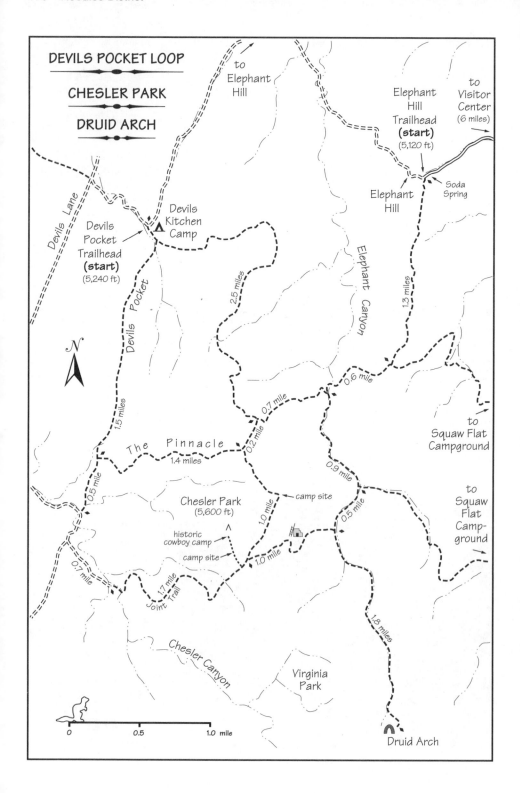

DEVILS POCKET LOOP

CHESLER PARK

DRUID ARCH

to
Elephant
Hill

Elephant
Hill
Trailhead
(start)
(5,120 ft)

to
Visitor
Center
(6 miles)

Soda
Spring

Elephant
Hill

Devils
Lane

Devils
Kitchen
Camp

Devils
Pocket
Trailhead
(start)
(5,240 ft)

Devils Pocket

2.5 miles

Elephant Canyon

1.3 miles

N

1.5 miles

0.6 mile

0.7 mile

0.2 mile

The Pinnacle
1.4 miles

0.9 mile

to
Squaw Flat
Campground

0.5 mile

camp site

1.0 mile

0.5 mile

Chesler Park
(5,600 ft)

to
Squaw
Flat
Camp-
ground

historic
cowboy camp

camp site

1.0 mile

0.5 mile

0.7 mile

1.7 mile

Joint Trail

1.8 miles

Chesler Canyon

Virginia
Park

0   0.5   1.0 mile

Druid Arch

of needles called the Pinnacle nearby and a fine view of the La Sal Mountain to the northeast. From the junction the trail climbs up through a narrow opening on the northeast side of the Pinnacle and reemerges on the northern edge of Chesler Park.

After hiking through the jumble of vertical sandstone monoliths that surround Chesler Park you will probably be astonished to see the flat, sandy meadowland south of the Pinnacle. What is the explanation for this geological oddity? The unlikely existence of Chesler Park is one of the many mysteries that make Canyonlands such a delightful place to visit.

My guess is that Chesler Park is an ancient sinkhole that has filled with sand. Most of Canyonlands lies above a deep subterranean layer of thick salt deposits called the Paradox Formation. The salt is very unstable, and forces in the earth often cause it to flow slowly from one place to another. It behaves as if it were an extremely viscous incompressible fluid trapped beneath a heavy overburden of sandstone. In some areas the shifting salt beds have pushed up the overlying rock, and in other places they have caused the land to drop. The nearby canyons of Devils Lane and Devils Pocket were both formed by movements in the Paradox Formation, and it is conceivable that Chesler Park was formed the same way.

Soon after dropping into Chesler Park the trail meets another path that circles the perimeter of the

see color photos, pages 149, 150

park. Turn right here and continue westward below the impressive spires of the Pinnacle. After 1.4 miles you will come to the Devils Pocket Trail where you must turn left, and 15 minutes later the trail ends at the Chesler Canyon jeep road. The sides of Chesler Canyon are lined with hundreds of stone needles. Like giant terrestrial pin cushions, even the hills above the road are

Needles north of Chesler Park

packed with clusters of needles.

When you reach the jeep road turn south, and within five minutes you will see a spur road leading to the Chesler Park Trailhead on the left. The trailhead is at the end of this spur, 0.5 mile from the fork. As mentioned earlier, if you have a 4WD vehicle it is possible to begin this hike at the Chesler Park Trailhead and avoid the 5.6 mile round trip walk in from Elephant Hill

The next mile is, for many, the most interesting part of this hike. After climbing out of Chesler Canyon the trail comes to another obstacle of heavily eroded sandstone. This barrier forms the southern wall of Chesler Park, and in order to get through it the trail is forced into a series of cracks and fissures that somehow lead to the flatland beyond. This section of trail is called the Joint Trail, because old-timers often refer to cracks in the sandstone as "joints". At one point you will be required to walk through the bottom of a joint that is nearly 300 yards long and, at times, less than two feet wide. The trail emerges from the sandstone wall at the bottom of a long flight of crude stone steps that climb back to the sunshine and blue sky on the southern edge of Chesler Park.

After climbing the steps the trail turns east along the southern side of Chesler. Soon you will come to a large island of sandstone in the center of the open meadow where backcountry campsites CP-2, -3, -4, and -5 are located. This is also where the cowboys once camped before Canyonlands National Park was created in 1964. Their camp is located on the west side of the island near CP-4 and CP-5.

When you reach the eastern side of the sandstone island the trail turns north and passes another trail to Elephant Canyon before finally coming to the junction with the Devils Kitchen trail on the northeastern corner of the park. From here you can retrace your steps the last 2.8 miles to Elephant Hill Trailhead.

Chesler Park

Druid Arch

☆ ☆ ☆   **day hike**

Distance:	10.2 miles (round trip)
Walking time:	6 hours
Elevations:	800 ft. gain/loss Elephant Hill Trailhead (start): 5,120 ft. Elephant Canyon: 5,220 ft. Druid Arch: 5,740 ft.
Trail:	Well marked, easy to follow
Vicinity:	The trailhead is at the Elephant Hill picnic area.
USGS Maps:	The Loop, Druid Arch

Follow the signs from the Needles Visitor Center to Elephant Hill where you will see the trailhead and parking area at the end of the graded road. The distance is 6.0 miles, with the last 3.0 miles unpaved.

High on the rim above Elephant Canyon, with nothing but blue sky behind it, stands the stately, chiseled profile of Druid Arch. The ancient arch reminds many people of Stonehenge in southern England; hence its name. (The Druids are the people who built Stonehenge.) In her book, *Desert Quartet*, Terry Tempest Williams shares with us her first impression of Druid Arch:

> *Red Rock. Blue sky. This arch is structured metamorphosis. Once a finlike tower, it has been perforated by a mas-*

see map, page 170

sive cave-in, responsible now for the keyholes where wind enters and turns. What has been opened, removed, eroded away, is as compelling to me as what remains. Druid Arch-inorganic matter-rock rising from the desert floor as a creation of time, weathered, broken, and beautiful. [5]

There are several possible hiking routes to Druid Arch: If you have a 4WD you can begin at the Chesler Canyon Trailhead and walk only 4.5 miles to the arch. Otherwise you must begin at the Elephant Hill Trailhead

---

[5] Terry Tempest Williams and Mary Frank, *Desert Quartet,* Pantheon Books, New York, 1995. (with permission)

or the Squaw Flat Trailhead and walk 5.1 miles or 7.2 miles respectively. Elephant Hill Trailhead is the most popular place to begin a hike to Druid Arch, and that is the route described below.

For the first 1.3 miles the trail winds across the slickrock in a southerly direction, threading its way through a forest of stone pinnacles and spires on the east side of Elephant Canyon. After 40 minutes will come to a junction where you must bear right, and from there the see color photos, pages 149, 150 trail turns west to begin its hunt for an easy descent route into Elephant Canyon. You will arrive at the sandy bottom of the ravine 10 minutes after leaving the junction.

Once inside Elephant Canyon the trail follows the bottom of the desert wash the rest of the way to Druid Arch. Along the way you will pass three more junctions where trails from Chesler Park and Squaw Canyon join the Elephant Canyon Trail. In each case be sure to take the trail that continues south along the bottom of the wash.

For 3.2 miles the trail along the canyon floor passes beneath a never ending spectacle of spires and needles that line the sides of Elephant Canyon. The ancient Cedar Mesa Sandstone, from which the pinnacles have been etched, was originally deposited in many distinct layers, and now the spires are heavily banded with horizontal stripes of red, white, orange, and pink. They present an awesome example of nature's handiwork. There are also numerous springs in the bottom of the canyon, and although there is not normally enough water to form a stream you should pass an occasional pool.

Druid Arch is located at the head of Elephant Canyon, and just before you get there the trail climbs up the eastern side of the ravine and circles around to a viewpoint on the east side of the arch. The best time to see it is before 10:00 a.m. when it is bathed in the morning sunlight.

Druid Arch

Devils Pocket Loop

4WD vehicle required
day hike

Distance: 5.6 miles (loop)

Walking time: 3¼ hours

Elevations: 450 ft. gain/loss
Devils Pocket Trailhead (start): 5,240 ft.
highest point: 5,650 ft.

Trail: Well marked, easy to follow

Vicinity: Off the Elephant Hill Road

USGS Maps: The Loop, Druid Arch

The trailhead is located at the Devils Kitchen Camp, 3.5 miles from the Elephant Hill Picnic Area along the Elephant Hill jeep road. (See page 103 for more information on the Elephant Hill Road.)

Note: This hike is particularly enjoyable when done in conjunction with a camp-out at the Devils Kitchen Camp. See pages 15-16 for information on how to make reservations for a night at Devils Kitchen.

Needles on north side of Chesler Park

Trail through The Pinnacle

lel walls of sandstone that rise along either side like bleachers for the imaginary spectators. The faulted valley continues in a southerly direction for about a mile before ending abruptly at the base of another prominent landmark called the Pinnacle. The huge jumble of stone needles that comprise the Pinnacle are clearly visible throughout the entire length of Devils Pocket, causing one to wonder what the trail might do when it reaches the end of the valley. But as you walk toward the Pinnacle you will begin to notice a narrow break on the left side of the seemingly impenetrable wall of stone, where a tiny sliver of daylight shines between two adjacent sandstone spires. This is the route the trail will follow through the barrier.

Near the end of the graben the trail leaves the valley floor and begins ascending to the west, finally passing through the Pinnacle after an elevation gain of 120 feet. When you exit on the south side of the Pinnacle a

Devils Pocket is the whimsical name given to an odd, flat-bottomed canyon that extends southward from the Devils Kitchen Campground. This canyon is one of many unusual depressions that occur east of the Colorado River in the Needles area. Geologists call them grabens, and they are formed in areas where the see map, page 170 surface of the land has dropped downward between two parallel faults. In Canyonlands this geologic activity is the result of a huge deposit of salt that lies several thousand feet below the surface. The fluid-like salt is continually being pushed and squeezed by movements in the earth's crust, causing the overlying rock to collapse into sinkholes and grabens or be pushed up into domes and horsts.

Walking south from Devils Kitchen through Devils Pocket is a little like walking down a long, wide racetrack, with paral-

Devils Pocket Trail

fine view of Chesler Canyon will open up before you, with hundreds more of the strange stone needles covering the hillsides in every direction. Then, 0.3 mile later the path comes to a junction where you must turn left into the southern leg of this loop.

This section of the trail skirts along the northern edge of Chesler Park, a large flat meadow that is surrounded on all sides by more of the needles. Before it became part of the national park Chesler Park was a favorite grazing area of local ranchers. The cowboys frequently camped on the west side of the large sandstone outcropping in the center of the park *see color photo, page 150* where some remnants of their camp can still be seen today. For a time in the late 1940s and early 1950s they even had a small landing strip in the park, but no trace of the runway is now visible.

After reaching the northeastern corner of the mile-wide meadow the trail comes to another junction, where you must turn north along a short segment of trail that passes out of Chesler Park through another small opening in the Pinnacle. Then, after only 0.2 mile, the short connecting trail meets another junction where the trail back to Devils Kitchen departs on the left.

As you walk along this final leg back to Devils Kitchen you will be treated to a stunning view of the LaSal Mountains, 40 miles to the northeast. The LaSals, which often keep their snow cover well into the summer, provide a shocking visual contrast to the hot desert country of Canyonlands. In Utah, only the Uinta Mountains on the Wyoming border have peaks that are higher than the LaSals. From the last junction the trail continues northward along the western rim of Elephant Canyon for 1.6 miles before turning west for the final 0.9 mile to Devils Kitchen where the hike began.

Toadstool formations on the rim of Elephant Canyon

Lower Red Lake Canyon

☆

4WD vehicle required
day hike

Distance: 8.4 miles (round trip)

Walking time: 5¼ hours

Elevations: 1,150 ft. loss/gain
Cyclone Canyon Trailhead (start): 4,840 ft.
Red Lake Canyon: 4,600 ft.
Colorado River: 3,850 ft.

Trail: Well marked, easy to follow

Vicinity: Off the Elephant Hill Road

USGS Maps: Spanish Bottom

To reach the trailhead you must first drive to the New Bates Wilson Camp on the Elephant Hill jeep road, then continue driving north for another 2.6 miles to the Confluence Overlook turnout. The trailhead is located 2.0 miles south of the turnout on the road into Cyclone Canyon. Look for a small sign on the right side of the road. (See page 103 for more information on the Elephant Hill and Cyclone Canyon Roads.)

For years the Park Service has been talking about closing the road through Cyclone Canyon, but as this book goes to press the road is still open. If in the future they do close this road then hikers will have to begin this hike at Devils Lane instead. The Devils Lane Trailhead is located 0.6 mile west of the Devils Kitchen Camp where the road first enters Devils Lane Canyon. The connecting trail between Devils Lane and the Cyclone Canyon Trailhead is 1.0 mile long; hence starting your hike at the Devils Lane Trailhead would increase the round trip distance to 10.4 miles.

Note: Since the Cyclone Canyon Trailhead is at least two hours by jeep from the nearest 2WD road, most people combine this hike with an overnight campout at either Devils Kitchen Camp or the New Bates Wilson Camp. (See pages 15-16 for more information on how to make reservations for these campsites.)

Red Lake Canyon provides the only feasible route for a good trail through the rugged Needles District of Canyonlands to the Colorado River; hence there has probably been a footpath through the canyon for hundreds or thousands of years. The existing path was improved by the Park Service after the mid-1960s, and now it provides an

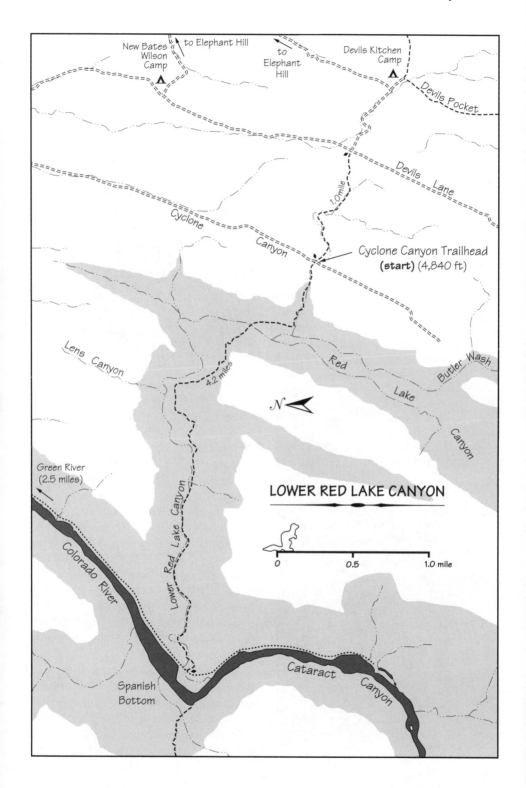

New Bates Wilson Camp

to Elephant Hill

to Elephant Hill

Devils Kitchen Camp

Devils Pocket

Devils Lane

1.0 mile

Cyclone Canyon

Cyclone Canyon Trailhead **(start)** (4,840 ft)

Lens Canyon

Red Lake

Butler Wash

4.2 miles

Lake

N

Canyon

Green River (2.5 miles)

Lower Red Lake Canyon

LOWER RED LAKE CANYON

0   0.5   1.0 mile

Colorado River

Spanish Bottom

Cataract Canyon

interesting way for hikers to see the Colorado River.

From the trailhead in Cyclone Canyon the trail immediately begins to descend westward through a small ravine that connects Cyclone Canyon to Red Lake Canyon. After a distance of 0.7 miles and an elevation loss of 240 feet the trail reaches the sandy bottom of Red Lake Canyon, a huge, graben that seems to go on forever in both directions. The trail then turns north and proceeds down the right side of the canyon for 0.3 mile before crossing to the opposite side and climbing out. In spite of what the name suggests, there is no water in Red Lake Canyon. There are signs, however, that on rare occasions after a heavy rain there might be standing water in the depression for a brief time. In some areas there is a great deal of dead

Lower Red Lake Canyon

juniper wood that appears to have been washed down from above.

0.3 mile after exiting Red Lake Canyon the trail climbs to the top of a ridge that looks west into the rugged chasm of Lower Red Lake Canyon. This heavily eroded gorge descends in a westerly direction from the northern end of Red Lake Canyon, and the trail follows it the rest of the way to the Colorado River. The path stays high on the south side of the rocky drainage for 0.7 mile before turning downward through an elevation loss of 500 feet to the canyon floor. The floor of Lower Red Lake Canyon at this point is only 200 feet higher than the Colorado, so the remaining 1.8 miles is a relatively easy walk.

Just before it reaches the river the trail passes through a field of low, light colored gypsum hills that are very different in appearance from the overlying sandstone, limestone and mudstone. At this point you are walking on the top layers of the deeply

Lower Red Lake Canyon

buried Paradox Formation; this is one of the few places in the park where the Paradox deposits are exposed.

The Colorado River itself is a disappointment to many hikers on this trail. The banks of the river are heavily overgrown with tamarisks; consequently it is hard to even see the river until you have walked a short distance upstream.

see color photo, page 160

When you finally come to an opening in the undergrowth you will see a smooth, flat river of muddy brown water, about 100 yards wide flowing lazily downstream between the walls of the 1,000-foot gorge of Cataract Canyon. Immediately opposite Lower Red Lake Canyon is a huge flat area called Spanish Bottom that is accessible by trail from the Maze District (see page 265). This huge, remarkably flat river bottom was formed by the same geologic event that exposed the Paradox formation in Lower Red Lake Canyon.

Side Trips along the Colorado River

There is a primitive trail along the east bank of the Colorado that extends from the mouth of Lower Red Lake Canyon to the confluence with the Green River 3.6 miles upstream. Even if you don't want to walk all the way to the confluence it is worthwhile to walk a mile upstream. Along the way you will pass several areas where the absence of tamarisk trees makes it possible to sit on a rock at the water's edge and enjoy the serenity of the canyon.

It is also possible to walk downstream a short distance into Cataract Canyon. Cataract Canyon is famous for its rapids—among the worst on the Colorado River. The rapids start about 0.7 miles downstream, but the really notorious rapids begin about 4.0 miles downstream in the vicinity of Y and Cross Canyons.

Cataract Canyon of the Colorado River

Thirteen Faces Pictographs

4WD vehicle required
short day hike

Distance: 1.6 miles (round trip)

Walking time: ³/₄ hour

Elevations: 20 ft. gain/loss
                    Thirteen Faces Trailhead (start): 5,240 ft.

Trail: Unmarked, but easy to follow

Vicinity: Horse Canyon

USGS Maps: South Six-shooter Peak

This trail is located in Horse Canyon; hence it is usually done in conjunction with a jeep ride on the Horse Canyon Road. (See page 109 for more information about the Horse Canyon jeep road.) The trailhead is located 1.2 miles before the end of the Horse Canyon Road, or 1.0 miles north of the Castle Arch Trailhead. As you approach the Thirteen Faces Trailhead the road enters a large grove of Cottonwood trees. Once inside the grove you come to a fork in the road where a short spur branches off into a small side canyon on the west side of Horse Canyon. After you have driven 150 yards into the side canyon you will encounter a barrier that has been erected by the Park Service to keep vehicles from going any further. This is where the foot path starts.

Note: A day-use permit for Horse Canyon is required to drive your vehicle to the trailhead. See pages 15-16 for more information on how to obtain a permit.

Don't expect to find any signs marking the Thirteen Faces Trailhead. This trail is not well advertised by the Park Service and does not appear on many maps. When you see the Thirteen Faces you will understand why. The ancient pictographs are extremely fragile and could be easily damaged by vandals, yet they are in surprisingly good condition after so many centuries of exposure. We really have no idea when they were painted, but the artist died at least 700 years ago, and probably much earlier.

Their style indicates that the Thirteen Faces were produced by the Fremont Culture, which is interesting because this canyon was heavily occupied by the Anasazi Indians. To date, no evidence has been discovered of any permanent Fremont settlements in the area. There appears to have been a great deal of intermingling between the two cultures in other parts of the Southwest, however, and perhaps the Fremonts were frequent visitors in Horse Canyon.

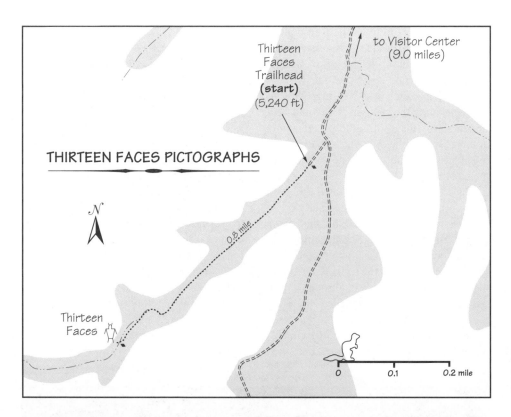

THIRTEEN FACES PICTOGRAPHS

Thirteen Faces Trailhead **(start)** (5,240 ft)

to Visitor Center (9.0 miles)

N

0.8 mile

Thirteen Faces

0   0.1   0.2 mile

Four of the Thirteen Faces

From the parking area the trail continues up the bottom of the sandy wash for 0.7 mile before climbing to the top of the left bank. Just beyond that point the wash is full of fallen oak trees, so it is impossible to continue along the bottom. The route continues above the south side of the sandy drainage for another 150 yards. Then, having bypassed the obstacle, it drops back into the streambed.

As soon as the trail rejoins the bottom of the wash you should immediately begin looking for a hiker-made path that again climbs out of the drainage on the north side. If you stay in the wash for more than 50 feet you have missed the trail. Once out of the streambed you must walk through a short stretch of heavy brush before arriving at the pictograph panel. The paintings are located at the bottom of a smooth, sandstone cliff just 60 feet north of the wash, but the veg-etation makes it impossible to see them from more than 20 feet away.

The Thirteen Faces are just that: a row of thirteen very ornately decorated faces drawn on the sandstone with white and reddish brown paint. Most of the figures are well defined, but a few of them are weathered and faint. I was able to positively identify only eleven of them; nevertheless the panel is very impressive. The white paint looks almost like thick plaster that has been smeared on the uneven rock with a artist's trowel, and the red paint appears to be some kind of iron-rich clay. Several of the faces look as though the paint was applied only weeks ago and might chip off at any time. The panel is somewhat protected from the elements by a 15-foot overhang in the canyon wall above them, but it still seems miraculous that the ancient art has endured for so long.

Four more of the Thirteen Faces

Castle Arch

4WD vehicle required
short day hike

Distance: 1.8 miles (round trip)

Walking time: 1 hour

Elevations: 210 ft. gain/loss
Castle Arch Trailhead (start): 5,290 ft.
Castle Arch Viewpoint: 5,500 ft.

Trail: Not well maintained, but easy to follow

Vicinity: near the end of the Horse Canyon jeep road

USGS Maps: South Six-shooter Peak

This trail is located in Horse Canyon; hence it is usually done in conjunction with a jeep ride on the Horse Canyon Road. (See page 109 for more information about the Horse Canyon jeep road.) The trailhead is located 0.2 miles before the end of Horse Canyon Road. Look for a small sign marking the trail on the west side of the road.

Note: A day-use permit for Horse Canyon is required to drive your vehicle to the trailhead. See pages 15-16 for more information on how to obtain a permit.

Castle Arch

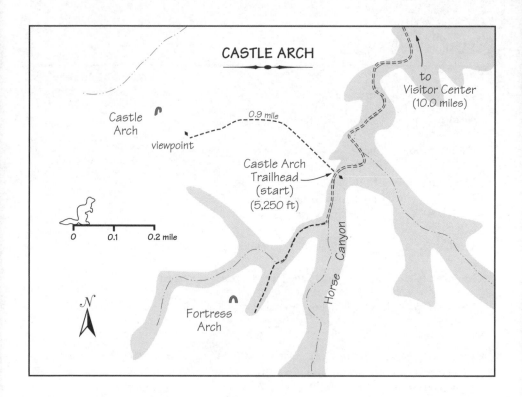

Castle Arch is certainly one of the most beautiful natural arches in Canyonlands. High and graceful, with only a thin sliver of sandstone at its apex, it is about 200 feet wide, 150 feet high, and perhaps 6 feet thick at its thinnest point. It is a very old arch with probably only a few centuries of existence left before it collapses.

see color photo, page 150

Castle Arch reminds me a great deal of Landscape Arch in Arches National Park, except that its location is much less accessible. It sits high on a ridge overlooking Horse Canyon with nothing but blue sky behind it.

From the road the trail immediately enters a heavily vegetated gully and begins to make its way westward through dense thickets of sagebrush and scrub oak. After just a few minutes, however, the path climbs up the south side of the depression allowing you to catch your first glimpse of Castle Arch. Over the next twenty minutes the arch comes into and out of view several times, until finally the trail ends at the bottom of a pouroff in the drainage.

For many this will be the end of the trail, but if you have an adventurous spirit I urge you to continue. It isn't too difficult to climb up a strategically placed log to the top of the 8-foot ledge, and once there you can follow a slickrock channel upward for another 200 yards to the bottom of a large sandstone bowl on the south side of the arch. This bowl is a great place to lean back and gaze at the slender sandstone span high above the canyon.

Fortress Arch

4WD vehicle required
short day hike

Distance:	1.5 miles (round trip)
Walking time:	³/₄ hour
Elevations:	160 ft. gain/loss Fortress Arch Trailhead (start): 5,320 ft. Fortress Arch viewpoint: 5,480 ft.
Trail:	Not well maintained, but easy to follow
Vicinity:	Off the Horse Canyon jeep road
USGS Maps:	South Six-shooter Peak

The trailhead is located in Horse Canyon and is usually done in conjunction with the Horse Canyon jeep ride. (See page 109 for more information on the Horse Canyon Road.) When you reach the end of the road walk down the streambed for another 100 feet and you will see a small sign on the right side of the drainage marking the trailhead.

Note: A day-use permit for Horse Canyon is required to drive your vehicle to the trailhead. See pages 15-16 for more information on how to obtain a permit.

Fortress Arch

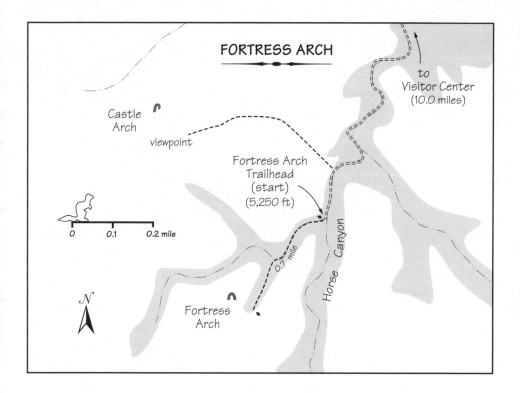

FORTRESS ARCH

Castle Arch

viewpoint

to Visitor Center (10.0 miles)

Fortress Arch Trailhead (start) (5,250 ft)

Horse Canyon

0.7 mile

0   0.1   0.2 mile

N

Fortress Arch

Fortress Arch is about as different from the nearby Castle Arch (page 185) as two arches can be. There is nothing graceful about this span. It is big and bulky, the way you would expect a fortress to be, with at least 150 feet of stone suspended above the opening. In comparing the two you can see that Fortress Arch is young and brawny, while Castle Arch is very old and fragile. Fortress Arch will continue to stand tall on the top of its ridge for many thousands of years after its neighbor has collapsed into a heap of rubble.

The trail begins by heading west out of Horse Canyon up the bottom of a minor side canyon. After 5 minutes the canyon forks and the trail turns left to follow the southern branch. You can't to see it yet, but Fortress Arch is situated at the top of the ridge that separates these two short canyons. The trail continues to climb up into the short, rocky canyon for another 15 minutes before arriving at a good viewpoint south of the arch. Be patient—the arch is hidden for most of the distance; it only comes into view near the end of the trail.

Actually the trail doesn't really end at the viewpoint. You can follow a route marked by cairns beyond the apparent end of the trail for another 15 minutes, but the crude trail eventually ends at the base of a cliff below the arch. An experienced rock climber could probably scale this 15-foot obstacle without too much difficulty and then scramble up the last 100 yards into the arch's opening, but there is considerable exposure below the pitch. It isn't something most hikers would want to attempt.

Salt Creek

☆ ☆ ☆ ☆ ☆

4WD shuttle required
4-day hike

Distance:	26.7 miles (including major points of interest) (plus 37 miles by 4WD shuttle car)
Walking time:	day 1: 2¼ hours day 2: 3 hours day 3: 5 hours day 4: 4 hours
Elevations:	2,130 ft. loss, 100 ft. gain Cathedral Butte Trailhead (start): 7,050 ft. Upper Jump: 5,600 ft. Peekaboo Camp: 5,020 ft.
Trail:	Generally easy to follow
Campsites:	SC-1, -2, -3, and -4 are the only backcountry campsites along the first 14.7 miles of this trail, and camping elsewhere is not allowed. For the last 7.7 miles, however, you will be in Zone 4 of the Needles District where you can camp anywhere. The only restrictions are that you must have a backcountry permit and you must be a reasonable distance from the trail or the creek. I suggest you try to reserve campsite SC-1 or -2 for the first night and SC-3 for the second night and spend the third night in Zone 4 at the Angel Arch Camp. See pages 15-16 for more information on how to obtain permits and reserve campsites.
Vicinity:	Begins in the Abajo Mountains near the southern boundary of the park.
USGS Maps:	Cathedral Butte, South Six-shooter Peak, Druid Arch

To get to Peekaboo Camp where the hike ends you must drive south from the Visitor Center following the signs to Cave Spring and Salt Creek. Just before the road ends at Cave Spring you will see the Salt Creek Road departing on the right. Turn here and drive 0.3 miles to the gate and parking area. The gate is normally locked, but when you obtain your backcountry permit from the visitor center you will be given the combination.

If your vehicle is not 4WD you will have to park at the gate. Otherwise continue driving beyond the gate for another 2.2 miles to the confluence of Salt Creek and Horse Canyon, then bear right for the final 1.0 mile to Peekaboo Camp. This is where the hike ends and where you must park your shuttle car.

To get to Cathedral Butte Trailhead where the hike begins you must return to Highway-211 and drive east out of the park. 13.7 miles beyond the national park entrance gate you will come to a gravel road and a sign that says "Beef Basin and Elk Mountain". Check your odometer at this point and turn south onto the Beef Basin Road. 9.2 miles after leaving the highway you will see another gravel road on the left. Bear right here. When you have driven 17.1 miles from the highway you will come to a turnout on your right that leads to the trailhead. Unfortunately the turnout is not marked, but it is not too difficult to recognize. First, the road at this point is only about 30 feet from the rim of Salt Creek Canyon; and second, the turnout is only 300 yards west of Cathedral Butte, an unmistakable landmark that can be seen for miles in every direction.

The trailhead is at the end of the turnout, only 200 feet from the main road. There is a signboard at the trailhead, but unfortunately it is blocked by the juniper trees and cannot be seen from the main road. If you arriving late in the day you will be pleased to know that there is a nice camping area at the trailhead. Furthermore, this is BLM land and campfires are permitted.

If you have a 4WD vehicle it is worthwhile driving to the end of Cathedral Point before beginning this hike. From there you can look down into the upper reaches of Salt Creek Canyon. The point offers an exquisite birds-eye view of the Big Pocket, a large side canyon that lies about five miles from the Trailhead. To get to the Cathedral Point Road you must backtrack 0.5 miles northeast of the trailhead. There, on the northwest side of Cathedral Butte you will see the two-mile jeep road that leads to the northern end of the promontory.

Salt Creek Canyon is one of those special places in Canyonlands National Park where water is generally available throughout the year. The canyon is a green oasis in the midst of a redrock desert, and the combination of the two ecosystems makes this hike unique. The trail alternately winds across the sage-covered benches above the creek, then drops down to carve a path through the willows and cottonwoods that grow nearer the water. The backdrop for the canyon greenery is a mural of red, white and black Cedar Mesa Sandstone, etched and sculpted into pinnacles, alcoves, natural arches, and a million other unusual shapes.

Perhaps the most interesting features on the canyon walls are the ancient cliff dwellings and rock art that were left behind by the Anasazi and Fremont Indians centuries ago. The cliffs are littered with their ancient pictographs, and dozens of prehistoric granaries and other structures lie hidden away in the dark recesses of the sandstone. Their's was a farming culture, and they must have found the sandy, flat-bottomed canyon an ideal place to grow their crops.

Salt Creek Canyon was also a grazing area for cattle during the first half of the twentieth century, and relics of the old ranching activity can still be seen occasionally along the trail. Probably the most interesting artifact from this era is an old log cabin near the head of the canyon that was once owned by a rancher named Rensselaer Lee Kirk. Kirk built the cabin sometime in the 1890s and worked an 80-acre ranch in the canyon until 1905.

see color photos, pages 151, 152

Rensselaer Lee Kirk's cabin

Campsites SC-1 & SC-2 (4.3 miles)

The trail begins descending almost immediately from the pinion and juniper forest on the rim down into the East Fork of Salt Creek Canyon. The path is initially quite steep in a few places, but soon the grade becomes more gradual. Finally, after an elevation loss of 1,000 feet, the trail crosses the national park boundary and begins following the sandy floor of East Fork Salt Creek Canyon. There is a trail junction at this point where the Bright Angel Trail departs to the west, but the old trail is seldom used now, and it is so faint you probably won't even see it.

After following the East Fork for 1.2 miles you will come to a marshy area where the trail is badly overgrown with grass and scouring rushes. The path is hard to follow in this area but the route is not difficult. If you can't find the trail just bear to the right along the east side of the marsh. After 0.4 mile you will come to a barrier of tamarisk trees, where you should see a clearly marked trail entering the thicket near the canyon wall. Before leaving the meadow, however, pause to study the sandstone cliffs 0.3 mile east of the trail. On a ledge about half way up the cliff there is a cliff dwelling with several small rooms. The site is so far away, though, that you will probably need binoculars to positively identify it.

The grass land surrounding the marsh was an important part of Kirk's ranch at the turn of the century. During the summer he would cut the grass and store it to feed his cattle during the winter months. According to Michael Kelsey[6] his old hay rake is still nearby, parked in an alcove on the west side of the canyon a short distance north of the

---

[6] Michael R. Kelsey, *Hiking, Biking and Exploring Canyonlands National Park and Vicinity*, Kelsey Publishing, Provo, Utah, 1992.

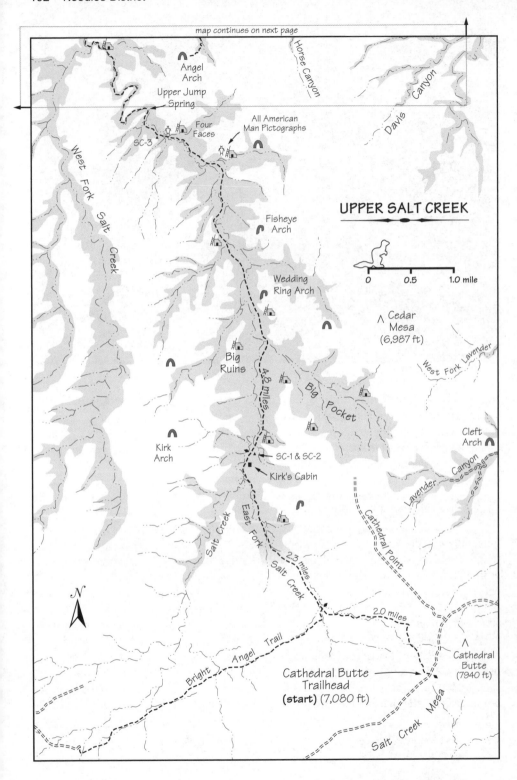

map continues on next page

Angel Arch

Upper Jump Spring

Horse Canyon

Davis Canyon

SC-3

Four Faces

All American Man Pictographs

West Fork Salt Creek

Fisheye Arch

Wedding Ring Arch

Cedar Mesa (6,987 ft)

UPPER SALT CREEK

0   0.5   1.0 mile

West Fork Lavender

Big Ruins

4.8 miles

Big Pocket

Kirk Arch

Cleft Arch

SC-1 & SC-2

Kirk's Cabin

Salt Creek

East Fork Salt Creek

Lavender Canyon

Cathedral Point

2.3 miles

2.0 miles

Bright Angel Trail

Cathedral Butte (7940 ft)

Cathedral Butte Trailhead **(start)** (7,080 ft)

Salt Creek Mesa

N

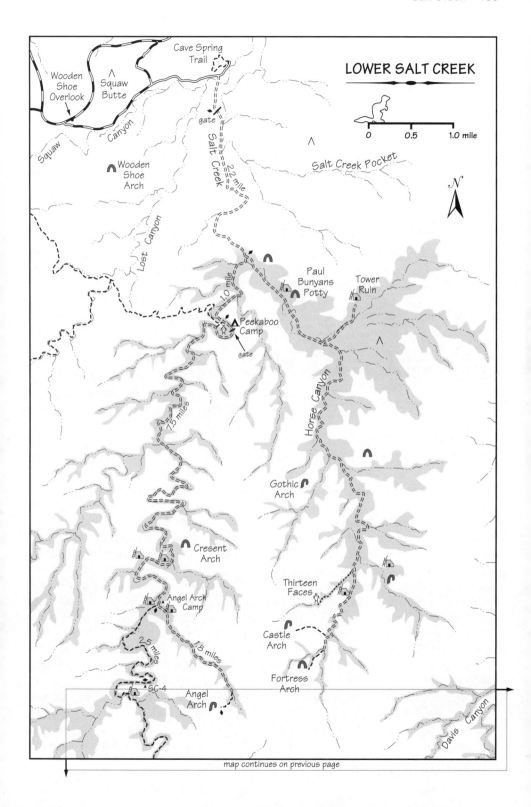

map continues on previous page

Waterslide near Kirk's cabin

marsh.

After entering the tamarisk trees on the southern end of the marsh the trail follows the canyon wall for a short distance, then it immerges from the trees above a waterslide near the junction of Salt Creek Canyon and the East Fork. The slide has a permanent stream of clear water flowing down it, and it is a great place to refill your canteens. The trail also passes a small pictograph panel about 4 minutes before it reaches the waterslide, so if you missed it you might want to backtrack a short distance to see it. The panel consists of 4 handprints and a small human-like figure.

150 yards beyond the waterslide you will see Kirk's 100-year-old cabin on the right side of the trail. The cabin is still in remarkably good condition considering its age. Its size is about 15 x 20 feet, and, amazingly, the roof is still intact. There is also an old wagon parked beside the cabin that Kirk probably used to haul supplies and family members from his winter home in Moab. The route he took through Salt Creek Canyon is basically the same route that the trail follows today.

Just after passing Kirk's cabin you will come to a short spur trail that leads to SC-1 and SC-2, the first two Salt Creek Canyon backcountry campsites.

Campsite SC-3 (4.8 miles)

Just north of the spur leading to SC-1 and SC-2 the trail passes an interesting fence that was probably originally built by Kirk. Notice the unique way in which he attached the horizontal rails to the fence posts. The wooden rails were laid on small pegs inserted between two parallel posts. This same kind of construction was used to build a corral near Kirk's cabin as well as several other fences along the trail. It is a mystery why Kirk choose to build these labor intensive wooden fences; barbed wire was invented 30 years before he settled the canyon.

0.4 mile north of the SC-1 and SC-2 camps the trail passes a small, easily accessible Anasazi ruin. The site is located in a small southwest-facing alcove only 100 yards from the right side of the trail. The ruins are easy to spot, and there is a primitive hiker-made trail leading from the main trail to a point just below the alcove.

As you continue northward past the Indian ruins watch the western horizon and soon a large natural arch will come into view above the canyon rim. This is Kirk's Arch. It is very impressive, but it lies in an inaccessible area nearly a mile west of the trail so you won't be able to get any closer. Also, it can be seen only intermittently as you walk along the path.

Keep watching the west side of the canyon and after about 15 minutes another ex-

Anasazi ruin in Big Pocket

tensive Indian ruin site will come into view. This site is called the Big Ruins, and indeed it contains the largest collection of Anasazi ruins in Canyonlands National Park. It is located 0.4 mile west of the trail on a ledge along the canyon wall. You will probably want to get a closer look at these impressive ruins, but Salt Creek flows through a deep gorge in this area that effectively blocks access from the trail. If you continue north a little further, however, you will come to a place where there is an easier way to cross the creek.

As the trail passes the Big Ruins on the left it also passes the mouth of a prominent valley on the right known as the Big Pocket. Look for a large diamond-shaped boulder, 30 feet across with one point buried in the ground, on the right side of the trail just north of the Big Pocket. A few hundred feet beyond that boulder there is a hiker-made

trail that crosses Salt Creek and continues on to the base of the Big Ruins. The ruins are a 15-minute walk from the main trail.

Big Ruins is the most impressive Anasazi ruin sight you will see on this hike. If possible you should try to see it in the morning light, since it faces east and is in deep shade in the afternoon. I counted at least 20 large dwellings at the sight plus many smaller granaries. Most of them are located on a narrow 250-foot-long ledge about 70 feet above the ground, but there are also remnants of a few additional structures at the base of the cliff. Looking at the dwellings so precariously perched on the very edge of the precipice makes one wonder how many Indian children over the years must have fallen to their deaths. The cliff below the ruins is a shear drop, with no way to reach the ledge except by ladder.

If you have the time for further exploration you might want to spend a morning checking out the Big Pocket; there are at least three more ruin sites in the large, flat-bottomed valley. The first site is situated just 250 yards from the trail on the south side of the canyon. It consists of at least 2 large rooms and several granaries, and it is also easily accessible. The second Big Pocket ruin is probably the most interesting of the three, but it cannot be reached without a ladder. It is situated in an east-facing alcove on the south side of the canyon about 1.3 miles from the trail. The third ruin is on the north side of the Big Pocket 0.8 miles northeast of the second one. This one is in the back of a deep, south-facing alcove, and the structures are in continual shade. Again, they can't be reached without a ladder.

The next few miles of trail through Salt Creek Canyon contain many interesting highlights of this hike. Just five minutes north of the mouth of Big Pocket you will see another small Anasazi ruin on your right, quickly followed by one of the most beautiful natural arches in the park: the Wedding Ring Arch. This arch is an almost perfectly symmetrical oval that looks just like a giant wedding ring. The opening is about 200 feet high and 150 feet wide, and it is located only 150 yards from the right side of the trail. Unfortunately there are no really good views of the arch from the trail; in fact you can easily miss it completely if you aren't paying attention. For the best view you must walk a short distance north of the arch, past an outcropping of sandstone, and then leave the main trail for a 200-yard walk back to it

0.6 miles north of Wedding Ring Arch the path passes another ruin in an alcove 250 feet off the left side of the trail. This ruin is near ground level, and there is an obvious hiker-made trail leading to it. The alcove contains only three small granaries, but for me it is one of the most exciting archeological sites in the canyon. The reason: a

Wedding Ring Arch

small squash patch growing immediately in front of the granaries. These squash almost certainly came from seeds originally planted by the people that built the granaries, yet today, over seven centuries later, they are still thriving! If you are there in September or October you will see dozens of small green squash scattered amidst the leaves of the hardy vines. In a good year the nearby granaries must have been filled to capacity with the vegetables.

About 0.5 mile beyond the squash patch Fisheye Arch comes into view. The Fisheye is situated high on the eastern rim of the canyon. It is not nearly as interesting as Wedding Ring Arch, and the trail never approaches closer to it than 0.4 mile; nevertheless it is very prominent and can be seen along a considerable stretch of trail. Finally, 1.2 miles north of the squash patch the trail arrives at the canyon's eastern wall and passes immediately below the next major point of interest: the All American Man Pictograph.

The trail also passes another Indian ruin just 100 yards before it reaches All American Man. Like All American Man this ruin is located in a small cave in the eastern canyon wall 40 above the ground. It contains at least five small dwellings or granaries.

With the exception of the pictographs in Horseshoe Canyon, All American Man is easily the most interesting piece of Indian rock art in Canyonlands National Park. The painting is done in three colors, red, white, and blue, and in truth it looks more like something a child would draw to commemorate American Independence Day than an ancient Indian pictograph. The man in the painting is about six feet tall, and his clothing includes a waist cloth with a design reminiscent of the American flag. To the eye the colors are vividly red, white and blue, but the blue color is actually an optical illusion. The true color is gray, but it appears

Four Faces pictograph panel

to be blue in the dim light against the reddish background of the surrounding sandstone. Like the preceding ruin, All American Man is located in a small cave about 20 feet above the ground. The trail passes directly under it.

200 yards beyond the All American Man the trail climbs up to take a shortcut through a crack in a large fin of sandstone that protrudes into the canyon. After 150 feet the trail emerges from the north side of the crack to continue down the canyon. Soon you will enter a section of canyon that is heavily vegetated with willow plants, and when you emerge from the dense undergrowth, 20 minutes after leaving All American Man one of the first things you will see is a fast flowing spring with excellent water.

This is also the location of another interesting pictograph panel called the Four Faces. If you will look to your right at the canyon wall just before you reach the spring the rock art and several dwellings or granaries are clearly visible about 200 feet east of the trail.

The Four Faces panel is in remarkably good condition, considering it is at least 700 years old. It is a fine example of Fremont art. According to the experts most of the ruins in Canyonlands were originally constructed by the Anasazis, but this pictograph panel and others like it prove that the Fremonts also maintained some sort of presence in the area.

The trail crosses to the west side of the canyon at Four Faces Spring and continues in a northwesterly direction on the flat plateau above the bottom of the drainage. After 200 yards you will see the spur trail on the left leading to the third Salt Creek backcountry campsite.

Campsite SC-4 (3.3 miles)

Fifteen minutes north of the SC-3 campsite the trail passes above the west side of a small waterfall known as the Upper Jump. The total drop in the creek bed at this point is about 25 feet, and at the bottom of the fall the water has formed a beautiful little pond surrounded by a dense growth of willows and cottonwood trees. Thankfully the area is still free of the noxious tamarisk trees that have invaded so much of the canyon.

Beyond the Upper Jump the canyon becomes significantly narrower and wetter, forcing the trail into the thicker vegetation that grows in the bottom of the drainage. Willows again dominate the sides of the stream, while a dense cover of sage and rabbit brush seems to thrive just above the creek. The trail cuts tunnel-like through the thick ground cover, with eight-foot walls of rabbit brush often lining the sides. For most of the summer the rabbit brush is covered with thousands of tiny yellow flowers, making the walk a delightful one.

2.3 miles downstream from the upper jump, just before reaching the confluence of West Fork and Salt Creek Canyon, the trail climbs out of the willows to a dry plateau on the northeast side of the streambed. The trail then proceeds in a westerly direction, passing within 100 feet of an impressive collection of Anasazi ruins. The ruins are about 100 feet above the trail on an easily accessible south-facing ledge. I counted at least 15 dwellings and granaries along the 150-yard-long ledge. On the western end of the ledge there is an interesting pictograph of several human figures that appear to be holding hands like a string of paper dolls.

Shortly after leaving the archeological site the trail drops down from the bench and turns 180 degrees to follow the canyon in an easterly direction. Within ten minutes after making the turn you should see SC-4, the last designated Salt Creek Canyon campsite on your right.

Angel Arch Camp (2.5 miles)

From SC-4 to the old Salt Creek Canyon jeep road is 2.1 miles. There is at least one more Indian ruin along the way and probably more, but nothing to compare with the previous ones. The first few hundred yards of the old road are fairly obscure now,

Salt Creek Canyon, below Angel Arch Camp

so it won't be immediately obvious when the trail turns into a road. However by the time you reach the side canyon leading to Angel Arch it will be very clear that you are on an old road. There, near a weathered signboard, an abandoned but still obvious jeep road leaves Salt Creek Canyon and turns east into the dry wash that ends near the arch.

There are at least two more Indian ruins near the junction of Salt Creek Canyon and what I will call Angel Arch Canyon. One is directly west of the canyon junction, in a south-facing alcove about 0.1 mile from the trail. The other is a short distance east of the junction on the north wall of Angel Arch Canyon.

You will surely want to see Angel Arch, which in my opinion is one of the most impressive arches in Canyonlands. But if you are planning to camp in the area I suggest you continue first to Angel Arch Camp, which is located just 100 yards north of the canyon junction. The camp is located in a flat area on the east side of Salt Creek beneath a grove of large cottonwood trees. If it can be arranged I urge you to spend a night at the Angel Arch Camp and take an early morning walk to the arch in time to see it illuminated by the sunrise. It is a scene you will not soon forget.

To get to Angel Arch you must return to the canyon junction and walk southeast along the Angel Arch Road for 1.5 miles. At the end of the road there is a marked trail that leads another 0.3 miles to a viewpoint below the east side of the arch. If you are feeling adventurous there is a cairned trail that continues from the viewpoint to the opening below the arch. The trail is easy to follow and it is not technically difficult, but a great deal of scrambling is required. It will take you about 30 minutes to reach the base of the arch.

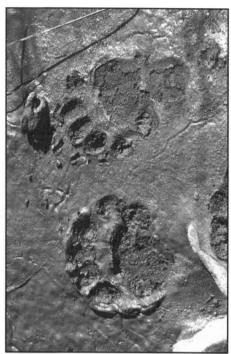
Black bear tracks in Salt Creek Canyon

Peekaboo Spring (7.5 miles)

Before 1998 it was possible to drive 4WD vehicles up Salt Creek Canyon as far as Angel Arch. But in June of that year, after a protracted legal battle between the National Park Service and the Southern Utah Wilderness Alliance, it was determined that motor vehicles in Salt Creek Canyon were causing unacceptable damage to the riparian area and the road was closed. The court decision was then appealed by a 4WD club known as the Utah Shared Access Alliance and the legal battle continued for another five years. Ultimately the original decision was upheld, and it now appears unlikely that motor vehicles will ever again be seen on the road to Angel Arch.

The closure of the Salt Creek Canyon road has affected the canyon in a number of interesting ways. The water in lower Salt Creek is clear again, the ground cover is slowly reclaiming the scared canyon floor, and wildlife of all kinds has moved back into the canyon. For me the most interesting change has been the return of the black bears. Now that the jeeps and motorcycles are gone the bears seem to have begun an annual late-summer migration down into the canyon from the nearby Abajo Mountains.

The bears seldom weigh over 250 pounds, and they are extremely shy of people. But as winter approaches their tracks and their scat can be seen everywhere along this trail. One of the bears' favorite canyon foods is cactus pears, and in early fall when the purple fruits are ripe they devour them by the hundreds. Look for their loosely formed piles of black or dark gray scat along the trail. They are usually filled with the undigested seeds of prickly pear cactus. In many parts of the canyon you can scarcely walk ten minutes without having to step over a pile of bear scat.

Within 30 minutes after leaving Angel Arch Camp you will see Crescent Arch coming into view high on the east side of the canyon. There is also a small granary on the south-facing side before you reach Crescent Arch, but the trail never comes closer than 200 yards from it. As you proceed down canyon several other small, unnamed arches will occasionally come into view, and if you are observant you may see another granary or two. There is also at least one old mine shaft near the creek bed, but in general this part of the canyon is not as interesting as the canyon above Angel Arch Camp.

see color photos, page 147

7.4 miles below Angel Arch Camp, after several miles of travel in a northerly direction, the trail turns southeast in order to get around a long fin that protrudes into the canyon. Look carefully at the base of the fin where the trail turns and you will see a window through to the other side. The trail leaves the road at this point and climbs up through the window to Peekaboo Camp on the other side. If you miss this shortcut you can still get to Peekaboo Camp by following the road, but the route through the window will save you a half-mile of additional walking.

The hike ends at Peekaboo Camp, but before leaving you should take a few minutes to see the nearby panel of Indian pictographs. They are located just west of the window above the camp. This panel was painted by the Fremont Indians sometime before 1300 AD. It is especially interesting because the figures were painted over the top of a much older mural laid down by the Archaic People who lived in Canyonlands at least a thousand years earlier. The older artwork is very faint now—it could be as much as 8,000 years old—but it is still easily distinguishable from the newer Fremont art.

View across Salt Creek Canyon from Angel Arch

Davis Canyon

☆

4WD vehicle required
day hike

Distance:	8.8 miles (round trip)
Walking time:	4³/₄ hours
Elevations:	100 ft. gain/loss Davis Canyon Trailhead (start): 5,300 ft. Log House Ruin: 5,360 ft.
Trail:	There is no trail for this hike. The route follows a series of sandy washes through the bottom of a dry canyon.
Vicinity:	Off Highway 211 in the southeastern corner of the park
USGS Maps:	South Six-shooter Peak

Drive 7.6 miles east of the Needles entrance gate on Highway 211, then turn right onto an unpaved road near a sign that says "Davis Canyon". Immediately after turning off the highway you will come to an unlocked gate, and after another 0.8 mile the road comes to an old corral where it passes through a second gate. Be sure to close both gates behind you. 1.4 miles after leaving the second gate the road drops into Davis Canyon and follows the bottom of the sandy wash the last 5.8 miles to the park boundary where you will see a sign marking the trailhead.

Davis Canyon is actually a complex labyrinth of canyons that have been etched out of the Cedar Mesa Sandstone on the southeast side of the Needles District. The network consists of two main canyons and at least a dozen minor ones. There are no developed trails in Davis Canyon and the area receives only a tiny fraction of the visitors that drive into the Needles District, so if you are looking for a more unstructured adventure with lots of solitude this may be just the place for you.

It is possible to get a backcountry permit from the Needles Visitor Center and spend several days backpacking in the Davis Canyon complex, but there is no water in the canyons so most people prefer to camp near the trailhead and walk into the canyons on day hikes. The road ends at the national park boundary and there are several nice campsites just out-

see color photo, page 152

side the park. Since this land is managed by the BLM no permits are required.

The best campsite is located 0.4 mile east of the park boundary. When you reach the end of the road turn around and drive back 0.4 mile until you see a spur road departing to the north. Turn here and drive north for another 200 yards to the end of the spur.

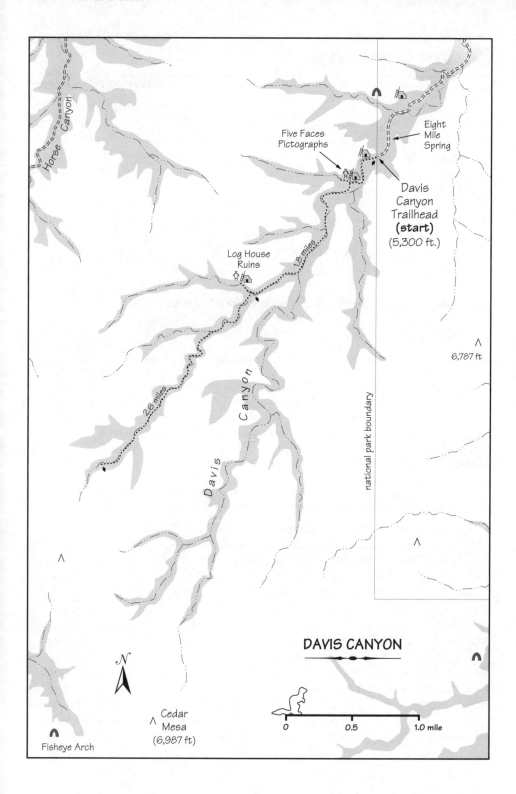

Horse Canyon

Five Faces
Pictographs

Eight
Mile
Spring

Davis
Canyon
Trailhead
(start)
(5,300 ft.)

Log House
Ruins

1.8 miles

2.6 miles

6,787 ft

national park boundary

Davis   Canyon

DAVIS CANYON

N

Cedar
Mesa
(6,987 ft)

Fisheye Arch

0   0.5   1.0 mile

The road ends at a beautiful campsite below the northern wall of the canyon, and as an added bonus there are two small Anasazi granaries on a ledge 20 feet above the camp. You can see one of the granaries from the camp, but if you want a closer look walk east along the base of the sandstone cliff for 150 yards. There you will find a break in the wall where it is possible to climb up to the ledge and backtrack to the granaries.

The hike described below is one that I found particularly interesting, but it explores just one section of the Davis Canyon complex. If you enjoy it I encourage you to walk up some of the other side canyons and see what you can discover on your own.

700 years ago there was a significant population of Anasazi Indians living near the Davis Canyon Trailhead. Eight Mile Spring is located in the bottom of the wash just east of the park boundary, and the number of ruins in the area indicate that the spring must have supported a sizable Indian community. Today the spring is completely overgrown with willows, tamarisk, and cottonwoods, but at that time this area was undoubtedly productive farmland.

As you walk into the national park from the trailhead you will soon begin to see the remnants of the ancient Anasazis. The first ruin is located in the back of a high alcove 200 yards from the traihhead on the north side of the canyon. The alcove is about 50 feet wide, 30 feet high, and 100 feet above the canyon floor. There are also a few remains of other small structures along the base of the cliffs west of the alcove, but most of them are so deteriorated they are hard to recognize.

200 yards beyond the alcove, or 0.2 mile from the trailhead, the canyon wall makes a 90-degree turn to the west. Continue following along the base of the cliff on your right and just 100 yards after making the

Five Faces Pictograph Panel

Anasazi Granary, Davis Canyon

painted by women? Why did they carry their corn up to this precarious ledge to grind? I can't imagine a more uncomfortable place to sit and mill corn than the narrow rocky ledge under the pictograph.

Continuing down the main canyon for 1.0 mile beyond the Five Faces will bring you to a junction where the canyon splits into its two divergent gorges. The larger canyon veers south from this point, and this is the direction most hikers take. But in my opinion the more interesting of the two canyons is the one that bears right in a southwesterly direction. This is the one I will describe here.

Turn right at the junction and within 0.4 mile you will come to an interesting side canyon on the right. Turn into this canyon and as you proceed west you will see another collection of Anasazi ruins on the northern wall of the canyon. These ruins

turn you will see a small south-facing granary in excellent condition not far above the canyon floor.

Keep walking west along the canyon wall for another 200 yards beyond the granary and you will come to one of the highlights of this hike. Just before the cliff turns to the south, in a shaded recess 30 feet above the canyon floor, is a fine example of Fremont rock art. It is a stylistic pictograph of five red and white faces, and it is in such amazing condition it looks like it was just painted yesterday. It was probably painted between 700 and 1,000 years ago, but it is so well protected from the rain and sun that it has been extremely well preserved.

On the ledge directly under the Five Faces Pictograph there are ten large depressions in the sandstone boulders where Indian women apparently ground their corn into flour. Also the rock face appears to have been smoothed with a grinding stone before the paintings were made. Were the faces

Davis Canyon

are quite extensive. But it is impossible to see them up close as they are situated on a ledge 150 feet above the base of the cliff. You should take a small pair of binoculars if you want to see the ruins in detail.

I counted no fewer than seven distinct structures at this site, as well as many broken walls where structures probably once stood. The ruins cover a span of about 100 yards along the cliff ledge. There are also remains of many granaries at the base of the cliff. There must have been at least 50 people living here at one time, but unfortunately the ruins at this site are not well preserved. Only a few of the dwellings are still intact.

I have called this site Log House Ruins because one of the dwellings is an unusual structure built entirely of logs. Some of the logs are over 15 feet long; the people who lived here must have struggled mightily to hoist the logs up the cliff to the ledge. Ob-

viously they possessed good ropes capable of supporting heavy loads. There is also a lot of rock art near the log dwelling, mostly handprints and small circles. The circles are arranged in orderly rows, almost as if they were being used to keep a running account of something. Some of the rock art is quite high on the cliff, indicating that the buildings below it must have been several levels high.

From Log House Ruins it is possible to continue up the canyon for another 2.5 miles to its head. There are probably more Anasazi ruins in the Davis Canyon complex, but the ones mentioned above are the only ones I have seen. One thing you will see in all of the branches of Davis Canyon, however, is natural arches. Watch the rims of the canyons carefully as you walk and you are bound to see at least a few arches hidden in the folds and recesses of the sandstone.

Davis Canyon Trail

Maze District

The Maze District of Canyonlands National Park was named after a large network of narrow canyons east of the Green and Colorado Rivers that have, over the last ten-million years, carved the land into a topless labyrinth of crazy winding passageways. The entire complex occupies an area of less than 35 square miles, but within this area 6 major canyons and dozens of smaller ones meander through the colorful Cedar Mesa Sandstone along their nonsensical routes to the rivers below.

This labyrinth of canyons actually comprises only about a third of the total area included in the Maze District. The national park boundaries extend for nearly 30 miles up the eastern shores of the Green and Colorado Rivers, from Waterhole Flat in the south to Horsethief Canyon in the north. Nevertheless, most of the hiking trails are located in the collection of canyons called the Maze.

Before the formation of the national park it was never imagined that the Maze District would one day become a tourist attraction. The area was virtually unknown to all but a few ranchers who ran cattle and sheep there. They called it Under the Ledge, because of its location east of the Orange Cliffs. The most common way to get there was to drive a wagon or truck to Flint Flat above the rim, and then descend into the canyons on horseback. Before the early 1950s there were no roads of any kind Under the Ledge—only horse trails.

The most popular Under the Ledge pastures for grazing livestock were in the southern half of the district, in Elaterite Basin, Ernies Country and Waterhole Flat, and oldtimers tell many stories about happenings there during the first half of the last century. Cowboys would frequently spend months tending their herds in the isolation of the canyons, then in the fall when it was time to market the cattle they would typically drive them up through North Trail Canyon to Hans Flat and on to the stock yards in Green River.

Most of the jeep roads in the Maze District were built during the 1950s when prospectors came flooding into Canyonlands in search of uranium. The road down from Flint Flat was built shortly after the completion of the White Rim Road in the Island in the Sky District. During the late 1950s there was also a crude ferry in operation that made it possible to travel from the Maze to the White Rim Road. The ferry crossed the Green River just above Anderson Bottom.

Much of the romance of the Maze District stems from its remoteness and isolation; the area hasn't really changed much since the Anasazi Indians left it 700 years ago. There are now a few jeep roads into the Maze but they haven't been upgraded since they were built 50 years ago, and they are still impassable to anything short of a 4WD vehicle. To its credit, the Park Service has dedicated itself to preserving the wild splendor of the land, and there are no plans to improve access to the Maze in the future. It is comforting to know that in this age of rapid development we can still count on some things staying the same. If you are willing to put up with hours of bone-rattling 4WD travel the Maze District of Canyonlands can provide a richly rewarding wilderness experience.

North Point Road

★ ☆

4WD vehicle required
1-day jeep ride

Distance:	25.6 miles (round trip to all points of interest)
Road conditions:	2WD pickups are sometimes driven on this road, but high clearance is a necessity.
Campsites:	The Park Service maintains 3 primitive campsites along this route, but camping elsewhere is not permitted. See pages 15-16 for more information about camping regulations and reservations.
Vicinity:	Near Hans Flat Ranger Station
USGS Maps:	Head Spur, Gordon Flats, Elaterite Basin, Cleopatra's Chair

This jeep ride begins at the Hans Flat Ranger Station. (See pages 13-14 for information on how to get to Hans Flat Ranger Station.)

North Point is the name given to a long, slender promontory of land that juts out in a northeasterly direction from Gordon Flats into the canyons on the west side of the Green River. The peninsula splits near its northern end, forming four separate fingers that protrude from the mesa like the prongs of a pitchfork. The road also divides here, with one spur continuing eastward to Panorama Point and the other turning west to an unusual sandstone formation called Cleopatra's Chair. The trip described here goes first to Cleopatra's Chair that then doubles back to Panorama Point on the east rim of North Point.

There are primitive campsites at both Cleopatra's Chair and Panorama Point, and many people do this trip as an overnighter. The Panorama Point Campsite is a particu- larly enjoyable place to spend a night. The site is situated high on the canyon rim above the Orange Cliffs, and the views into Elaterite Basin and Horse Canyon below are remarkable. The Millard Canyon jeep road runs across the benches directly below Panorama Point, so if you are planning a jeep ride to the Maze Overlook or the Green River there is no finer place to survey the route.

Drive east from Hans Flat Ranger Station on the Gordon Flats Road towards the Flint Trail. After 2.3 miles you will pass the road to French Spring, and 0.2 mile later you will see the beginning of the North Point Road where you must turn right. Along the way you might want to check out French Spring as well as French Cabin and the

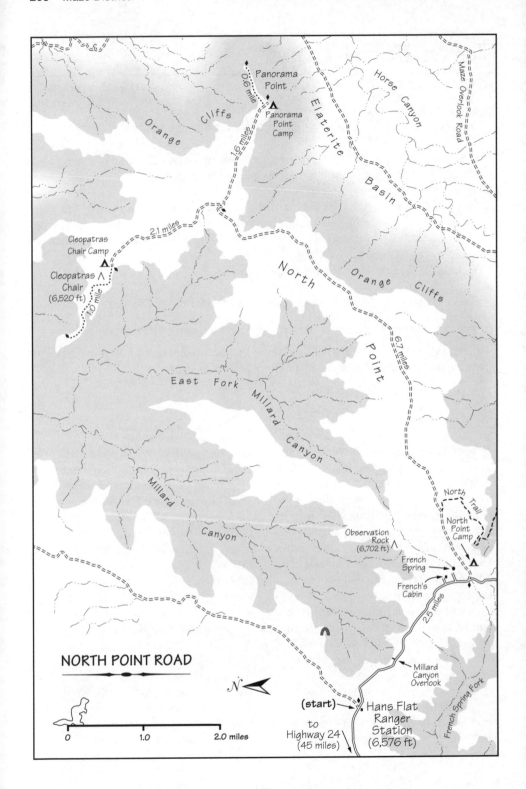

Panorama Point

0.6 mile

Panorama
Point
Camp

Orange   Cliffs

Elaterite

Horse   Canyon

Maze Overlook Road

1.6 miles

2.1 miles

Basin

Cleopatras
Chair Camp

Cleopatras ∧
Chair
(6,520 ft)

1.0 mile

North   Orange   Cliffs

Point

6.7 miles

East   Fork   Millard   Canyon

Millard

Canyon

North   Trail

North
Point Camp

Observation
Rock
(6,702 ft) ∧

French
Spring

French's
Cabin

2.5 miles

French Spring Fork

Millard
Canyon
Overlook

NORTH POINT ROAD

N

0   1.0   2.0 miles

(start)

to
Highway 24
(45 miles)

Hans Flat
Ranger
Station
(6,576 ft)

Cleopatra's Chair

Millard Canyon Overlook. Read more about these points of interest on pages 212-213.

Within 300 yards after turning onto the North Point Road you will see the North Point Campsite on the east side of the road, and another 0.9 mile will bring you to the North Point Trailhead. This trail is often used by people who do not own a 4WD vehicle as an access route into the canyons of the Maze. With care ordinary cars can usually get as far as the North Point Trailhead, but the road is still very rocky and difficult for low clearance vehicles. Beyond the North Point Trailhead the road is definitely for high clearance vehicles only.

Soon after leaving North Point Trailhead the road begins a long, gradual turn to the north. As you bounce along through the pinion and juniper forest you will occasionally catch glimpses of the canyons below the right side of the road. The views get better and better as the top of the mesa narrows.

Cleopatra's Chair, a prominent outcropping of Navajo Sandstone, is frequently visible in the distance on the left side of the road. The huge block of white stone really does look like an enormous chair rising above the forest. Finally, 6.7 miles after leaving the Gordon Flats Road, the route veers away from the rim and drops down to a junction where you must turn left to get to Cleopatra's Chair.

From the junction the Cleopatra's Chair spur heads out across the top of the mesa in a northwesterly direction for another 2.1 miles, finally ending at Cleopatra's Chair Camp at the base of the formation. The Chair poses a tantalizing challenge for rock climbers. The formation is surrounded by 200-foot cliffs, but there is a prominent crack angling up the vertical wall from the campsite that looks like it might be scalable by an experienced climber.

A primitive trail continues on to the end of the point 1.0 mile beyond Cleopatra's

Chair. At one time it was possible to drive a car most of this distance, but the road west of the camp was closed in the 1990s and now it is open to foot traffic only. From the end of the point you can see almost the entire length of Millard Canyon, a 15-mile-long ravine that extends from Hans Flat all the way to the Green River.

In order to get to Panorama Point you must retrace your journey back to the Cleopatra's Chair junction and drive east for 1.6 miles. Again the road ends at the campsite, but this time the campsite is only 20 feet from the edge of the rim. The view is fantastic. The Standing Rocks are clearly visible 7 miles to the southeast. Elaterite Butte, 4 miles south, seems to be only a stone's throw away, and the road to the Maze Overlook, 3 miles away, is easily distinguishable.

But the best part of Panorama Point is the short walk to the extreme eastern end of the point. One hundred yards before the end of the road you will pass a small parking area where the trail begins. Follow the cairns eastward for 200 yards to the first good viewpoint, then continue for another 0.5 mile to the end of the point. On the south side of the point the view is much the same as from the camp, but on the north side of the point you can see the Green River gorge meandering northward all the way to Anderson Bottom.

The canyon just below the north side of the point is Deadhorse Canyon. If you look northeast to where Deadhorse Canyon meets the Green River you will see the Turks Head, a low lying butte in the middle of one of the river's meanders. 700 years ago the fertile land surrounding Turks Head was farmed by a community of Anasazi Indians that lived near the river.

Panorama Point

Flint Trail—Green River

☆ ☆ ☆ ☆

4WD vehicle required
4-day jeep ride

Distance: 110.4 miles (round trip to all points of interest)

Road conditions: Ordinary cars can usually make it to the top of the Flint Trail, 12.2 miles from the Hans Flat Ranger Station, but beyond that point this road is for 4WD vehicles only.

Campsites: The Park Service maintains 8 primitive campsites along this route, but camping elsewhere is not permitted. None of the campsites have water or toilet facilities, and you must carry a portable toilet in your vehicle in order to obtain a camping permit. See pages 15-16 for more information on obtaining camping permits and reservations.

Vicinity: The southwestern corner of Canyonlands

USGS Maps: Head Spur, Gordon Flats, Clearwater Canyon, Teapot Rock, Elaterite Basin, Cleopatras Chair, Turks Head, Horsethief Canyon

This jeep ride begins at the Hans Flat Ranger Station. (See pages 13-14 for information on how to get to Hans Flat Ranger Station.)

"Under the Ledge" is a term local cowboys once used to identify the canyon country east of the Orange Cliffs in Canyonlands National Park. The area has subsequently been renamed the Maze District, but this jeep ride will clearly demonstrate how appropriate the older term was. From Hans Flat Ranger Station the road heads south along the top of the mesa, occasionally approaching the edge of the rim for dramatic views into the canyons below. Then, after 12.4 miles of relatively easy driving, the road abruptly turns east to descend through a series of steep, rocky switchbacks that lead into the Under the Ledge country.

This steep section of road, known as the Flint Trail, is the only place where it is possible to descend with a car below the Orange Cliffs. The trail was well known during most of the last century; it was frequently used by cattle ranchers to gain access to the pastures

see color photos, pages 153, 154

Under the Ledge. It was improved enough to accommodate 4WD vehicles during the uranium boom that hit Canyonlands in the early 1950s, but the Park Service has not done much to improve it since then.

Once below the rim the road turns north to meander across a series of canyons and benches for the next 41 miles before finally ending at the Green River near the mouth of Millard Canyon. Most of the route is through dry, barren desert country, but the canyons and the buttes provide panoramas that are often breathtaking. The harshness of the dry, waterless land Under the Ledge may be too alien for some city dwellers to enjoy, but for me the vast land is full of wonder.

The Park Service has established 8 primitive campsites along the route described here, and in order to preserve the pristine condition of the land camping is not allowed elsewhere. The trip could conceivably be done in 2 days with an overnight stay at the Millard Canyon Camp, but I wouldn't recommend doing it in less than 4 days.

Most people following this route get only as far as the Maze Overlook. There are two very pleasant campsites at the Maze Overlook, and a trip there and back can provide a fine Under the Ledge experience. However, if time permits I would encourage you to extend your trip an additional 43 miles, round trip, and drive all the way to the Green River.

Flint Seep Camp (11.2 miles)

From Hans Flat Ranger Station the road continues in a southeasterly direction across Hans Flat for only 0.9 mile before coming to the first point of interest: the Millard Canyon Overlook. Look for a sign marking the parking area and the 200-foot trail from the road to the overlook point. Millard Canyon is a 15-mile-long canyon that extends all the way from Hans Flat to the Green River where this jeep ride ends, and from the overlook you can see about two-thirds of that distance. Notice the small natural arches about a mile from the viewpoint on the up-

per west rim of the canyon. Also Cleopatra's Chair, a prominent sandstone formation on the east rim of Millard Canyon is clearly visible 6 miles from the viewpoint.

1.4 miles after leaving the Millard Canyon Overlook you will come to another short spur road on the left that leads to French Cabin. The Park Service calls this cabin French Cabin because it is near French Spring, but actually the cabin was built by a man named T. C. Conley who worked as a wildcat oil driller here in the 1920s. Of the several artifacts in the area the most interesting is an old boiler that was used provide power for Conley's drilling rig. A major factor in his selection of this drill site must have been the availability of water for the boiler at nearby French Spring.

The road to French Spring is just 0.1 mile beyond the turnout to French Cabin. To reach the spring you must again turn left

Millard Canyon Overlook

French Cabin

and drive 0.2 mile to a parking area just above the water. This is the most reliable spring for many miles around, and it has been used at least since the 1890s as a waterhole for livestock. At that time most of the domestic animals in the area were sheep and many of the sheep herders were French; hence the name French Spring. The spring has been developed over the years by a succession of ranchers, and now their broken troughs, cables, and pipes make it look more like a junk yard than a spring. But the water still flows.

0.2 mile after passing the turnout to French Spring you will see the road to North Point departing on the left. Continue driving south from this point across Gordon Flats, and after another 6.5 miles you will come to another overlook point above Bagpipe Butte. Again, the parking area is well marked with a small sign and a 200-foot path leads from the road to the viewpoint. Bagpipe Butte rises up from the bottom of the canyon only a mile from the rim, and with its jagged, multi-pinnacled summit it really does look like a set of bagpipes. Elaterite Butte is the large formation northeast of Bagpipe, and on the distant eastern horizon are the LaSal Mountains.

Another 2.2 miles beyond the Bagpipe Butte Overlook will bring you to Flint Seep Camp, the first campsite along this road.

There is also a spring here, but it has all but dried up in recent years. According to oldtimers Flint Flat, where the seep is located, was once covered with flakes of flint. Centuries ago it was apparently an Anasazi chipping site where the Indians made points and other stone tools. Unfortunately the chips have been picked up over the years to the extent that by the time the site became a protected area there were very few left.

You might want to check out the Flint Cabins before you leave Flint Seep. The cabins can't be seen from the road and there is no trail going to them, but they are not difficult to find. To reach the Flint Cabins park your car at the Flint Seep turnoff and continue down the main road on foot for another 250 feet to the edge of a large treeless meadow south of the campsite. When you reach the meadow turn right and begin walking through the sagebrush near the trees on the west side of the meadow. Five minutes, or 300 yards, after leaving the road you will come to an old, broken-down corral in a

Bagpipe Butte

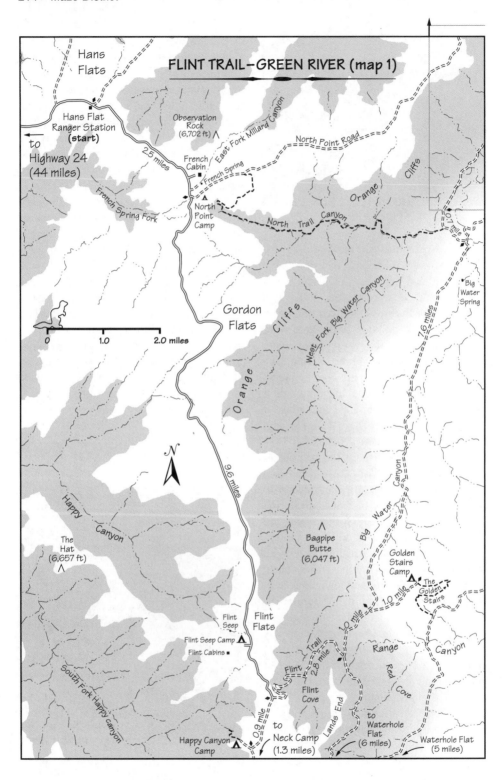

FLINT TRAIL–GREEN RIVER (map 1)

Hans
Flats

Hans Flat
Ranger Station
(start)

to
Highway 24
(44 miles)

2.5 miles

French Spring Fork

Observation
Rock
(6,702 ft)

French
Cabin

French Spring

East Fork Millard Canyon

North Point Road

North
Point
Camp

North   Trail   Canyon

Orange

Cliffs

0.1 mile

Big
Water
Spring

7.6 miles

Gordon
Flats

Orange

Cliffs

West Fork Big Water Canyon

0   1.0   2.0 miles

N

9.6 miles

Happy

Canyon

The
Hat
(6,657 ft)

Bagpipe
Butte
(6,047 ft)

Big   Water   Canyon

Golden
Stairs
Camp

The
Golden
Stairs

1.0 mile

Flint
Seep

Flint
Flats

Flint Seep Camp

Flint Cabins

Flint   Trail

2.8 mile

Range   Canyon

Red

Cove

South Fork Happy Canyon

Flint

Flint
Cove

1.0 mile

Lands End

to
Waterhole
Flat
(6 miles)

Waterhole Flat
(5 miles)

0.9 mile

to
Neck Camp
(1.3 miles)

Happy Canyon
Camp

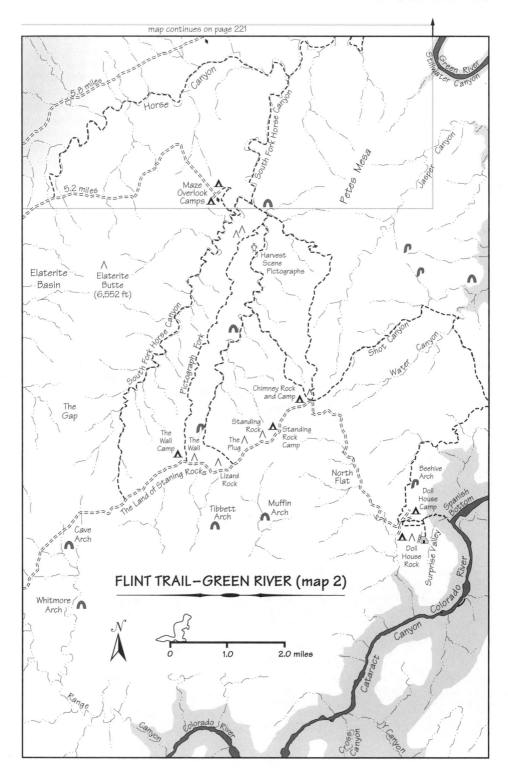

map continues on page 221

Green River

Stillwater Canyon

Horse Canyon

5.8 miles

South Fork Horse Canyon

Jasper Canyon

Petes Mesa

5.2 miles

Maze
Overlook
Camps

Harvest
Scene
Pictographs

Elaterite
Basin

Elaterite
Butte
(6,552 ft)

South Fork Horse Canyon

Pictograph Fork

Shot Canyon

Water Canyon

The
Gap

Chimney Rock
and Camp

Standing
Rock

The
Wall
Camp

The
Wall

The
Plug

Standing
Rock
Camp

Lizard
Rock

North
Flat

Beehive
Arch

Doll
House
Camp

Spanish Bottom

The Land of Standing Rocks

Cave
Arch

Tibbett
Arch

Muffin
Arch

Doll
House
Rock

Surprise Valley

Colorado River

FLINT TRAIL—GREEN RIVER (map 2)

Whitmore
Arch

Cataract Canyon

N

0   1.0   2.0 miles

Range

Canyon

Colorado River

Cross Canyon

Y Canyon

grove of trees on the edge of the meadow. When you reach the corral turn into the trees and walk directly away from the meadow for a distance of 500 feet to the three cabins. They are located in a small open area near the top of a low hill about 50 feet higher than the corral. You will know you are getting close when you start seeing a collection of old tin cans and other debris that has washed down the hill from the cabins.

These cabins were originally built in 1919 to serve as a base of operations for the Nequoia Oil Company, a consortium of wildcat drillers headed by a man named E. T. Wolverton. They never found oil and it wasn't long before Wolverton ran out of money, but the Flint cabins continued to be used by cattlemen for many years afterward. Eventually one of the cabins burned down, and the roof has collapsed on another one. But the third cabin is still in amazingly good condition.

Happy Canyon Camp and Neck Camp (3.8 miles)

Within 0.8 mile after leaving Flint Seep Camp the road passes the Flint Trail Overlook, where there is a fine view of the Flint Trail making its way down the Wingate cliffs to Under the Ledge. The overlook is marked by a small sign where a 50-foot trail leads to the edge of the rim. Then continuing

Flint Cabins

down the road for another 0.2 mile will bring you to a junction where the road to Happy Canyon and Big Ridge branches off to the right.

Happy Canyon is actually a large network of canyons that drain into the Dirty Devil River west of the national park. These canyons are not as spectacular as the canyons above the Green and Colorado Rivers, but they are interesting nevertheless. The Park Service maintains two primitive campsites in this area, Happy Canyon Camp and Neck Camp, where you can spend a night. To reach the Happy Canyon Camp drive 0.9 mile from the junction with Flint Trail and turn right onto a short spur road that drops down to the west. After another 200 yards you will see the camp on your left.

Continuing down the spur road past Happy Canyon Camp for another 0.2 mile will bring you to a terrific view over the South Fork of Happy Canyon with the Henry Mountains on the western horizon. The road ends just 20 feet from the rim near another old jeep road that descends on down into the gorge. The road below the rim has long been closed to vehicles, but if you are in the mood for a hike you can use it as a trail to gain access to the bottom of the Happy Canyon complex. The old track descends 800 feet over a distance of 1.5 miles.

The Big Ridge is a long narrow finger of land that extends westward for many miles above Happy Canyon and Under the Ledge. Big Ridge Road follows the top of the narrow mesa for at least 15 miles beyond Happy Canyon Camp, and the views on both sides are often dramatic. Just 1.3 miles past the spur to Happy Canyon Camp, at a particularly narrow point along the top of the Big Ridge, the Park Service has designated another campsite called Neck Camp.

I would definitely classify Neck Camp as one of the more interesting camps in Canyonlands. The mesa is only 100 feet wide at this point, with the road on the west side of the constriction and the camp on the east side. From Neck Camp you can look 1,400 feet down into Waterhole Flat and Teapot Canyon. The gorge of Cataract Canyon is clearly visible 5 miles to the east, and directly below the camp are the jeep roads that lead to the Flint Trail and the Land of Standing Rocks. It is a very inspirational place to spend some time.

Golden Stairs Camp (7.0 miles)

After you have driven back to the junction where the Big Ridge Road departs from the main road it is only 0.2 mile to the beginning of the Flint Trail. There are two parking areas just before the beginning of the steep descent, marked by a sign that says "High Clearance 4WD Required Beyond This Point". With care it is usually possible to drive most 2WD cars from Hans Flat Ranger Station to the beginning of the Flint Trail, but I would never attempt the Flint

Trail itself with anything less than a 4WD.

The Flint Trail existed as a cow trail for most of the last century, but it was only in the early 1950s that it was improved enough for wheeled vehicle use. This road, like most of the other jeep trails in Canyonlands was constructed by uranium prospectors during the post-war uranium boom, and it is still the only place where it is possible to drive a car from the top of the Orange Cliffs down into the Maze. The road drops 800 feet in the first mile and then levels out slightly as it enters an area called Flint Cove at the head of Big Water Canyon. There are very few places wide enough for two cars to pass, so before you start down you should listen and look for any vehicles that might be coming up.

Finally, 2.6 miles from the top of the Flint Trail, the road comes to the Flint Trail Junction, where the Millard Canyon Road begins and the road to Waterhole Flat branches off to the right. Occasionally

Flint Trail

someone will go down the Flint Trail with a 2WD vehicle and turn right at this junction, arriving at a paved road 41 miles later near the town of Hite. It is sometimes possible to do this with a high clearance 2WD truck, but it is risky.

Turning left at the Flint Trail Junction onto the Millard Canyon Road will take you across 1.0 mile of easy driving to the Golden Stairs turnoff. When you arrive at the turn-off turn right for the last 1.0 mile to the Golden Stairs Camp. If you plan to spend the night here and if it is still early in the day you might what to spend a few hours walking down the 2.0-mile-long Golden Stairs Trail. The trail begins just east of the campsite and leads to the Dollhouse Road and Ernie's Country 800 feet below. (See page 239 for more information on this hike.)

Maze Overlook Camps (13.8 miles)

From the Golden Stairs Camp you must drive 1.0 mile back to the Millard Canyon Road and turn right. Along the way the road passes an impressive overlook on the south side of the road where you might want to stop and enjoy view. The wide expanse to the east is Ernie's Country, with a rugged area known as The Fins on its north side. To the south you can clearly see the gorge of Cataract Canyon, although from this perspective you can't see the Colorado River at its bottom.

Within 0.4 mile after rejoining the Millard Canyon Road you will begin a descent down Big Water Canyon to Elaterite Basin, and for the next mile the road is very steep. It is again obvious at this point that you are in 4WD country. A 2WD vehicle might be able to get down this road, but it would never make it back out. As you drive into Big Water you will have an impressive view of Bagpipe Butte on the canyon's west rim. The road passes within 0.9 mile of the butte. Finally the route drops into the dry,

sandy streambed for a mile, then climbs out again and continues northward along the west side of the drainage. 3.7 miles later it arrives at the Maze Overlook Junction.

During the early and mid-1900s Ernie's Country and Elaterite Basin were important grazing areas for local ranchers, and they would often drive their livestock between the two pastures over much the same route that the road follows today. From Ernie's Country the cows were driven up the Golden Stairs Trail, across the China Neck, and then down Big Water Canyon to Elaterite Basin. A key factor in determining where and when the cattle drives took place was the availability of water. The cowboys all knew where they could find water, and one of the most important springs in Elaterite Basin was the Big Water Spring in lower Big Water Canyon.

The best way to find Big Water Spring is to backtrack south from the Maze Overlook Junction 0.7 mile to another old jeep

Descending into Big Water Canyon

road on the east side of the main road. Park here and walk east for 300 yards to a grove of cottonwood trees growing in the bottom of the drainage. The trees are fed by water seeping from Big Water Spring. In the old days cowboys would often camp in this area and today it is still possible to see a few examples of the graffiti they left behind. If you walk down canyon from the Big Water Spring for a ten or fifteen minutes you should see a few remnants of the old cowboy etchings on the rocks.

To get to the Maze Overlook you must turn right at the Maze Overlook Junction and drive 5.2 miles to the end of the road. For the first 0.3 mile the road continues north along the side of the Big Water drainage, then it crosses and turns east to follow the south rim of Horse Canyon to the overlook. 1.4 miles from the junction, just east of the national park boundary, you will see a slickrock trail marked by a line large cairns that heads north from the road into the desert. This is the beginning of the Horse Canyon Trail, an old livestock trail once used to get cattle in and out of the lower canyons of the Maze.

The Horse Canyon Trail is also sometimes used by hikers wishing to gain entry into the Maze. A possible loop hike into the Maze begins by walking down Horse Canyon to the South Fork, and then following that canyon to the bottom of the Maze Overlook Trail. From there one can climb back out of the canyons to the Maze Overlook Road and walk 3.9 miles back to the starting point. The total length of the loop is 17.0 miles. In my opinion, however, the upper part of Horse Canyon does not have much to offer. A more interesting way to see the Maze is to camp at the Maze Overlook and make day trips down into the canyons.

At two points, 0.9 mile and 1.5 miles beyond the Horse Canyon Trailhead, the road passes very close the rim of Horse Canyon, providing exceptional views down into its depths. If you are contemplating a hike into the canyon I recommend checking it out from these two vantage points before you begin. The canyon bottom is dry and sandy, but walking is relatively easy with few obstacles to impede your progress.

You are in for a real treat at the Maze Overlook. The view down into the Maze is certainly one of the finest panoramas in the national park. Directly below lies an incredible jumble of canyons and side canyons that have over the millennium been etched into the bedrock of Cedar Mesa Sandstone. In the five miles from the overlook to the Green River the unrelenting forces of erosion have carved out five major canyons and dozens of smaller ones, all connected together like a giant labyrinth with the top removed. The

Elaterite Butte above Horse Canyon

Land of Standing Rocks lies immediately to the south, and most of its distinctive landmarks are also clearly visible form the Maze Overlook. Most impressive is the Chocolate Drops formation, where four enormous rectangular-shaped pillars of deep read Organ Shale rise some 200 feet above the top of the mesa less than a mile away.

The two Maze Overlook camps are the most popular campsites in the Maze District, so if you plan to stay in one of them you should call for reservations at least several weeks in advance. Be sure to spend one morning watching the sun rise over the canyons. Both sites are located just west of the rim and the sunrises are often dramatic.

Ekker Butte Camp (14.4 miles)

Continuing north on the Millard Canyon Road from the Maze Overlook Junction for 0.6 mile will bring you to the North Trail, a historic trail that leads from Elaterite Basin to North Point Road near the ranger station. The trailhead is well marked on the left side of the road. (See page 234 for a description

of this hike). This area is also of historic interest because it was the primary drilling location for E. T. Wolverton's Nequoia Oil Company in 1920-21. (The same company that built the Flint Cabins in 1919.) You can still see the iron boiler that was used to power Wolverton's drilling rig nearby. It is located beside the North Trail about 150 yards west of the road.

That boiler, along with the rest of Wolverton's drilling rig, was disassembled and slid off the rim where the Flint Trail is today and lowered down to Big Water Canyon on the snow. It was then transported to Elaterite Basin, where the boiler sits now, and reassembled. Wolverton's crew drilled in the area for an entire year; the men lived in tents and spent most of their days cutting down trees to fuel the boiler and hauling water for the operation. Most of them made it to town only two or three times during the whole project. They drilled many holes but they never struck oil, and when the year was up the company was bankrupt. Few of the men were ever paid for their work.

The Chocolate Drops, seen from the Maze Overlook

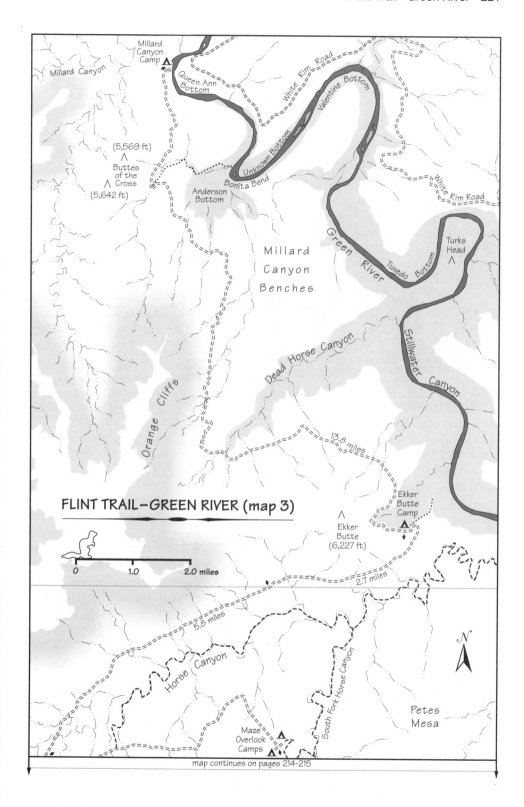

Millard Canyon Camp

Millard Canyon

Queen Ann Bottom

White Rim Road

Valentine Bottom

Unknown Bottom

(5,569 ft)
Λ
Buttes
of the
Λ Cross
(5,642 ft)

Anderson Bottom

Bonita Bend

Millard

Canyon

Benches

Green River

Tuxedo Bottom

Turks Head
Λ

White Rim Road

Dead Horse Canyon

Orange Cliffs

Stillwater Canyon

13.8 miles

FLINT TRAIL—GREEN RIVER (map 3)

Ekker Butte Camp

Λ
Ekker
Butte
(6,227 ft)

0   1.0   2.0 miles

2.7 miles

5.8 miles

Horse Canyon

South Fork Horse Canyon

Petes

Mesa

N

Maze
Overlook
Camps

map continues on pages 214-215

Ekker Butte above the White Rim Sandstone Formation

Wolverton was right in one respect: there is a massive deposit of oil under the ground in the Maze District of Canyonlands. But what he didn't know is that the oil is not in liquid form; it is present in the form of elaterite or tar sand. The only feasible way to get the oil out of the ground would be liquefy it by injecting superheated steam into the deposit, and that technology did not exist in 1920 when the ill-fated Noquoia Oil Company was in operation.

Soon after leaving the North Trail Trailhead the road begins following the north rim of Horse Canyon, and it continues to do so for the next 7.0 miles. Most of the time the road is several hundred yards form the edge of the rim, but occasionally it approaches to within a few feet of the precipice. When you are looking into Horse Canyon notice the thick, uniform layer of sandstone just below the road. This is the White Rim Formation, after which the White

Rim Road in the Island in the Sky District was named. In this area, however, it is not really white. The intrusion of oil into Elaterite Basin has stained it to a dirty yellow color.

The tableland above the Orange Cliffs on the left side of the road is North Point Mesa, where the North Point jeep road is located (see page 207). As you approach the eastern side of the mesa you will pass directly under Panorama Point Camp, the most popular campsite on the North Point Road, and if there is anyone staying there they will probably be watching you as you drive by beneath them. The large butte directly in front of the road, three miles east of Panorama Point, is Ekker Butte. The Ekker Butte Camp is located just east of the butte on the rim above the Green River.

Ekker Butte Camp is considered by many to be one of the least desirable campsites on this jeep ride, but personally it is

Green River below Ekker Butte Camp

one of my favorites. The campsite is on bare slickrock, and there are very few trees in the area, but it does have one unique quality. Within a 15-minute walk of Ekker Butte Camp there is an extraordinary view of the Green River.

Although the campsite is located very close to the rim of Stillwater Canyon you can't actually see the river from the camp. However, if you will walk northeast along the canyon rim for 0.3 mile you will come to a long narrow finger of land that extends outward from the plateau for a quarter-mile into the Green River gorge. Walk out onto this promontory and you will be treated to a view that will take your breath away. If you have a panorama camera this is the place to take some prize-winning photographs! You can see the river below for almost 180 degrees, and on the other rim of the canyon many prominent features of the Island in the Sky embellish the skyline. If you are there around the second week of April you can watch the sun rise directly behind the notch between Grandview Point and Junction Butte.

Millard Canyon Camp (13.7 miles)

From Ekker Butte Camp the road swings around to the west and proceeds directly away from the river for four miles in order to get around the head of Deadhorse Canyon. When you finally turn north again you will be driving just below the Orange Cliffs on the northernmost extremity of North Point. Then, as you approach the end of North Point two more well known buttes come into view three miles to the north. These two formations are called the Buttes of the Cross. It is not apparent from this angle how they got their name, but when you reach the end of the road you will see why they are called the Buttes of the Cross.

The flat desert country between North Point and the Buttes of the Cross reminds me of a scene out of a 1950s western movie.

As you drive across this flat, called the Millard Canyon Benches, you can see buttes rising from the desert in almost every direction. Candlestick, Junction, Ekker, Buttes of the Cross, plus at least a half-dozen unnamed buttes. One almost expects to see a team of horses pulling a stagecoach down the road. This impression is oddly appropriate because the river bottoms below the Millard Canyon Benches saw a great deal of human activity during the era of cattle ranching in Canyonlands.

As you approach the Buttes of the Cross stop to look down into Anderson Bottom on the west side of the Green River. Anderson Bottom was inhabited off and on from 1909 until 1964 when it became part of the national park. Many attempts were made during that time to homestead Anderson Bottom and farm its fertile land. At one time there were 100 acres of cultivated land on the bottom, complete with irrigation ditches, a tractor, and a cabin. All of that is gone now, however, and today there are few remnants left of the old homesteads. If you are in the mood to explore there is a trail that goes into Anderson Bottom from the Millard Canyon Road. See page 246 for more information about the trail and the bottom.

From Anderson Bottom the road proceeds along the eastern side of the Buttes of the Cross and then drops down the last 200 feet to the mouth of Millard Canyon at the Green River. Millard Canyon Camp is located just above the water at the end of the road, or if you prefer there is a short spur that goes downstream another 200 yards to a more sheltered site. If you look back to the southwest from Millard Canyon Camp you will see how the Buttes of the Cross got their name. From this prospective the two buttes are aligned in such a way that they form a cross. John Wesley Powell was the first one to notice this; he named the buttes during his famous expedition down the Green and Colorado Rivers in 1869.

Green River at the mouth of Millard Canyon

Land of Standing Rocks

☆ ☆ ☆ ☆

4WD vehicle required
overnight jeep ride

Distance: 42.0 miles (round trip from Waterhole Flat)

Road conditions: There is a particularly rough section of road beginning just north
of Waterhole Flat where the route crosses the upper reaches of
Teapot Canyon. If you don't have a 4WD vehicle with high
clearance you won't get beyond this point. Pickup trucks with a
long wheel base may also have some difficulty.

Campsites: The Park Service maintains 8 primitive campsites along this
route, but camping elsewhere along the road is not permitted.
None of the campsites have water or toilet facilities, and you
must carry a portable toilet in your vehicle in order to obtain a
camping permit. See pages 15-16 for more information on
obtaining camping permits and reservations.

Vicinity: The southwestern corner of Canyonlands

USGS Maps: Clearwater Canyon, Teapot Rock, Elaterite Basin, Spanish
Bottom

The best way to reach Waterhole Flat, where this jeep ride begins, is from High-
way 95 near Hite. Drive 1.1 miles north of the Hite turnoff on Highway 95 to
the bridge across Lake Powell. After you cross this bridge drive another 1.0
mile until you see a gravel road departing on the right. This is the road to
Waterhole Flat. The distance to the flat is 34 miles along a road that can usu-
ally be driven by most cars. There are numerous side roads along the way, mostly built by
local ranchers, but if you just stay on the best-traveled road you should have no trouble.
You will know you have arrived at your destination when you come to the Waterhole Flat
Junction, a 4-way intersection with signs indicating the way to the Dollhouse, Flint Trail,
and Hatch Canyon.

If you are starting from the Hans Flat Ranger Station it will be easier to drive to Waterhole
Flat by way of the Flint Trail. 15 miles south of the ranger station, or 2.6 miles below the
point where the Flint Trail begins its descent from the canyon rim, the road comes to the
well-marked Flint Junction. Turn right here and drive another 6.9 miles to the Waterhole
Flat Junction. See page 211 for a detailed description of this road. See pages 13-14 for
more information on how to get to Hans Flat Ranger Station.

Although the end of this road is only 51 miles from a paved highway it can take as much as 6 hours of driving to get there. The first 34 miles, from Highway 95 near Hite to Waterhole Flat, can usually be driven by almost any vehicle, but beyond that point the road is definitely for 4WD vehicles only. You will probably be stopping frequently to get out and study the road before venturing ahead with your jeep.

Most people drive all the way from the highway to Dollhouse Rock at the end of the road in a single day, but you may want to take two days for the trip. Long distance driving on 4WD roads is very tiring, and there is so much to see along the way it is a shame to rush. The Park Service maintains 8 primitive campsites along this route, and the trip will be much more enjoyable if you make use of them. During the spring and fall seasons the sites are often full, so it is best to plan ahead and make reservations.

The jeep ride described below begins at Waterhole Flat, a wide grassy meadow south of the national park that was once considered prime grazing land for cattle. As mentioned earlier, the easiest way to get to Waterhole Flat is from the town of Hite on the shore of Lake Powell. There is, however, a 6.9-mile connecting road from the Flint Trail to Waterhole Flat, which makes it possible to drive there from the Hans Flat Ranger Station.

see color photos, pages 157, 158

This connecting road is very scenic with great views of Teapot Rock, the Fins, Ernie's Country, Waterhole Flat, and the Cataract Canyon gorge. In some places the road passes within 10 feet of the Moenkopi and Organ Shale cliffs below. After 3.5 miles the road makes an abrupt descent to the bottom of the cliffs, and soon afterward it arrives at Waterhole Flat.

The drive from Hans Flat Ranger Station to Waterhole Flat is very steep in places, and the route is definitely not recommended

Waterhole Flat near the Chaffin Cowboy Camp

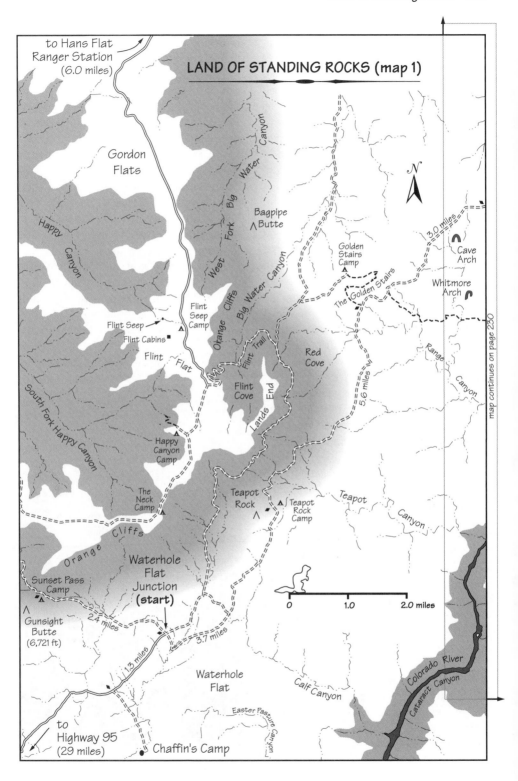

to Hans Flat
Ranger Station
(6.0 miles)

LAND OF STANDING ROCKS (map 1)

Gordon
Flats

Happy Canyon

West Fork Big Water Canyon

Big Water Canyon

Bagpipe
∧ Butte

N

3.0 miles

∩ Cave
Arch

Golden
Stairs
Camp
∧

The Golden Stairs

Whitmore
Arch ∩

Flint
Seep
Camp
∧

Orange Cliffs

Flint
Seep

Flint Cabins ■

Flint Trail

Flint   Flat

Red
Cove

5.6 miles

Range Canyon

Flint
Cove
∧

Lands End

Happy
Canyon
Camp
∧

South Fork Happy Canyon

The
Neck
Camp
∧

Teapot
Rock
∧

Teapot
Rock
Camp
∧

Teapot Canyon

Orange   Cliffs

Waterhole
Flat
Junction
(start)

Sunset Pass
Camp
∧

∧
Gunsight
Butte
(6,721 ft)

2.4 miles

1.3 miles

3.7 miles

Waterhole
Flat

Calf Canyon

Colorado River

Cataract Canyon

Easter Pasture Canyon

to
Highway 95
(29 miles)

Chaffin's Camp

0   1.0   2.0 miles

map continues on page 230

for 2WD vehicles. Occasionally, however, someone will drive a high-clearance 2WD vehicle *down* the Flint Trail, across to Waterhole Flat, and on to Hite. If you don't own a 4WD vehicle this can be an interesting alternative to the trip described below. Just don't try it in a low-clearance passenger car and don't attempt to do the trip in reverse. It is probably impossible to get up the Flint Trail with anything less than 4WD.

Sunset Pass Camp and Teapot Rock Camp (3.7 miles)

These two camps are located within a few miles of Waterhole Flat. In order to reach Sunset Pass Camp you must turn west at Waterhole Flat Junction and drive up the 2WD road to the saddle on the north side of Gunsight Butte. The camp is located at the summit of the pass 2.4 miles from the junction. If you happen to be in Waterhole Flat at the end of the day look up toward Sunset Pass and you will see immediately how the pass got its name. At certain times of the year the sun sets directly behind the opening between Gunsight Butte and the Orange Cliffs.

The road to Sunset Pass is actually the beginning of a much longer road called the Poison Springs Road. This is a little used jeep trail that extends all the way from Waterhole Flat, through North Hatch and Hatch Canyons, across the Dirty Devil River, up Poison Springs Canyon, and ultimately back to Highway 95. The route is extremely rough. It also requires a ford of the Dirty Devil River which is possible only after a long dry spell when the river's flow rate is lower than normal.

Before leaving Waterhole Flat you might want to visit the old Chaffin Cowboy Camp. The Chaffin family ran cows Under the Ledge from 1919 until they sold out in 1944. There were sheep ranchers in the area before that, but their's was the first sizable cattle operation in the Maze District. They ran their cows in Waterhole Flat, Ernie's Country and Elaterite Basin, but their operation was mostly centered in Waterhole Flat, and that is where their primary camp was. There isn't much left of their camp today but an old corral; however it is still fun to visit.

To get to the Chaffin Camp you must drive back towards Hite from the Waterhole Flat Junction for 1.3 miles until you see a primitive road departing on the left. Turn here and drive southeast for 1.3 miles, where the road ends at an old stock pond. The Chaffins built the pond simply by making a 150-foot-long dam across the drainage in the upper part of Waterhole Canyon. 150 yards below the dam is an old corral that is still in amazingly good condition. Their living quarters were a tent cabin that stood about halfway between the corral and the dam on the opposite side of the canyon.

Chaffin Camp

Teapot Canyon

There is nothing left of the cabin now, but you can still see a few relics in the area, including a small trough for collecting water and parts of an old stove. A cowboy's life was very simple in those days, supplemented by lots of hard work.

Another 150 yards down the wash from the corral you can see several old names that were scratched into the sandstone long before even the Chaffins were here. Two of the signatures, Ella Butler and Geo. E. Felton were carved in 1897. To get there walk down the sandy bottom of the wash until you see a small overhang above the low cliffs on the right. The overhang is 100 feet north of the bottom of Waterhole Canyon, on the east side of a minor side canyon that comes in from the north. The old signatures are on the rock face below the overhang.

Teapot Rock Camp is located 3.7 miles east of the Waterhole Flat Junction. Turn right at the junction and follow the road marked "Dollhouse". The road makes a long sweeping turn to the left as it proceeds through the wide, grassy flat, finally heading directly toward Teapot Rock on the northern edge of the meadow. The camp is located 200 yards east of the base of Teapot Rock, just beyond the point where you can no longer proceed with a 2WD vehicle.

The Wall, Standing Rock, and Chimney Rock Camps (13.5 miles)

Immediately after leaving Teapot Rock Camp you will be confronted by the most formidable obstacle on the Dollhouse Road: Teapot Canyon. Teapot Canyon is a 4-mile-long canyon that runs east from Teapot Rock to the Colorado River. At its head it spawns at least 6 separate drainages that fan out to the west and end along a 2-mile arc of very rugged country. Beyond Teapot Rock Camp the road turns northwest and follows the arc all the way around to the east, all the while trying to stay as far above the canyons as

Mother and Child Rock

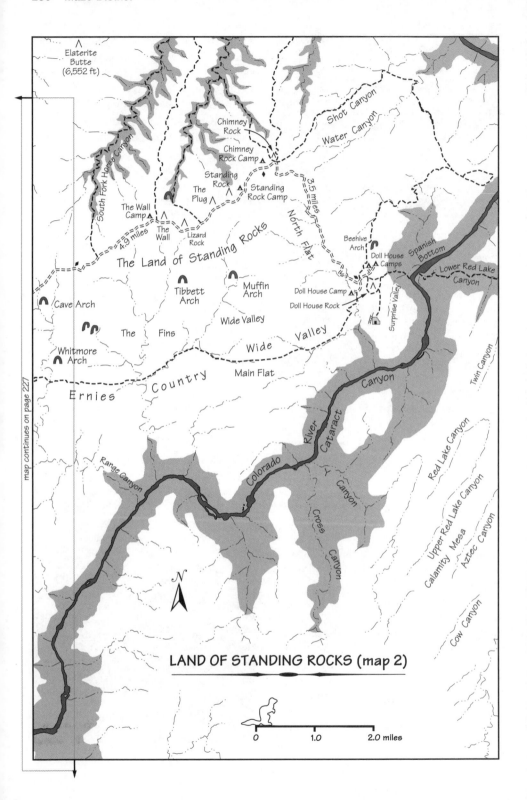

LAND OF STANDING ROCKS (map 2)

0   1.0   2.0 miles

map continues on page 227

The Land of Standing Rocks

possible. The problem is that there are vertical cliffs northwest of canyon, so there is only a narrow band of land left for road building. For the next two miles you can expect some very rough driving as the road climbs out of one drainage and drops into another.

5.6 miles after leaving Teapot Rock Camp the road crosses a shallow wash that the Park Service has marked with a large cairn. This is the lower trailhead for the Golden Stairs Trail (see page 239). Cattle and sheep ranchers often used this trail in the early 1900s for the purpose of getting their animals from Ernie's Country and Waterhole Flat to Elaterite Basin. These three areas were the primary grazing pastures Under the Ledge, and ranchers often drove their animals from one to the other to meet their demands for water and feed. Today the Golden Stairs Trail is used primarily by hikers who want to get down to Ernie's Country and The Land of Standing Rocks but don't have a vehicle that can get across Teapot Canyon.

Notice the unusual pinnacle of Organ Shale a half-mile in front of the car as you pass the Golden Stairs Trailhead. This 100-foot-high pillar is called the "Mother and Child". The reason for the name is not obvious from this perspective, but when you look at it from the north it does look like a mother with a small child clinging to her leg. When you reach the base of the Mother and Child, 0.8 mile beyond the Golden Stairs Trailhead, you will see a small parking area on the right side of the road that is bordered by a rectangle of stones. This carpark marks the beginning of the trail into Ernie's Country. (See page 272 for a description of the Ernie's Country Trail.)

Continuing north for another four miles will bring you to the Land of Standing Rocks, where The Wall, Standing Rock, and Chimney Rock Camps are located. This is a very scenic area, and as you drive along it will become obvious why it was named the Land of Standing Rocks. In the three miles between The Wall and Chimney Rock Camps the road passes no fewer than six vertical sculptures of dark red mudstone that rise up to 250 feet above the surrounding plane. Looking out across the canyons to the north you can see at least a half-dozen more of the unlikely pinnacles decorating the landscape like candles on a birthday cake. Some have been given whimsical names like Lizard Rock, Chimney Rock, and the Chocolate Drops, but most remain unnamed.

These odd formations are all remnants of the thick strata of rock called the Organ Shale Formation that was deposited in this region some 255 million years ago. In the last 25-30 million years, since the birth of the Colorado and Green Rivers, most of the ancient stone near the rivers has been washed away; however through some quirk of geological fate there still remain in the Land of Standing Rocks a few scattered remnants of the crumbly red Organ Shale. Probably the best way to see the standing rocks up close is to hike to the Chocolate Drops, an 8.8-mile hike that passes seven of the shale pinnacles. (See page 251.) The trailhead is located just east of the turnoff to The Wall Camp or 2.0 mile west of the turnoff to the Standing Rock Camp.

In my opinion the best of the three campsites in the Land of Standing Rocks is The Wall, just because it has the best views of the standing rocks north of the road. The Wall is located 10.6 miles from the Teapot Rock Camp. Chimney Rock Camp is also a favorite because of its proximity to the Chimney Rock Trailhead. This trailhead is the beginning point for two great loop hikes into the Maze: Pictograph Fork (see page 253), and Shot and Water Canyons (see page 257).

Dollhouse Camps 1, 2, and 3 (3.9 miles)

From Chimney Rock Camp the road turns south, loosing 360 feet as it descends to the Dollhouse. After 3.3 miles you will come to a junction where a 0.6-mile spur branches off to Dollhouse Camp 3. This camp is far removed from the other two Dollhouse camps, and it is somewhat more private. Few people bother to drive there

Dollhouse Road

unless they are planning to camp. From its elevated location it also boasts a memorable view of the Dollhouse and the nearby Sentinels. The Ernie's Country Trailhead is just 0.1 miles east of Dollhouse 3 on the south side of the road.

If you are headed for Dollhouse Camp 1 or 2 you must bear left at the junction and continue another 0.7 miles to the end of the road. Dollhouse 1 is particularly attractive; it is nestled in a cozy, well-shaded opening in the rocks north of the Dollhouse. It even has a short private trail that goes a few hundred feet from the camp to a good viewpoint north of the Sentinels.

see color photo, page 155

There are several interesting hiking trails near Dollhouse Camps 1 and 2. 0.2 mile before arriving at the camps you will pass a small parking area on the left, and directly

across from this parking area is the trailhead for the Spanish Bottom Trail (see page 265), and the Granary Trail (see page 269). The Colorado/Green River Overlook Trailhead is just 100 feet west of the parking area where the road crosses a small, sandy wash.

But even if you don't plan to do any hiking you should stop and take in the scenery. The famous Dollhouse formation is located just 150 yards from the Spanish Bottom Trailhead, and it really is a sight to behold. It is a large outcropping of Cedar Mesa Sandstone that has been weathered into a fantastic array of towers and spires that challenge the imagination. The Dollhouse is especially attractive just before sunset when the last rays of the western sun shine directly on the red and pink horizontal bands in the sandstone, igniting them to a fiery glow.

Dollhouse Rock

North Trail

☆   **day hike**

Distance:	12.4 miles (round trip), or 6.2 miles (one way to Millard Canyon Road)
Walking time:	7³/₄ hours (round trip) 3¹/₂ hours (one way)
Elevations:	1422 ft. loss (one way) North Trail Trailhead (start): 6,506 ft. Millard Canyon Road: 5,084 ft.
Trail:	Primitive, but well marked by cairns
Vicinity:	Off North Point Road
USGS Maps:	Gordon Flats, Elaterite Basin

Drive south from the Hans Flat Ranger Station towards Flint Trail for 2.5 miles to the North Point Road. Turn left here and continue towards Panorama Point for another 1.0 mile to the trailhead.

The hike ends at the Millard Canyon Road, 0.6 mile north of the Maze Overlook Junction. (See page 211 for more information on the Millard Canyon Road.)

North Trail, which descends from North Point into Elaterite Basin, was one of the first trails to penetrate the Under the Rim country. The first known person to use the trail was a sheep rancher named John Boline who was using Elaterite Basin as a winter grazing pasture as early as the 1890s. The story goes that when he brought his sheep up from Under the Ledge each spring he would roll rocks onto the trail so other sheepmen couldn't find it.

At that time there was no Bureau of Land Management and no laws governing grazing on public land. Many of the ranchers did not even own any land of their own, and success was heavily dependent on finding pastures that the other ranchers did not know about. Under the Ledge was ideally suited to sheep, and by the 1930s sheepmen had penetrated nearly every canyon in the area. By the time the Taylor Grazing Act was passed in 1935 it is estimated there were at least 15,000 sheep grazing Under the Ledge. After the 1930s cattle ranching became more prominent, and eventually the sheep ranchers disappeared altogether.

see color photo,
page 155

The trail begins by meandering gently downward through the trees in a southeasterly direction for 0.4 mile until it reaches a small outcropping of Navajo Sandstone. Then, after finding a way down through this minor barrier, it turns west and doubles back along a bench for the next 0.9 mile to the head of North Trail Canyon. When the path finally reaches the head of the canyon it makes a sharp left turn and begins a 150-foot descent through a series of short, steep switchbacks that lead to the bottom of the drainage.

As you make your way down pause to look at the sloping orange cliffs on each side of the canyon where it cuts through the Wingate Sandstone Formation. Normally the Wingate Sandstone is a very hard material that tends to fracture into long vertical cracks and form sheer cliffs, but here for some odd reason the rock has eroded into a smooth V-shaped opening that forms a natural corridor through the Wingate barrier. The orange rock slopes up at a 45-degree angle on each side of the canyon leaving a

North Trail Canyon

10-foot wide corridor at the bottom.

Almost every other canyon above the White Rim Plateau in Canyonlands dead-ends against the Wingate Cliffs, but here, because of this unusual feature, North Trail Canyon continues all the way to the rim above. This was the discovery that so excited John Boline that he decided to roll rocks onto the trail so that other sheepmen wouldn't find it. The narrow passageway was the key to the development North Trail.

Just 50 feet upcanyon from the V there is a small pouroff in the canyon floor where you can often find water. The water collects in a 4-foot diameter pothole at the bottom of the pouroff, sometimes to a depth of 12-15 inches. The pond is well shaded so it evaporates very slowly.

Below the V the trail becomes less steep and rocky as it leaves the Wingate Formation and enters the crumbly shale and mudstone of the Chinle. You can see several blind arches in the cliffs above as the trail makes its way down the sandy bottom of the drainage. The large picturesque butte in front of you is Elaterite Butte on the east side of Elaterite Basin. You will be walking towards this butte for almost the entire length of this hike.

Over the next two miles you can see several seeps in the walls of North Trail Canyon where water oozes out of the mudstone on either side of the drainage. The water from these seeps is heavily saturated with alkali that leaves an ugly white crust on the ground when it evaporates. I don't know what the water tastes like—I am not brave enough to try it—but there is seldom enough to drink anyway. You will also pass a couple of fence posts where one of the old sheep ranchers must have had a fence across a narrow part of the canyon to corral his animals.

As you enter Elaterite Basin the North Trail Canyon becomes little more than a shallow, sandy desert wash, and for the last

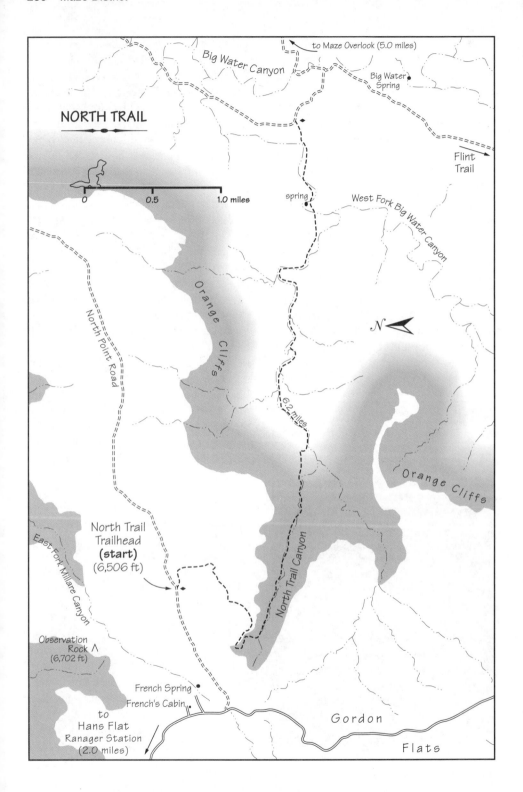

Big Water Canyon

to Maze Overlook (5.0 miles)

Big Water
Spring

NORTH TRAIL

Flint
Trail

0   0.5   1.0 miles

spring

West Fork Big Water Canyon

Orange Cliffs

N

North Point Road

6.2 miles

Orange Cliffs

North Trail
Trailhead
(start)
(6,506 ft)

North Trail Canyon

East Fork Millare Canyon

Observation
Rock ∧
(6,702 ft)

French Spring
French's Cabin

to
Hans Flat
Ranager Station
(2.0 miles)

Gordon

Flats

two miles the trail crosses a grassy flat that must have been a wonderful winter grazing pasture for sheep. You can see all around for long distances in this area, and as you approach the Millard Canyon Road you will probably be wondering what the black object lying on the ground far in front of you is. It is an old steam boiler that lies near the trail about 150 yards from the trailhead. It was once part of an oil-drilling rig that operated in the basin.

There are many signs of underground oil in this part of Canyonlands. In some places on a hot day you can actually see it seeping out of the sandstone. This evidence of oil was a hot topic of discussion in the early 1900s and many claims were filed. Around 1919 a company called the Nequoia Oil Company was formed, and in 1920 a drilling rig was brought to Elaterite Basin, then called Big Water, to search for the black gold. The company spent an entire year drilling in the area, but they never struck oil. By the end of 1921 the Nequoia Oil Company was bankrupt, and most of the men who worked for it lost an entire year's wages.

Today we know that although there is a great deal of oil in Canyonlands it is not in liquid form. Rather it is in the form of elaterite, a solid mixture of sandstone and petroleum that looks something like dirty asphalt. The only feasible way to extract the oil from elaterite is with heat, and the process is prohibitively expensive.

Backpacking into the Maze

North Trail is often used by hikers who want to visit the Maze but don't own a 4WD vehicle. With care it is usually possible to get ordinary cars to the trailhead. The hike from the North Trail Trailhead to the Maze Overlook is 12.0 miles one-way, but once you get to the overlook you will probably want to go down the Maze Overlook Trail

Steam boiler of the Nequoia drilling rig

at least as far as the Harvest Scene Pictograph Panel. (See page 242.) This would add 2.9 miles one-way onto your hiking distance, for a total of 29.8 miles round trip.

This is a long, dusty hike, and water can be a big problem in the summer. The only places you are likely to find water are 1.5 mile from the trailhead in the upper reaches of North Trail Canyon and 1.7 miles before the Harvest Scene in South Fork Horse Canyon, which means you will have to walk 11.7 miles before refilling your canteens. I would only attempt this hike in the spring from about mid-March to mid-May.

The hike down North Trail to the Maze and back is best done as a 3 or 4 day backpack trip with camps in lower North Trail Canyon and below the Maze Overlook. A good plan is to hike 5.5 miles down North Trail on the first day and spend the night in Elaterite Basin near the confluence of North Trail Canyon and West Fork Big Water Canyon. (A detailed description of this segment of the hike is given above.) Each person should carry an extra half-gallon jug of water that can be cached at the campsite for the return trip. There is a small spring in the bottom of the West Fork Big Water drainage just north of where the trail crosses it 0.7 mile before the Millard Canyon Road. Don't depend on it though. You might not see it, and even if you do it might be dry.

On the second day of the hike you can walk the final 0.7 mile of the North Trail to the Millard Canyon road, then walk 5.8 miles along the road to the Maze Overlook Trailhead. (see page 218 for a description of this road.) From there it is a 2.9-mile walk down the Maze Overlook Trail to the Harvest Scene Pictograph Panel. Unless it is a very dry year you should find a small pond of water in the bottom of South Fork Horse Canyon. There is a spring just 50 feet upcanyon from the point where the trail first reaches the canyon floor. There are many good places to camp in the area. My favorite spot is right at the mouth of Pictograph Fork Canyon. (See page 242 for a more detailed description of the hike from the Maze Overlook to the Harvest Scene Pictographs.)

On the last day you can refill your canteens at the spring in South Fork Horse Canyon and retrace your steps 7.7 miles back to your water cache at the North Trail Canyon campsite. From there it is another 5.5 miles back to the North Trail Trailhead.

Elaterite Butte above North Trail Canyon

Golden Stairs Trail

☆

Distance:	4.0 miles (round trip), or 2.0 miles (one way to Dollhouse Road)
Walking time:	3 hours (round trip) 1¼ hours (one way)
Elevations:	800 ft. loss (one way) Golden Stairs Trailhead (start): 6,052 ft. Dollhouse Road: 5,260 ft.
Trail:	This is a primitive trail, very steep and rocky in a few places, but it is well marked by cairns.
Vicinity:	Near the bottom of the Flint Trail
USGS Maps:	Elaterite Basin

The trailhead is located at the Golden Stairs Camp on the Flint Trail–Green River Road. (See page 211 for more information on the Flint Trail–Green River jeep road.)

Note: This hike is often done in conjunction with an overnight stay at the Golden Stairs Camp, but you must have a permit if you intend to camp in the area. See pages 15-16 for more information on how to make reservations and obtain a permit.

The Golden Stairs Trail was originally built by sheep and cattle ranchers around the turn of the 20th century to facilitate moving their animals from Ernie's Country to the pastures in Elaterite Basin. Today the trail is sometimes used as an alternative way to access Ernie's Country by people who want to avoid the difficult 4WD road through Teapot Canyon. With care 2WD trucks can sometimes be driven to the Golden Stairs Trailhead via Waterhole Flat, but it is almost impossible to get a 2WD vehicle through Teapot Canyon to Ernie's Country. It is only a 0.8-mile walk along the Dollhouse Road from the lower Golden Stairs Trailhead to the Ernie's Country eastern trailhead. Neither trailhead is marked with a sign, but both are well marked with stone cairns.

From the trailhead the path heads down a gentle slope through an open forest of pinion and juniper and out onto the top of a long, narrow mesa. After 200 yards the mesa narrows to a thin neck of land only 10 feet wide and 150 feet long. The trail proceeds across this land bridge and climbs to the top of the ridge on the other side. The most

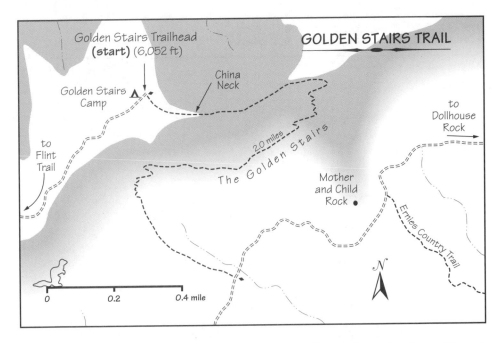

striking thing about the narrow neck of land is that it is composed of a monolithic block of pure white sandstone while the rest of the mesa is mostly made of crumbly reddish-brown shale. The contrast is such that the bridge looks almost as if it were made

China Neck, Golden Stairs Trail

of white porcelain; hence the name China Neck.

From the eastern side of China Neck the trail continues along the top of the mesa for another 0.2 mile, then veers off to the right and descends through a series of short switchbacks to a ledge about 350 feet below the mesa top. Your goal, the Dollhouse Road, is easily visible on the flat desert terrain below, but it is also clear from this perspective that the trail will have difficulty finding a feasible route down the cliffs of Organ Shale that rise above the road.

The deep red Organ Shale is prominently displayed in an interesting formation just below this part of the trail. It is called the Mother and Child, and in consists of a prom-

ontory of shale that juts out above the Dollhouse Road with a single 100-foot pillar of stone punctuating its southern extremity. Looking at the Mother and Child you will probably wonder how the trail will ever find its way down through the Organ Shale.

That question is answered when the trail turns to begin a traverse back to the west along a ledge just above the Organ Shale Formation. It stays at this elevation for 0.6 mile before finally coming to a place where it is feasible to descend the rest of the way to the road. Finally the trail turns south again and starts down another series of switchbacks that end in a dry wash. The last 0.3 mile of the hike is through the bottom of this shallow drainage to the road.

Mother and Child Rock (right center), from the Golden Stairs Trail

Maze Overlook Trail

☆ ☆ ☆   **4WD vehicle required**
day hike

Distance: 5.8 miles (round trip to the pictographs)

Walking time: 3¹/₂ hours

Elevations: 580 ft. loss/gain
Maze Overlook Trailhead (start): 5,160 ft.
Harvest Scene Pictographs: 4,580 ft.

Trail: The route from the Maze Overlook to the bottom of South Fork
Horse Canyon is down a steep slickrock trail, and some scrambling
is necessary. If you are carrying backpacks into the Maze you
should have a 30-foot length of rope to lower them down in a few
places.

Vicinity: Off the Flint Trail—Green River jeep road

USGS Maps: Elaterite Basin, Spanish Bottom

---

*The Maze Overlook Trailhead is located at the end of a spur 5.2 miles east of the
Flint Trail—Green River jeep road. The spur branches off from the main road 7.6
miles north of the turnout to the Golden Stairs Camp. (See page 211 for more
information on the Flint Trail—Green River Road.)*

*Note: You must get a permit at the visitor center if you intend to camp at the Maze
Overlook Camp near the trailhead. See pages 15-16 for more information on how to make
reservations and obtain a permit.*

There is no better place in Canyonlands to view the incredibly rugged expanse of the Maze than the Maze Overlook. The loneliness and serenity of this point, combined with the tortuously etched canyons below make it one of the grandest panoramas in the park. The five-mile stretch of land between the overlook and the Green River is an amazing work of art, tenaciously sculpted by eons of rainwater searching for a way to the sea.

Given enough time almost anything is possible, but it has taken the forces of nature an unimaginable length of time to produce this scene. They began by washing away thousands of vertical feet of sedimentary rock that had been deposited during earlier times to get down to the layer of ancient sandstone that we now call the Cedar Mesa Formation. The excavation of the massive overburden is almost complete now, but here and there one can still see isolated pinnacles of the reddish-brown mudstone that once covered the Cedar Mesa Sand-

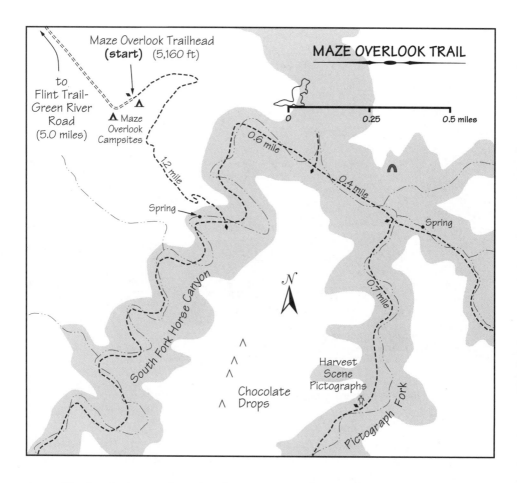

stone. The lonely outcroppings rise above the barren slickrock landscape like weary soldiers who have somehow survived an epic battle. They too will ultimately fall, but for the moment they are still standing.

After ten million years spent removing the rock above the Cedar Mesa Formation the stage was set for excavating the Maze itself, and now the task of etching out the labyrinth in the underlying sandstone is well underway. Again, the tools of nature are nothing more than the wind and the rain, with the Colorado River serving as the transport system for removing the cuttings. The carving of the Maze is a work in progress, and there is much left to be done. The dramatic scene below the Maze Overlook rep-

resents but one phase of the ongoing evolution of the Colorado Plateau.

One can hardly look into the canyons below the Maze Overlook without experiencing a compelling urge to explore, and this trail offers a way to get down into the depths of the labyrinth. The route described explores two major canyons of the Maze and also visits the Harvest Scene Pictographs. This famous panel of rock art was painted at least 2,000 years ago by the Archaic People of Canyonlands. (See photograph on page 256.)

From the parking lot at the end of the road a well marked trail proceeds across the slickrock to the edge of the abyss. Then,

South Fork Horse Canyon, seen from the Maze Overlook

after finding a break in the hard, white sandstone that defines the rim, the trail starts downward. Upon loosing just a few feet of elevation the path turns south to traverse around a large mushroom-shaped formation called the Nuts and Bolts, then it continues along a shale bench for several hundred yards before again turning downward. From there the route to the bottom of South Fork Horse Canyon is an exciting scramble from one ledge to the next as the cairn-marked trail searches for the easiest way down.

If you exercise reasonable care the route is not really dangerous, but it presents just enough difficulty to make it fun. Fortunately, the Cedar Mesa Sandstone that forms the canyon walls does not typically form steep vertical cliffs as does the overlying layers of Wingate and Navajo Sandstone. Rather, it is stratified into a series of flat, narrow benches, separated by short pitches of smooth, sloping slickrock. The route is well marked by stone cairns, and in one or two places the Park Service has chiseled footholds into the rock to help with the descent.

Unless you are very short of time you will probably want to check out a few of the canyons once you reach the bottom of the Maze. The nearest item of interest is the Harvest Scene Pictograph Panel, located 2.9 miles from the Maze Overlook Trail in a nearby canyon called Pictograph Fork. To get there turn left at the bottom of the trail and walk north through the South Fork of Horse Canyon for 0.6 mile to a junction with another unnamed canyon. Bear right (east) at the junction and continue for another 0.4 mile to the mouth *see color photos, pages 156, 157* of Pictograph Fork. This junction is easily recognizable. The mouth of Pictograph Fork is nearly 200 yards wide, and also there is a fine view of the Chocolate Drops formation that rises from the canyon rim above the southwest side of the junction.

If you turn into Pictograph Fork and walk for another 0.7 mile you will come to the famous prehistoric rock art panel called the Harvest Scene. The panel is located at the bottom of the cliffs, about ten feet above the west side of the sandy stream bed. Most archeologists believe that the Harvest Scene was painted by the Archaic People who inhabited Canyonlands from 8,000 to 2,000 years ago. The faded painting was so named because one of the figures appears to be holding a sheaf of rice grass, an important food source for the prehistoric peoples of the area.

The trails in the bottom of the Maze are not well marked, so when you return be sure to watch carefully for the point where the route exits South Fork Horse Canyon and begins climbing back to the canyon rim. You should see a large cairn at the exit point. There is also a spring nearby, and there is usually a large pool of muddy water in the bottom of the canyon where the trail starts up.

Maze Overlook Trail below the Nuts and Bolts Formation

Anderson Bottom

☆ ☆

4WD vehicle required
day hike

Distance:	3.8 miles (round trip)
Walking time:	2¼ hours
Elevations:	250 ft. loss/gain Anderson Bottom Trailhead (start): 4,222 ft. Anderson Bottom: 4,040 ft.
Trail:	This is a primitive, seldom-used trail. You may have difficulty following it for the first 0.8 mile, but after that it is well marked.
Vicinity:	Off the Flint Trail—Green River jeep road
USGS Maps:	Cleopatras Chair

Drive north from the Ekker Butte Camp on the Flint Trail—Green River jeep road for 11.3 miles, or if you are coming from the other direction drive south from Millard Canyon Camp for 2.3 miles. (See page 211 for more information on the Flint Trail—Green River jeep road.) Just east of the Buttes of the Cross the road turns southwest in order to get around a shallow slickrock wash, and then turns sharply north again on the other side. The trail into Anderson Bottom begins at the head of this wash. Although there are no signs marking the trailhead you should see several cairns beside the road.

Note: This hike is usually done in conjunction with an overnight camp along the Flint Trail—Green River jeep road, but you must get a permit at the ranger station if you intend to spend a night in the area. See pages 15-16 for more information on how to make reservations and obtain a permit.

Most of the bottom land along the Green River in Canyonlands National Park was farmed or homesteaded at one time or another during the early 1900s, but none of the river bottoms saw as much human activity as Anderson Bottom. At least seven different families attempted to establish ranches or farms here. They all failed not because the land was infertile but because it was too remote, too hard to supply, and too lonely.

Albert Issac Anderson, the first settler on Anderson Bottom, lived there for three summers between 1909 and 1911. He intended to homestead the bottom, but eventually moved away because his sons didn't want to live there. Anderson was followed by a succession of ranchers who ran sheep and cattle in the area before it became part of Canyonlands National Park.

One reason there were so many attempts

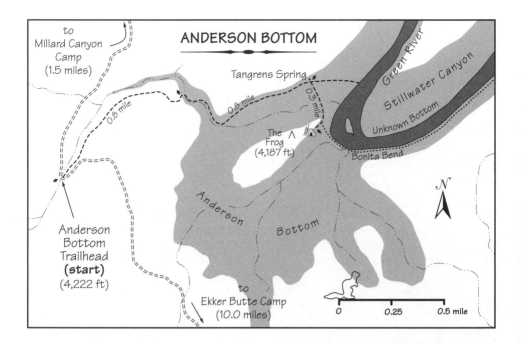

to settle Anderson Bottom is because it is the only place south of Millard Canyon where it is possible to get to the Green River by horseback. Access to the water is blocked by the White Rim Formation, a thick strata of hard sandstone that tends to form sheer cliffs above the river throughout the length of Stillwater Canyon. Only at Anderson Bottom is there an easy way to get below the White Rim Sandstone.

The wash at the trailhead is the beginning of Anderson Canyon, a small ravine that runs into the northwest side of Anderson Bottom. It is not possible to follow the short canyon all the way from the road to Anderson Bottom because there are several dropoffs in the canyon floor. But if you will walk for 0.7 mile along the southern rim of the ravine you will come to an old trail that was built down into the bottom by one of the early homesteaders.

It will take you about 20 minutes to walk along the slickrock on the south side of Anderson Canyon to the trail. You will find it a little easier if you stay 200 feet from the edge, as the rock is very uneven near the rim of the canyon. You may see an occasional cairn along the way, but don't count on it. They are few and far between. As you follow the ravine you will initially be walking towards a large pillar of rock in the distance that has separated

> see color photo, page 156

from the Wingate Cliffs on the other side of the river. It stands out from the adjacent cliff like some kind of a giant erection. But the small canyon makes a long 90-degree bend to the south, and as you near the end you will see Grandview Point and Junction Butte far in front of you.

After 20 minutes the trail comes to a 40-foot depression in the slickrock where another minor slickrock canyon drains into Anderson Canyon. If you will follow the bottom of this gully down to its mouth above Anderson Canyon you will find a constructed trail that leads the rest of the way to down.

Anderson Canyon, near the trailhead

From the mouth of the gully the trail turns left along a ledge and stays at that level for 50 yards before descending the last 100 feet through a series of rocky switchbacks to the sandy canyon floor below. At the foot of the trail you will see an old iron gate that was erected in the late 1950s by Karl Tangren, the last person to occupy Anderson Bottom before it became a national park.

When you reach the old gate proceed across to the opposite side of Anderson Canyon and you will see a rock face that contains a lot of cowboy rock art. Many of the etchings replicate the brands that the old cowboys used to brand their cattle.

From there a hiker-made trail follows the north wall of Anderson Bottom for another 1.0 mile to the Green River. About 200 yards before reaching the river the trail passes by Karl Tangren's Spring. In the early 1960s the spring provided running water for a nearby cabin, but all of that is gone now. All that remains is an old rusty pipe with water dripping out of it above a small grove of cottonwood trees.

Just east of Tangren's Spring is a small room that the Park Service has blasted out of the sandstone cliff for the purpose of storing supplies, mostly portable toilets, for an annual event called the Friendship Cruise. This is a two-day outing, sponsored by the cities of Green River and Moab, that takes place each year during the Memorial Day weekend. Typically a hundred or more boats float down from Green River on the first day for an evening of feasting and dancing at Anderson Bottom. On the second day they continue the float to the confluence and then motor up the Colorado River to Moab. The Friendship Cruise dates back to the 1950s when Tangren was still ranching at Anderson, and it has since become a well established Memorial Day tradition.

Several cabins, boat docks, irrigation canals, and at least one granary were built on Anderson Bottom during the 56 years that it was ranched and cultivated by white settlers, but today there is no trace of any of the old structures. Ironically however, there still exists a small granary that was built by another group of settlers that were growing corn on Anderson Bottom 700 years before the arrival of the white men. These people were the Anasazi Indians that lived there before 1300 A.D.

The Anasazi granary is located on the northeast corner of the mesa that rises in the center of the bottom. This mesa was called the Frog by early settlers. Follow the trail from the spring to the corner of the Frog nearest the river and continue around its south side. The granary is located 150 feet southwest of the end of the mesa about 80 feet above its base. There is a pile of rubble below the granary so it is easy to climb up to it. It is located in a tiny south-facing al-

North Butte, Buttes of the Cross, from Anderson Bottom

cove right where the White Rim Sandstone meets the Organ Shale. The granary is very small, only 3 feet wide and 1 foot high, and it cannot be seen from the ground below the Frog.

Backpacking south of Anderson Bottom

As mentioned earlier there is no easy way to get from the top of the White Rim Formation to the other river bottoms south of Anderson Bottom. However it is possible to visit some of the bottoms by walking south from Anderson along the river. There is actually an old trail along the west bank of the river called the Lower Trail that was probably made centuries ago by the Indians who lived in the area. There are still many Anasazi dwellings and granaries in the alcoves above the banks of the Green River, and the Anasazis probably traveled frequently along its shore. One member of John Wesley Powell's second expedition down the Green River in 1871 reported finding fragments of pottery when they stopped on the river bottoms. Unfortunately the pottery shards are long gone now.

The first bottom the Lower Trail comes to, 3.0 miles downstream from Anderson Bottom, is Valentine Bottom. This bottom was named after the Valentine family who attempted to settle there around 1892. The Valentines built a log cabin and lived on the bottom for at least a year, but there is now no sign of their old cabin. There are at least six Anasazi granaries on Valentine Bottom, and more are visible on the other side of the river, but none of them can be reached without a ladder.

Another 3.0 miles below Valentine Bottom is Cabin Bottom, where you can see the remains of an old cabin that burned down around 1935. The cabin was reportedly built by Bill Tibbets and Al Portus, two trappers who worked along the Green River around 1920. The fate of most of these old cabins was fire. Few of them had stoves, and their small fireplaces were inherently dangerous.

Beyond Cabin Bottom the Lower Trail veers away from the river into Dead Horse Canyon, but just before doing so it passes between two large truck-sized boulders that are almost covered with Indian pictographs. These pictographs provide strong evidence that the Lower Trail was well traveled by the Anasazi Indians that lived in the area before 1300 A.D.

After you see the petroglyphs you will probably want to leave the trail and walk east along the benches of the Cutler Formation for a mile to the Turks Head. The Turks Head is a large butte topped with a block of White Rim Sandstone that looks somewhat like a Turkish turban. It is located in the center of one of the meanders of the Green River. This area is interesting because there is a great deal of chert in the area which the Indians used to make stone tools, and there are thousands of flint chips lying all over the ground. The land below Turk's Head is well known among archeologists for its extensive chip-ping sites. There are also a few Anasazi dwellings or granaries above the river on the northeast side of the Turk's Head. The Indians undoubtedly lived in the area and had farms on the fertile bottomland near the river.

From the petroglyph boulders east of the Turk's Head the Lower Trail traverses westward to get around Deadhorse Canyon, then turns south until it meets Horse Canyon. From there you can follow Horse Canyon westward to South Fork Horse Canyon and on to the Maze Overlook Trail, which ends at the Maze Overlook Road. This is a long, dusty trip on a poorly marked trail, and there is little water after you leave the Green River. But for a well-prepared party with an extra car to leave as a shuttle at the Maze Overlook it can provide a memorable backpacking experience. If you are interested I suggest you read Michael Kelsey's book, *Hiking, Biking and Exploring Canyonlands National Park and Vicinity*. He has thoroughly explored this route and discusses it at length in his book.

Anasazi Granary on Anderson Bottom

The Chocolate Drops

☆ ☆

4WD vehicle required
day hike

Distance:	8.8 miles (round trip)
Walking time:	5 hours
Elevations:	540 ft. loss/gain Chocolate Drops Trailhead (start): 5,460 ft. Chocolate Drops: 5,080 ft.
Trail:	This is a slickrock trail, well marked by stone cairns. There is no water, so be sure to carry plenty.
Vicinity:	The Land of Standing Rocks
USGS Maps:	Spanish Bottom, Elaterite Basin

The Chocolate Drops Trailhead is located in the Land of Standing Rocks 3.0 miles west of the Chimney Rock Trailhead, or 14.1 miles east of Waterhole Flat on the Dollhouse Road. (See page 225 for more information on the road to the Dollhouse Road.)

Note: This hike is usually done in conjunction with an overnight camp in the Land of Standing Rocks, but you must have a permit if you intend to spend a night in the area. See pages 15-16 for more information on how to make reservations and obtain a permit.

What shall we name those four unnamed formations standing erect above this end of The Maze? From our vantage point they are the most striking landmarks.... In a far-fetched way they resemble tombstones, or altars, or chimney stacks, or stone tablets set on end.[7]

When Edward Abbey first wrote these words he was standing near the Maze Overlook (page 242) looking at what we now call the Chocolate Drops. Little has changed in the Maze since Abbey's observation forty years ago; hence it is still possible to share the feeling of wonderment he must have experienced.

The Chocolate Drops formation consists of four vertical rectangular shaped columns of Organ Shale that rise almost 200 feet above the ridge separating the South Fork of Horse Canyon from Pictograph Fork Canyon. They are one of the most prominent

---

[7] Edward Abbey, *Desert Solitaire, a Season in the Wilderness*, Simon & Schuster, New York, 1968. (with permission)

landmarks in the Maze and can be seen for miles around. The trail described here also

see map, page 255

passes by a half dozen other pillars of Organ Shale on its way to the Chocolate Drops. These formations are all part of an area known as the Land of Standing Rocks.

Follow the cairns from the parking area around the east side of the large monolith beside the road, then on towards the other spires farther out on the plateau. All of these formations are the unlikely remains of a 200-foot-thick layer of Organ Shale that once covered Canyonlands. By now, however, the unrelenting forces of erosion have almost completely removed the crumbling rock from the area, and only a few pinnacles of red shale still remain. After about thirty minutes the trail passes by the next group of Organ Shale formations, including one particularly pic-

see color photos, page 157

turesque mound that is topped by an enormous balanced rock. So precarious is the capstone that it is hard to pass beneath it without unconsciously walking a little faster.

From the balanced rock to the first Chocolate Drop is about three miles. The route is well marked with cairns and not difficult to follow. It is generally an easy walk across level ground, however at one point some minor scrambling is necessary to get to the bottom of a low spot on the ridge. If you look to the right when you reach this point you will find an easy way down the slickrock to the bottom of the incline (about

50 feet lower), and beyond this point there are no additional obstacles.

As you walk northward along the ridge you can frequently peer into the bottom of Pictograph Fork on your right. At one point you can look directly down at the Harvest Scene Pictograph Panel (page 256). From the trail, however, the panel is over a mile away—too far to recognize any of the pictographs. When you finally reach the last Chocolate Drop on the end of the plateau you will also have a clear view of the trail down from the Maze Overlook.

The Chocolate Drops

Pictograph Fork

☆ ☆ ☆

4WD vehicle required
day hike

Distance:	9.3 miles (loop)
Walking time:	5¹/₂ hours
Elevations:	1,560 ft. loss/gain Chimney Rock Trailhead (start): 5,460 ft. Harvest Scene Pictographs: 4,580 ft.
Trail:	The portion of the trail in the sandy bottom of the Maze is unmarked, but the route is not difficult to follow. The slickrock part of the trail above the Maze is marked with cairns. There is no water on this trail, so be sure to carry plenty.
Vicinity:	The Land of Standing Rocks.
USGS Maps:	Spanish Bottom, Elaterite Basin

The Chimney Rock Trailhead is located beside Chimney Rock Camp in the Land of Standing Rocks. (See page 225 for more information on the road to the Land of Standing Rocks.)

Note: This hike is usually done in conjunction with an overnight camp in the Land of Standing Rocks, but you must have a permit if you intend to spend a night in the area. See pages 15-16 for more information on how to make reservations and obtain a permit.

This hike provides an opportunity to explore four intersecting canyons of the Maze, that crazy labyrinth of canyons after which the Maze District of Canyonlands was named. As a bonus, the trail also passes by the Harvest Scene, an impressive panel of ancient Indian pictographs near the mouth of Pictograph Fork. The Harvest Scene was probably painted by the Archaic People who lived in the canyons from about 6,000 B.C. until the time of Christ. They tended to live

see color photos, pages 157-159

further inland from the Colorado and Green Rivers than the Anasazi and Fremont Indians who came to the area much later. Why the preferred to live so far from the rivers is a mystery, but their distinctive red, purple, orange, and gray pictographs can be found at a number of sites in the upper reaches of the dry desert canyons of Canyonlands National Park.

There are four cairned trails leaving from the Chimney Rock parking area. The first trail on the left, bearing around the west

Elaterite Butte and the Maze, as seen from the Pictograph Fork trail

side of Chimney Rock, leads directly to the bottom of Pictograph Fork. When you return to the trailhead at the end of the loop you will be on this trail. The second trail from the left passes by the east side of Chimney Rock and heads north across the plateau above Pictograph Fork. The hike starts on this trail. (The third and forth trails from the left lead to Shot Canyon and Water Canyon, respectively.)

As you walk northward across the slickrock from Chimney Rock you will see Petes Mesa directly in front of you. The large butte behind Petes Mesa is Ekker Butte. If you loose track of the cairns just stay high on the ridge as you continue towards Petes Mesa. When you get to within a half mile of the mesa, however, be sure to watch more carefully for the cairns so you will not miss the turn when the trail begins its descent down into the Maze. Also, be on the lookout for mountain sheep in this area. They are often sighted on the plateau near Petes Mesa.

Once you reach the bottom of the Maze you will be on the sandy floor of a small side canyon leading in a northwesterly direction. Soon you should see three large red rocks that look like a cluster of giant mushrooms growing out of the edge of the rim about a mile down the canyon. This rock formation lies just below the Maze Overlook (page 242).

Within fifteen minutes after you spot the mushroom rocks you will pass by another major canyon entering the drainage from the south. This is Pictograph Fork, the canyon containing the famous Harvest Scene Pictograph Panel. There are several other side canyons in the area, but Pictograph Fork is the largest one. It is nearly 200 yards wide at the junction, with a 150-foot-wide span of slickrock in the center of the stream bed. Also the Chocolate Drops formation, a row of 200-foot-high shale pillars that rise above the canyon's west rim, is clearly visible from the streambed.

This junction is a very pleasant place to

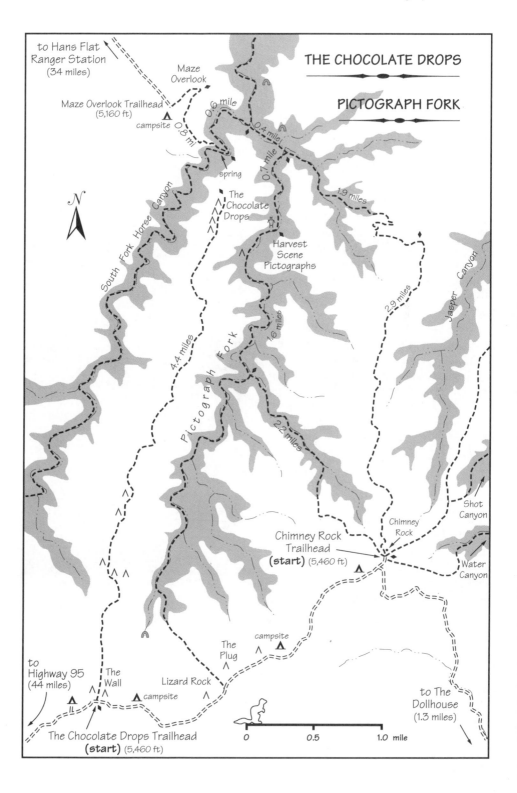

to Hans Flat
Ranger Station
(34 miles)

Maze
Overlook

Maze Overlook Trailhead
(5,160 ft)

campsite 0.8 mi

0.6 mile

0.4 mile

0.7 mile

spring

The
Chocolate
Drops

Harvest
Scene
Pictographs

1.9 miles

THE CHOCOLATE DROPS

PICTOGRAPH FORK

South Fork Horse Canyon

4.4 miles

Pictograph Fork

1.6 miles

2.2 miles

2.9 miles

Jasper Canyon

N

Chimney
Rock

Chimney Rock
Trailhead
(start) (5,460 ft)

Shot
Canyon

Water
Canyon

The
Plug

campsite

Lizard Rock

to Highway 95
(44 miles)

The
Wall

campsite

The Chocolate Drops Trailhead
(start) (5,460 ft)

to The
Dollhouse
(1.3 miles)

0   0.5   1.0 mile

stop for the night if you are doing this hike as an overnighter. There are several good campsites in the area. If you have the time you might also want to consider a side trip to the top of the Maze Overlook. The walk from Pictograph Fork to the Maze Overlook and back will take you about 2 hours. (See page 242 for a description of this hike.)

From the mouth of Pictograph Fork it is 0.7 miles up the dry, sandy canyon to the Harvest Scene Pictograph Panel. The panel is located at the bottom of the cliffs, about ten feet above the west side of the stream bed. There is a thumb-shaped pillar of sandstone in the bottom of the canyon about 300 yards upcanyon from the Harvest Scene, so if you see this formation you have gone too far.

No reliable method has yet been developed for dating Indian rock art, but most archeologist believe that the Harvest Scene was painted by the Archaic People who lived in Utah from 8,000 to 2,000 years ago. These are the same people who produced the famous Great Gallery Pictograph Panel 18 miles to the north in Horseshoe Canyon (see page 279). The Archaic People, who predated the better known Anasazi, left few other remnants of their ancient culture for us to study; hence archeologist have long struggled to interpret their art. But deciphering the paintings has proven just as difficult as dating them, and we still know little about what they mean. In this panel, one of the figures appears to be holding a sheaf of rice grass; hence the name Harvest Scene.

Continuing up the canyon from the Harvest Scene for another 1.6 miles will bring you to another junction with a major side canyon. The trail splits at this point. If you bear right you will be continuing up Pictograph Fork on a little used trail that finally ends near the east end of Lizard Rock. Most hikers, however, turn left at this junction and follow the cairns up an easier route to the rim that finally ends at the Chimney Rock Trailhead.

Harvest Scene Pictograph Panel

Shot and Water Canyons

☆ ☆ ☆

4WD vehicle required
day hike

Distance:	7.7 miles (loop)
Walking time:	5¼ hours
Elevations:	1,160 ft. loss/gain
	Chimney Rock Trailhead (start): 5,460 ft.
	Shot Canyon: 4,540 ft.
	Water Canyon Spring: 4,620 ft.
Trail:	Primitive, cairned trail. The scramble out of Water Canyon requires some minor rock climbing. It is not a particularly difficult climb, but if you are afraid of heights you may have a problem. Carry a 30-foot length of rope so you can pull your backpack up behind you in one or two places.
Vicinity:	The Land of Standing Rocks
USGS Maps:	Spanish Bottom

Chimney Rock Trailhead is located beside Chimney Rock Camp in the Land of Standing Rocks. (See page 225 for more information on the road to the Land of Standing Rocks.)

Note: This hike is usually done in conjunction with an overnight camp in the Land of Standing Rocks, but you must have a permit if you intend to spend a night in the area. See pages 15-16 for more information on how to obtain a permit.

These two interesting canyons run roughly parallel for a distance of four miles east of the Land of Standing Rocks; hence they present a fine opportunity for a loop hike into the Maze. Be cautioned, however, that the seldom-used trails are primitive, and at one point a good deal of scrambling is required. If you are a seasoned hiker looking for something more challenging than usual this might be just the hike you are looking for. But if you haven't had much experience climbing in and out of canyons I wouldn't recommend it.

Shot Canyon was grazed by livestock in the early 1900s; consequently the trail into this canyon is not too bad. But the trail out of Water Canyon is another story. Water Canyon ends at the 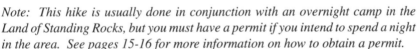 see color photos, pages 158, 159 base of a 400-foot cliff of Cedar Mesa Sandstone that appears at first glance to be almost unscalable. You will find a feasible route to the top, however, if you follow the cairns carefully. The circuitous trail passes

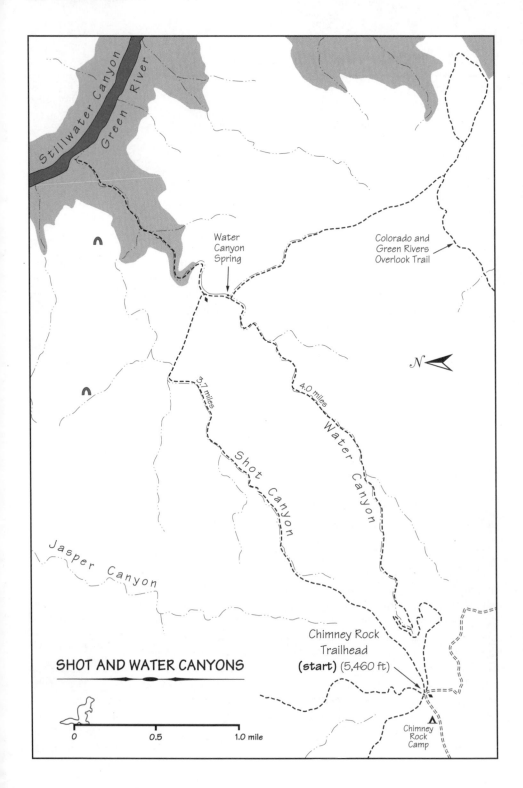

Stillwater Canyon

Green River

Water
Canyon
Spring

Colorado and
Green Rivers
Overlook Trail

N

3.7 miles

4.0 miles

Shot Canyon

Water Canyon

Jasper Canyon

Chimney Rock
Trailhead
(start) (5,460 ft)

Chimney
Rock
Camp

SHOT AND WATER CANYONS

0   0.5   1.0 mile

along a series of ledges that eventually lead to the rim on the south side of the canyon. Some hand-over-hand scrambling is required in a few places, but anyone with some agility and a small amount of climbing experience should be able to handle it. The only caveat is that you should not be unduly afraid of heights. There are several places along the way with a fair amount of exposure, and a misstep could be disastrous.

If you are carrying a backpack on this hike be sure to include a 30-foot length of rope for pulling up your gear in a few places. It is much easier to climb if you are not encumbered by a pack. Also, your shoes should have good rubber soles for maximum traction on the slickrock. There are a couple of places where you will be required to friction walk up a 30-degree incline of smooth sandstone. Finally, don't attempt the climb out of Water Canyon if the weather is bad or if there is ice on the trail.

There are four trails leaving Chimney Rock Trailhead. They are all marked by cairns, but there are no signs so be sure you

Shot Canyon

are on the right one. The last trail on the left leads down into Pictograph Fork (see page 253). The next trail leads to South Fork Horse Canyon. The second to last trail on the right is the Shot Canyon Trail, and the last one goes to Water Canyon. Of the four trails the one to Water Canyon is the least well marked and many people do not even notice it. The Shot Canyon trail is probably the best marked of the four.

Begin by walking east on the Shot Canyon Trail. The route meanders across the slickrock below Chimney Rock for 0.6 mile before reaching the rim of Shot Canyon. After you have walked about half of that distance you will see another deep narrow canyon directly north of the trail. That is Jasper Canyon. Before the mid-1990s there was another trail that branched off of the Shot Canyon Trail into Jasper, but the Park Service has since closed Jasper Canyon to hikers. The canyon was closed in order to preserve its pristine condition for future scien-

Water Canyon

tific study. Jasper was never grazed by cattle and sheep ranchers; consequently the distribution of native plants within its confines is very close to what it was in all of Canyonlands before the arrival of white men in the late 1800s.

Soon the trail arrives on the rim of Shot Canyon and starts working its way down to the bottom. Notice the crude stairs made from rocks piled up against a long sloping face of slickrock not far from the top. This part of the trail was probably built by an old forgotten sheepherder a century ago. It has been in place as long as anyone now alive can remember. Below the slickrock the trail switchbacks a few times and continues its steady descent to the canyon bottom 400 feet below the rim. Once it reaches the bottom it strikes out in a northeasterly direction across a wide, open flat of grass and sage towards the Green River.

As mentioned earlier, Shot Canyon was used by local ranchers in the early 1900s as a pasture for livestock. There was plenty of feed in the canyon at that time but, unfortunately, no reliable water. In order to get water the animals had to walk across a low pass near the end of Shot Canyon to an excellent spring in nearby Water Canyon. In the late 1920s the ranchers dynamited a few sections of the trail across the pass to make it easier for cows to get into Water Canyon, and my guess is that is how Shot Canyon got its name.

This hike also goes across the pass from Shot Canyon to Water Canyon. As you approach the turning point the trail begins spending more time in the sandy wash at the bottom of Shot Canyon and less time on the flat above the wash. Finally, 2.8 miles after entering the canyon you will see a line of cairns exiting the wash and turning south onto the slickrock above the canyon. The trail gains and then looses about 250 feet over the next 0.9 mile as it traverses into Water Canyon. The climb is relatively easy, espe-

cially if you are a human, not a four-legged cow, and the traverse is quite scenic. The route will take you across several more slickrock inclines and then down a narrow chute near Water Canyon.

When you reach Water Canyon you will usually see water right away. Sometimes there is running water all the way to the river, but even in dry years there will be intermittent pools of water in the canyon. The trail turns south and follows the west side of the drainage for another 0.1 mile to the source of the water. Soon you will come to a wide shelf of hard, flat limestone that extends across the floor of the canyon. Below the limestone the canyon floor drops abruptly for 30 feet to a spring, the first of many places where water can be seen seeping out of the canyon walls. Above the limestone boundary the canyon is generally dry.

When you reach the top of the limestone shelf you will be at a trail junction. If you turn left at this point and walk to the east side of the shelf you will see another trail continuing on to the southeast. That well-used trail eventually connects with the Green

Pass between Shot and Water Canyons

and Colorado Rivers Overlook Trail. But in order to complete this loop hike you must bear right at the junction and take the trail that leads into upper Water Canyon. 200 yards after leaving the limestone shelf the Water Canyon Trail passes through a small grove of cottonwood trees and then continues up the sandy wash toward the head of the canyon.

The trail up Water Canyon generally follows the bottom of the sandy drainage along the northern side of the canyon. This is mildly frustrating because the canyon opens up to some nice views to the south in a few places, and it is difficult to see anything from inside the wash. 2.5 miles after leaving the spring the trail reaches the head of the canyon. It will be obvious that you have reached the end because Water Canyon ends in a box with cliffs on three sides.

As you follow the sandy wash into the box start looking for cairns on the left side of the drainage. Soon you will see the obvious departure point where a line of cairns marks the way up an outcropping of sandstone on the south side of the canyon. This is followed by a 20-foot scramble where you will probably want to use your rope to pull your pack up behind you.

From the south side of the canyon the trail circles along a series of benches to the north side and then back to the south side again, each time gaining a few more feet as it climbs to successively higher layers of rock. At one time you will be required to walk 20 feet up a steep slickrock incline, at another you will be crawling for 15 feet beneath an overhang with only 3 feet of headroom. If you follow the cairns carefully the climb is not technically difficult, but at times it may be a bit unnerving. Finally, after 40 minutes of climbing you should break out onto the rim of the canyon where you will once again be on flat ground. From that point it is just 0.6 mile more along the cairned path back to Chimney Rock Trailhead.

Other Trails

There is a primitive trail that follows Water Canyon all the way to the Green River. The distance from the spring to the river is only 2.1 miles, but the elevation loss is 750 feet. If you are careful the route is not particularly dangerous, but it is very steep and rocky. After you have gone 0.6 mile downcanyon, before you come to the steepest part of the trail, you will come to a point where there is a good view of the Green River below, and many people choose to go at least that far.

As indicated earlier there is also a connecting trail that goes from Water Canyon to the Green and Colorado Rivers Overlook Trail. The overlook point is only 1.7 miles from the spring along this trail, or if you wish you can follow it all the way to the Overlook Trailhead and end your hike at the Dollhouse Road. (See page 262 for a complete description of the Green and Colorado Rivers Overlook Trail.)

Green River at mouth of Water Canyon

Green and Colorado Rivers Overlook

☆ ☆   **4WD vehicle required**
                                                       day hike

Distance: 8.9 miles (round trip)

Walking time: 5 hours

Elevations: 300 ft. loss/gain
                     Green and Colorado Rivers Trailhead (start): 5,100 ft.
                     Overlook point: 5,000 ft.

Trail: Easy, well marked trail, but there is no water so be sure to carry
                     plenty.

Vicinity: The Land of Standing Rocks

USGS Maps: Spanish Bottom

The trailhead is located 0.3 mile from the end of the Dollhouse Road near Dollhouse Rock and Dollhouse Camps 1 and 2. (See page 225 for more information on the Dollhouse Road.)

Note: This hike is usually done in conjunction with an overnight camp in the Land of Standing Rocks, but you must have a permit if you intend to spend a night in the area. See pages 15-16 for more information on how to obtain a permit.

For colorful desert scenery it is hard to beat this popular hike. The normally light colored Cedar Mesa Sandstone has a rich red layer running through it in this area, which makes it much more colorful than the same formation in the nearby Maze. Beginning with the impressive Dollhouse, at the beginning of the trail, the rock formations along this hike are truly magnificent. They are particularly pretty in the late afternoon when the sunlight tends to enhance the red bands in the sandstone.

From the trailhead the trail winds northward, through clusters of sandstone formations similar to those found on the other side of the Colorado in the Needles District of Canyonlands. Within 0.8 mile you will see the small Beehive Arch on your left. The trail winds down the slope a little ways and then back, passing right beside it.

About a mile beyond the arch start watching for pieces of flint scattered on the ground, particularly at the base of the sandstone cliffs on the left side of the trail. This glassy stone was brought here by prehistoric Indians from other locations in the park. Look carefully at the smaller pieces and you will see that most of them are actually flakes that have been chipped from larger stones. These flakes are espe-

see color photos, page 159

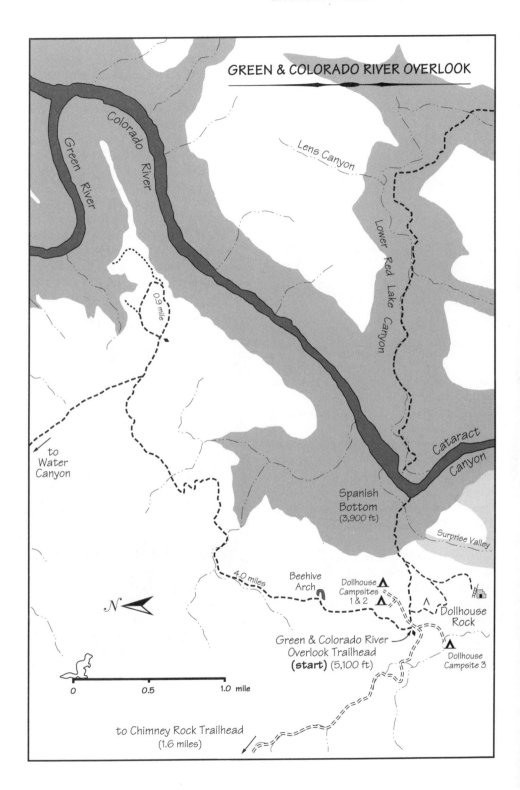

GREEN & COLORADO RIVER OVERLOOK

Colorado River

Green River

Lens Canyon

Lower Red Lake Canyon

0.9 mile

to
Water
Canyon

Cataract Canyon

Spanish
Bottom
(3,900 ft)

Surprise Valley

4.0 miles

Beehive
Arch

Dollhouse
Campsites
1 & 2

Dollhouse
Rock

N

Green & Colorado River
Overlook Trailhead
(**start**) (5,100 ft)

Dollhouse
Campsite 3

0   0.5   1.0 mile

to Chimney Rock Trailhead
(1.6 miles)

Green and Colorado Rivers Overlook Trail

Continue east and soon the overlook trail splits into a 0.9 mile loop that goes past the overlook points. If you bear right here for another 0.4 mile you will arrive at the western rim of the Colorado River gorge. The river is only about 400 yards away at this point, at the bottom of a nearly vertical wall. From there the path bends around to the west again, passing by a fine view of the Green River. You might want to do a little off-trail hiking before you leave this loop in order to achieve better views of the rivers.

Soon after the trail leaves the Green River viewpoint it drops back into the meadow to complete the loop. From that point back to the trailhead is 4.0 miles.

cially prevalent in a few alcoves along the trail where prehistoric Indians must have worked, chipping the hard rock into points, scrapers, and other tools.

Halfway to the overlook point the trail skirts past the head of a large canyon. Although you can't see it from this perspective the Colorado River is below you, over a thousand feet down at the northern end of Cataract Canyon in an area called Spanish Bottom.

A mile beyond the canyon the trail enters a large open meadow similar to Chesler Park in the Needles District. In the center of this meadow you will encounter another trail coming in from the northwest. This trail leads to Water and Shot Canyons, and ultimately back to the Chimney Rock Trailhead. (See the trail description on page 257.)

Green River

Spanish Bottom

☆ ☆

4WD vehicle required
day hike

Distance: 2.8 miles (round trip)

Walking time: 2 hours

Elevations: 1,260 ft. loss/gain
Spanish Bottom Trailhead (start): 5,100 ft.
Colorado River: 3,840 ft.

Trail: Steep and rocky, but well marked and easy to follow

Vicinity: Near Dollhouse Rock

USGS Maps: Spanish Bottom

The Spanish Bottom Trailhead is located 0.2 mile from the end of the Dollhouse Road near Dollhouse Rock and Dollhouse Camps 1 and 2. (See page 225 for more information on this road.)

Note: This hike is usually done in conjunction with an overnight camp in the Land of Standing Rocks, but you must have a permit if you intend to spend a night in the area. See pages 15-16 for more information on how to obtain a permit.

Cataract Canyon has a well-deserved reputation as one of the most imposing canyons on the Colorado River. The walls of the canyon rise steeply from the water's edge to a height of 1200 feet, and the whitewater rapids in the narrow channel below are often formidable. Yet, oddly, in the midst of this rugged canyon there is an unusually flat swath of river bottomland where the shore widens into a broad sandy plain that extends west from the water's edge to the base of the canyon wall 600 yards away. This geological anomaly is called Spanish Bottom.

How was this strange depression formed? Most of Canyonlands lies above an ancient salt bed called the Paradox Formation. Salt tends to flow like a very dense liquid when it is under pressure, and Spanish Bottom is one of many interesting formations in the area that were formed by movements in the Paradox Formation. At some time in the past 100 million years the salt was squeezed out of the strata beneath

see color photo, page 160

Spanish Bottom causing the layers of heavy rock it supported to collapse. Spanish Bottom is essentially what is left of an ancient sinkhole. The river has certainly contributed to its present appearance, but the bottom was actually created long before the birth of the Colorado River.

This area is one of the few places in Canyonlands where the Paradox Formation is actually visible on the surface. Look

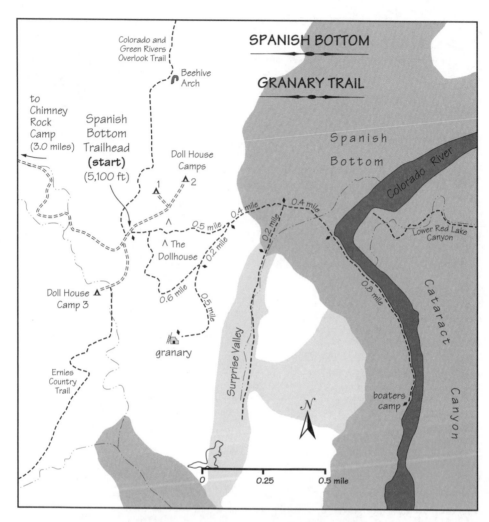

across from Spanish Bottom at the east side of the river and you will see a jumble of light tan-colored hills that are obviously different from the surrounding rock. These hills are composed of gypsum that has migrated upward from the subterranean Paradox strata. The hills are a sample of the material that undoubtedly underlies Spanish Bottom.

From the trailhead the Spanish Bottom Trail proceeds eastward towards Dollhouse Rock. After only 150 yards you will come to a junction where the Granary Trail departs on the right. Bear left here, following the trail through a narrow opening between the pinnacles of the Dollhouse. Soon the trail emerges on the east side of the Dollhouse and begins a gradual descent over the next 0.4 miles that will take it to the lower junction with the Granary Trail. As before, you must bear left here to reach Spanish Bottom. Soon after the second junction the trail gets considerably steeper as it makes its way down off the rim. The trail descends 900 feet through a series of short switchbacks over the last 0.5 mile, and eventually reaches the river on the southern side of the bottom. Though the path is steep and rocky, the views

Colorado River at Spanish Bottom

of the Colorado River and Cataract Canyon from the trail are awesome. You can see the river below you for almost the entire distance.

Looking down at Spanish Bottom from the trail you will probably marvel at how flat the bottom of the valley is. It is roughly the shape of a half-moon 0.6 mile long and 0.3 mile wide, yet the elevation never varies more than 30 feet. Other than a few cottonwoods growing near the river the land is also treeless. The soil is probably fertile but unlike many of the other river bottoms upstream on the Green River it was never settled. The land was frequently used as a pasture for sheep and cattle during the early 1900s, but as far as anyone today knows there has never been a cabin or even a corral on Spanish Bottom. The trail down to the bottom has been there at least since the turn of the twentieth century.

In 1890, 21 years after John Wesley Powell discovered it; there was an attempt to build a tourist hotel on Spanish Bottom. The idea was eventually shelved because of

the difficulty floating boats up and down the Green River, but eleven years later another entrepreneur from Denver began raising money to build a sanatorium on the bottom. His project lasted about a year before his money ran out and his boat was destroyed in an accident near Moab.

Down Cataract Canyon

There is another trail that begins on the southern end of Spanish Bottom and follows the river for several miles. The first brief section of rapids is located 0.8 mile downriver, and the trail is quite good until then. Beyond the first rapid, however, the trail frequently disappears into the rocks. The first rapid is by no means one of the worst, but it is still an interesting walk. There is also a camping area on the sandy beach just below the first rapid where you may see some boaters.

Surprise Valley

If you walked the Granary Trail (page 269) before descending to Spanish Bottom you will remember looking off the upper rim of Cataract Canyon at the Colorado River and seeing another sunken valley, or graben, about 800 feet above the west side of the water. This is Surprise Valley, another flat-bottomed depression in the landscape that was formed by the same geologic process that produced Spanish Bottom. There is a primitive trail that branches off of the Spanish Bottom Trail and climbs into the north end of Surprise Valley. Although the trail is primitive it isn't hard to follow. It is a little less than 0.2 mile long and climbs 200 feet before reaching the valley.

As you walk down the Spanish Bottom Trail you will be walking below the north side a low ridge for about half the distance. This ridge effectively blocks your view of the terrain south of the trail. But after the trail has descended to within about 0.5 mile of the river the ridge ends, enabling you to see the rim south of the trail. When you reach this point you will notice that the skyline south of the trail dips down briefly and then rises up again before descending abruptly into Cataract Canyon.

Watch the right hand side of the trail carefully when the skyline behind the ridge first comes into view. Soon you will see a faint cairned trail that leaves the Spanish Bottom Trail and climbs 250 feet to the low point on the skyline. The length of this short trail is about 300 yards. Although the trail is very rocky it is well marked with cairns, and if you are observant you shouldn't have any trouble following it. Some minor scrambling is required at the very end but nothing too difficult. When you cross through the notch you will be on the northern end of Surprise Valley.

There is a good trail through the mile-long Surprise Valley, and at the southern end of the valley there is another cairned route down to the river. This trail is seldom used, but if you are looking for something different you might want to walk the loop through Surprise Valley, down to the river, and back up the Spanish Bottom Trail.

Boaters in Cataract Canyon below Spanish Bottom

Granary Trail

☆ ☆ ☆ ☆ ☆

4WD vehicle required
day hike

Distance: 2.3 miles (loop)

Walking time: 1¹/₂ hours

Elevations: 230 ft. loss/gain
Spanish Bottom Trailhead (start): 5,100 ft.
Granary: 5,000 ft.

Trail: Easy, well maintained

Vicinity: Near Dollhouse Rock

USGS Maps: Spanish Bottom

The Spanish Bottom Trailhead is located 0.2 mile from the end of the Dollhouse Road near Dollhouse Rock and Dollhouse Camps 1 and 2. (See page 225 for more information on this road.)

Note: This hike is usually done in conjunction with an overnight camp in the Land of Standing Rocks, but you must have a permit if you intend to spend a night in the area. See pages 15-16 for more information on how to obtain a permit.

The Granary

This short loop trail is full of surprises. The Anasazi granary at the end of the trail would be enough on its own to make the hike worthwhile. But as you walk to the granary you will pass several other points of interest that combine to make this a truly extraordinary hike. In particular there is a spectacular view of the Colorado River from the upper rim of Cataract Canyon. Also from the rim you can look down into Surprise Valley, a large sunken valley on a plateau between the rim and the bottom of Cataract Canyon.

Walk east from the Spanish Bottom Trailhead for 150 yards until you come to a trail junction where the Granary Trail departs from the Spanish Bottom Trail. Turn right here. The Granary Trail heads south along the base of the Dollhouse for a short distance, then it turns left along the southeast side of the formation. Here it seems that the trail must soon end, because there is nothing in front of you but an impregnable barrier of sandstone. But just before reaching the barrier the path suddenly makes a sharp right turn and climbs 25 feet through a small opening between the pinnacles. On the south side of the opening the trail drops down again to immerge on the west side of a small walled valley called a graben.

Grabens are a fairly common feature in Canyonlands, particularly in the Needles District, but when you first see one you will probably think it an odd formation indeed. Typically they are long, narrow valleys with flat, featureless bottoms surrounded by sheer sandstone cliffs. There is usually no outlet for water and no well-defined drainage in the bottom. What forces of nature could have formed these unusual valleys? That was a bewildering question for early geologists until it was discovered that a deep layer of salt underlies most of Canyonlands. This salt, called the Paradox Formation, is noto-

riously unstable, and when it moves it sometimes causes the land above it to sink.

The trail descends into this graben by way of a 150-foot-long crack that in places is only 18 inches wide. After loosing 30 feet of elevation the trail reaches the flat bottom of the sunken valley and turns north for the next 0.2 mile. Near the northern end of the valley you will come to another trail junction where you must turn right to see the granary. Here the trail climbs up the eastern side of the graben and doubles back in a southerly direction for the next 0.5 mile.

The amazing views along this last half-mile of trail before the granary make it, in my opinion, the most interesting part of the entire loop. The trail follows closely along the rim of Cataract Canyon, and not only is the Colorado River clearly visible below but, amazingly, you will find yourself looking

see map, page 266

Granary Trail

down into another much larger graben between the upper rim of the canyon and the Colorado River. This lower graben is called Surprise Valley; it is about 170 yards wide and 0.9 mile long. Surprise Valley parallels the Colorado River along a plateau that is 350 feet below the level of the Granary Trail and 800 feet above the water. From your vantage point you can see another well-defined path running along the bottom of Surprise Valley. This trail is not often used, but it is possible to access it from the Spanish Bottom Trail (see page 265).

The Granary Trail finally turns away from the canyon rim and ends 3 minutes later in front of a small alcove that shelters two prehistoric granaries. One of the granaries is particularly interesting. In is about 8 feet long and it is divided into three separate compartments. My guess is that it was probably used by three different families for storing their foodstuffs.

From the granaries you must retrace your steps 0.5 mile back to the trail junction in the bottom of the first graben and turn north toward the Spanish Bottom Trail. This 0.2-mile connecting trail between the Granary Trail to the Spanish Bottom Trail is also interesting in its own right. It traverses the east side of the Dollhouse, giving you an opportunity to see the impressive formation from another angle. When you reach the Spanish Bottom Trail you must turn left to return to the trailhead. Finally, after climbing about 180 feet over 0.5 mile the trail emerges through a small opening on the west side of the Dollhouse and ends at the road.

Surprise Valley, from the Granary Trail

Ernie's Country

☆ ☆

4WD shuttle car required
day hike

Distance: 10.7 miles (including side trips to points of interest)
(plus 10.9 miles by 4WD shuttle car)

Walking time: 7 hours

Elevations: 1,150 ft. gain, 950 ft. loss
Ernie's Country East Trailhead (start): 5,120 ft.
Clell's Spring: 5,140 ft.
Ernie's Country West Trailhead: 5,320 ft.

Trail: Slightly confusing in a few places, but if you pay attention to the cairns you shouldn't have any trouble.

Vicinity: Near the Dollhouse

USGS Maps: Spanish Bottom, Elaterite Basin

Drive 6.4 miles north of the Teapot Rock Camp, or 4.2 miles south of the Wall Camp, on Dollhouse Road until you see the Mother and Child rock formation. Although there are no signs, you will find a small parking area on the east side of the road, directly across from the Mother and Child Rock. This is the Ernie's Country West Trailhead where the hike ends and where you should leave your shuttle car. (See page 225 for more information on the Dollhouse road.)

To get to the Ernie's Country East Trailhead where the hike begins drive east on the Dollhouse Road, following the signs to the Dollhouse. 3.4 miles beyond the turnoff to Chimney Rock Camp you will come to the turnoff to Dollhouse Camp 3. Turn right here. 0.1 mile before you arrive at Camp 3 you will see a small parking area on the left bordered with a row of rocks. This is the Ernie's Country East Trailhead.

Note: This hike is usually done in conjunction with an overnight camp in the Land of Standing Rocks, but you must have a permit if you intend to spend a night in the area. See pages 15-16 for more information on how to obtain a permit.

No one now remembers who Ernie was, or how Ernie's Country got its name, but this part of the Under the Ledge country has long been a favored grazing area for sheep and cattle. From 1919 until 1944 it was used by the Chaffin family as a pasture for their cattle. It has not been grazed since 1944, however, and since then it has recovered to near pristine condition. The two springs along this trail, Lou's Spring and Clell's Spring were both named after members of the Chaffin family. They were developed by the federal government during the 1930s as a WPA project.

This hike is often done as an overnighter with a camp near Clell's Spring or Lou's Spring. Clell's Spring, 6.8 miles from the beginning trailhead, is relatively close to the halfway point on the trail, but unfortunately the campsites near Clell's Spring are not nearly as nice as those near Lou's Spring.

The hike described below begins at the Ernie's Country East Trailhead, near the Dollhouse, and ends at the west trailhead 4.2 miles south of the Wall Camp. Try to get an early start so the sun will be low and behind you as you walk through Main Flat at the beginning of the hike. This area is particularly pretty early in the morning.

If you aren't able to arrange a shuttle and you plan to begin and end your hike at the same trailhead I suggest hiking in from the west trailhead. In my opinion the most interesting part of the hike is the western portion.

For the first 0.1 mile the trail winds down through the boulders south of the road, then after dropping 80 feet it levels out on the northeastern side of a huge sage-covered meadow. This area is called Main Flat, and as you walk into it you will see why it was once a popular grazing area. The Main Flat is a huge sandy plain, some three miles long and a mile wide. It would have been ideal for a large herd of cattle or sheep.

The biggest obstacle to raising cattle on this flat was the problem of finding water; the Chaffins sometimes had to drive their cattle all the way down to Spanish Bottom to drink from the Colorado River. I expected to see more grass on the flat, especially in light of the fact that it has not been grazed for over 60 years. But there are many indications that Canyonlands is generally hotter and more arid now that it was in the early 1900s. Many of the springs mentioned by the old timers are now nearly or completely

dry, and there was once significantly more winter ice on the rivers than there has been in recent years. I would imagine that places like Main Flat had a good deal more grass in the early years than they do now.

Once on Main Flat the trail generally sticks to the north side of the valley, following the sandy washes most of the time. At one time the trail stayed on the flat above the washes, but in an effort to preserve the ecology the Park Service has rerouted it through the bottoms of the washes. Finally, after 1.5 miles of trudging through the loose sand, the trail climbs back onto the flat as it begins the transition out of Main Flat and into Wide Valley.

3.3 miles from the trailhead the route passes near the western end of a rocky wall that marks the northwestern boundary of Main Flat. Then 0.4 mile later you will come to the bottom of another wide, sandy drain-

Main Flat

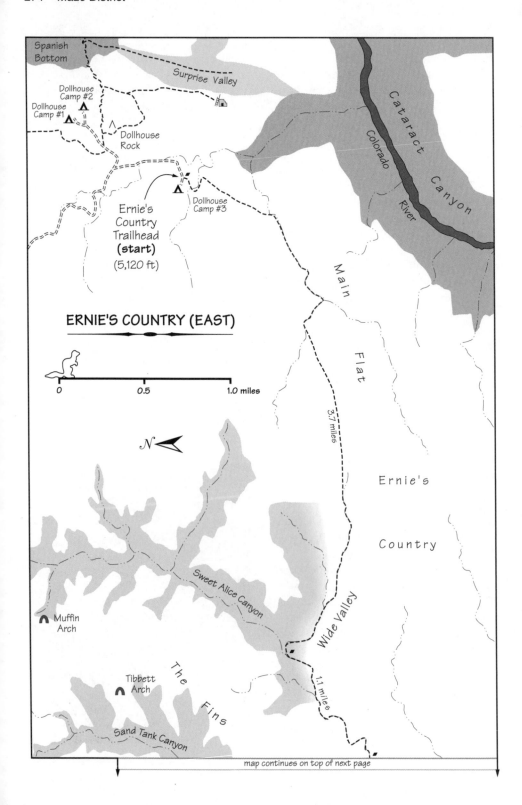

Spanish Bottom

Surprise Valley

Cataract Canyon

Dollhouse Camp #2

Dollhouse Camp #1

Dollhouse Rock

Colorado River

Ernie's Country Trailhead **(start)** (5,120 ft)

Dollhouse Camp #3

Main Flat

ERNIE'S COUNTRY (EAST)

0   0.5   1.0 miles

𝒩

3.7 miles

Ernie's

Country

Sweet Alice Canyon

Wide Valley

Muffin Arch

Tibbett Arch

The Fins

1.1 miles

Sand Tank Canyon

map continues on top of next page

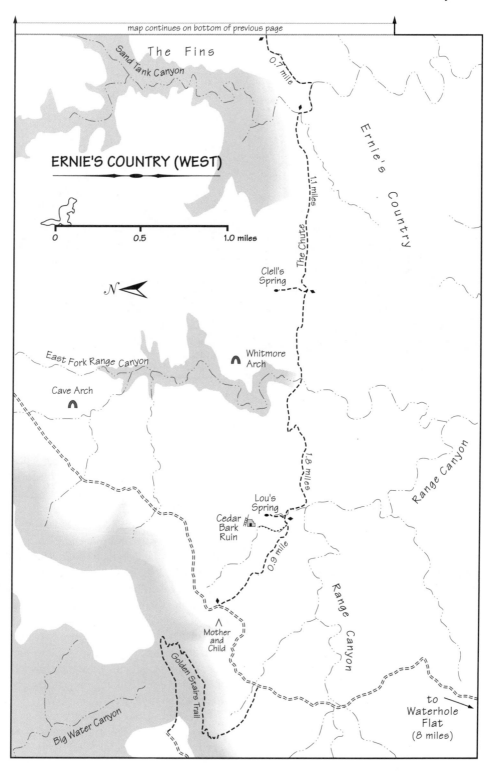

map continues on bottom of previous page

The Fins

Sand Tank Canyon

0.7 mile

Ernie's Country

ERNIE'S COUNTRY (WEST)

0   0.5   1.0 miles

1.1 miles

The Chute

N

Clell's
Spring

East Fork Range Canyon

Whitmore
Arch

Cave Arch

1.8 miles

Range Canyon

Lou's
Spring

Cedar
Bark
Ruin

0.9 mile

Range Canyon

Mother
and
Child

Golden Stairs Trail

to
Waterhole
Flat
(8 miles)

Big Water Canyon

Ernie's Country, above Range Canyon

age where you must turn left. This is Sweet Alice Canyon; it was named after Lou Chaffin's wife, Alice. The trail follows Sweet Alice Canyon for the next 1.6 miles.

The turn into Sweet Alice Canyon is very straightforward if you are hiking in the direction described here. But if you are hiking in the opposite direction it is easy to miss the turn out of Sweet Alice Canyon. The sandy wash is nearly 100 feet wide at this point, and the trail out of its east side is not well marked. If you are hiking from the west trailhead to the Dollhouse watch carefully for the cairn marking the exit out of Sweet Alice Canyon.

The rugged country on the north side of the trail as you walk west down Sweet Alice Canyon is called The Fins, and if you look to your right you will see how it got its name. Four enormous fins of sandstone and many smaller ones protrude upward 0.3 mile north of the trail. This is the kind of country where one is likely to find arches, and indeed there

are at least a half dozen natural arches in the sandstone between Ernie's Country and The Land of Standing Rocks. It is a great place for some off-trail exploration.

After walking 1.6 miles in Sweet Alice Canyon you will come to another junction where you must turn right into Sand Tank Canyon. Watch carefully for the cairns on the right side of Sweet Alice. If you miss this turn you will end up heading directly south towards the Colorado River. The trail into Sand Tank Canyon bears due west for five minutes, then turns north for another two minutes, and finally arrives at another cairn on the left marking the exit point. This is where the trail leaves the network of dry washes that characterize Ernie's Country and begins climbing out into the more rocky terrain to the west. At this point you are approximately half way through the hike.

After leaving the last wash the trail starts heading across the flat towards a wall of rocks on the west side of Sand Tank Canyon. After ten minutes the path enters a fault in the wall and begins to climb into an area known as the Chute. At one point the Chute is only 18 inches wide, but it soon widens out into a small canyon. Finally, 0.9 mile and 240 feet of elevation gain after leaving Sand Tank Canyon, the trail reaches the western side of the Chute and begins a long descent down through the small canyon towards the northern arm of Range Canyon.

Just 3-4 minutes after leaving the top of the Chute you will see a spur trail leaving the right side of the main trail. This is the trail to Clell's Spring. There is a deep cove on the north side of the canyon at this point, and Clell's Spring is located at the back of the cove about 250 yards from the main trail. The spur trail to the spring is well marked by cairns. Clell's Spring consists of two small water collection troughs that are fed by an old rusty pipe buried under the sand. The flow rate is very slow, but I have never heard of the spring being completely dry.

From Clell's Spring the main trail continues west for another 0.6 miles before dropping into the East Fork of Range Canyon. Whitmore Natural Arch is located just 0.4 mile north of the point where the trail crosses the East Fork, but unfortunately it can't be seen from the bottom of the wash. The arch is situated high above the east side of the canyon near the top of the mesa, and to get to it from the trail would require some serious scrambling up the canyon wall. Probably the easiest way to get to the arch would be to hike in on top of the mesa from the Dollhouse Road south of The Wall Camp.

After the trail crosses the East Fork of Range Canyon it immediately starts climbing again to the top of another high point between Range Canyon and the East Fork. At the top there is a brief respite of level ground, but the route back down to Range Canyon is the most strenuous part of this hike. Some scrambling is in order as the cairned trail drops 150 feet down a steep,

Lou's Spring

narrow gully that ends near the eastern side of Range Canyon.

When it reaches Range Canyon the trail immediately turns right into a minor tributary and heads north for 0.2 mile. At that point the path climbs out of the left side of the small wash for the climb up to the trailhead. But before you exit the wash you should stop and look back. 100 feet before the trail exits the wash it passes another cairned trail on the right, and if you follow that side trail for 200 yards you will come to Lou's Spring.

Lou's Spring is a much nicer spring than Clell's Spring; not only is the flow rate greater, but there are some nice campsites nearby for backcountry campers. The spring is located under a pleasantly shaded alcove, and at the bottom of the feeder pipe there are three small storage troughs full of clear water.

There is also an interesting Anasazi granary not far from Lou's Spring. Return to the point where the main trail climbs out the left side of the wash, but instead of climbing out continue walking up the wash for an-

other 4-5 minutes. You will come to a place where the drainage makes an abrupt 90-degree turn to the left. Continue in the bottom of the wash for another 200 feet and then turn around and look back at the northern side of the canyon. 300 feet behind you, about 200 feet north of the canyon bottom, you should see a small alcove with a granary inside.

From the point where you first see the granary it is possible to climb up the slickrock to a bench 20 feet above the canyon bottom and walk back along the bench to the granary. Alternatively, it may be a little easier to climb up to the bench below the granary from the junction where the trail to Lou's Spring first leaves the wash. This granary is unusual because the roof has been thatched with juniper bark. For that reason it is sometimes called Cedar Bark Ruin.

From the point where the main trail leaves the wash it is a 0.8-mile walk up to the Ernie's Country West Trailhead. This stretch of trail involves a 320-foot climb mostly over slickrock. Expect just enough scrambling to make it interesting.

Cedar Bark Ruin

Horseshoe Canyon

☆ ☆   **day hike**

Distance: 7.4 miles (round trip)

Walking time: 4¼ hours

Elevations: 540 ft. gain/loss
Horseshoe Canyon Trailhead (start): 5,340 ft.
Great Gallery Pictograph Panel: 4,800 ft.

Trail: The descent into the canyon is made on a slickrock trail with rock cairns. Inside the canyon a vague trail winds along the bottom of the sandy wash.

Vicinity: West of Hans Flat Ranger Station

USGS Maps: Sugarloaf Butte

Drive east from Highway 24 as if you were going to the Hans Flat Ranger *Station. (See pages 13-14 for more information on how to reach the Hans Flat Ranger Station from Green River or Hanksville). 24.0 miles after leaving the highway, or 20.7 miles before arriving at the ranger station, you will come to a signed fork in the road with the left fork leading to Horseshoe Canyon. Turn left and after another 5.1 miles you will come to a smaller road on the right near a sign that says "Horseshoe Canyon Foot Trail". Follow this road for the last 1.8 miles to the trailhead.*

Horseshoe Canyon contains what is probably the finest display of prehistoric Indian rock art in the United States. The famous Great Gallery, largest of several Horseshoe Canyon sites, is 200 feet long, 15 feet high, and contains dozens of intriguing red, brown and white pictographs. The paintings are at least 2,000 years old, and possibly as old as 8,000 years. Rock art is notoriously difficult to date accurately, but from the style we can be reasonably certain that the work was done by the so called Archaic People who lived in the area before the arrival of the Anasazi and Fremont Indian cultures. Archaic clay figurines that closely mimic the pictographs have been found about nine miles away in Spur Fork, a tributary of Horseshoe Canyon, and the figurines have been dated to about 4700 B.C.

For years archaeologists have struggled to interpret the strange anthromorphs that are depicted in the Great Gallery. In addition to many smaller figures, the huge panel contains about twenty life size human shapes, all of which

> see color photo,
> page 160

have a strange mummy-like appearance. They lack arms or legs, and often have huge insect-like eyes and bucket-shaped heads.

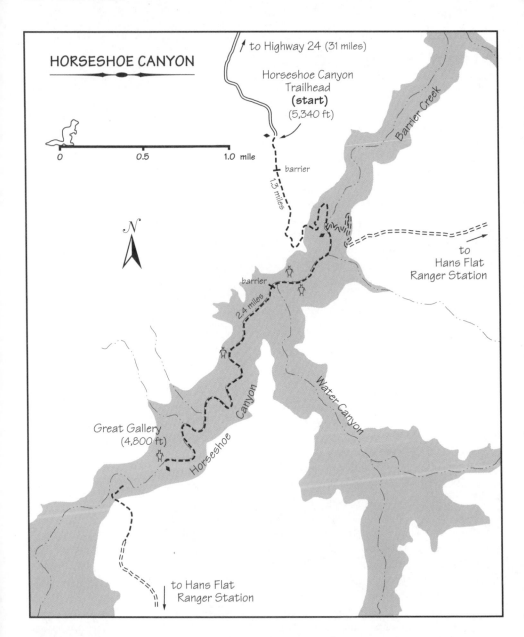

HORSESHOE CANYON

to Highway 24 (31 miles)

Horseshoe Canyon
Trailhead
(start)
(5,340 ft)

0   0.5   1.0 mile

barrier

1.3 miles

Barrier Creek

to
Hans Flat
Ranger Station

N

barrier

2.4 miles

Great Gallery
(4,800 ft)

Horseshoe Canyon

Water Canyon

to Hans Flat
Ranger Station

Most intriguing of all is the figure known as the "Holy Ghost". This seven-foot-high painting stands out among the others because of its size and its ethereal appearance. Perhaps it was intended to portray a revered ancestor, or a mythical deity.

From the car parking area, the trail pro-

ceeds into the canyon along an old jeep road that was originally built in the 1920s by the Phillips Petroleum Company. Phillips was one of many oil companies that drilled unsuccessfully for oil in the area during the first half of the last century. 0.2 mile from the trailhead you will pass an old iron gate that has since been erected to keep vehicles

Horseshoe Canyon

out of the canyon, and another 0.4 mile beyond the gate the trail passes on old water tank. The watertank was part of a pumping system built by sheep ranchers in the early 1940s to bring water up to the pastures above Horseshoe Canyon. The system never worked well, however, and it was abandoned after just a few years.

There are several fossilized dinosaur tracks in the slickrock near the old watertank. They are located near the trail 400 feet before the tank, or 200 feet beyond the point where the watertank first comes into view. Watch the left side of the trail as you approach the tank and there, in a flat slab of limestone just 3 feet from the side of the path, you can see the clear impression of a 3-toed monster that once passed this way. The track is 10 inches long and 8 inches wide. There are several more tracks another 20 feet from the trail, but the footprint near the trail is the most obvious one. Prior to 1997 it was also possible to see dinosaur tracks at another site on the canyon floor 0.2 mile above the Great Gallery Pictographs. However a flood in that year covered those tracks with debris and, to my knowledge, no other tracks are now visible inside the canyon.

As you continue down into the canyon you can see another section of the old Phillips jeep road descending downward from the opposite rim. Until recently it was still possible to drive a jeep down that harrowing road, but in the late 1990s the road was damaged by floods to the extent that it is now impassible by any wheeled vehicle. When you reach the bottom you must turn south and walk down the sandy streambed of Barrier Creek. This section of the trail was also once used by vehicles. When it was still possible to drive down the old Phillips Road from the east rim cars would often continue of 0.6 mile up the canyon floor as far as Water Canyon where a barrier was in place. Now, however, you won't have to worry about encountering any vehicles in Horseshoe Canyon.

As you approach Water Canyon be sure to watch for the first two pictograph sites, one on each side of the canyon. The trail passes right by them. These sites, like the other two that you will see later, were painted by the Archaic People between 2,000 and 8,000 years ago. The third site is situated in a huge alcove on the west side of the stream, about 0.6 mile up-canyon from the first two. Unfortunately the alcove site has sustained substantial damage, both natural and man-caused, and it is not as impressive as the others.

Finally, 1.3 miles from the alcove site, or 3.7 miles from the beginning of the trail, you will come to the Great Gallery. This display of rock art has been called the Louvre of the Southwest, and, indeed, it is a phenomenal relic of the past. Dozens of intricate human and animal figures decorate the panel, mostly in red with some brown and white. The pigments were made from finely ground minerals, mostly hematite, and then mixed with a liquid base, perhaps animal tallow or vegetable juices, to form a crude paint. After thousands of years all traces of the base have disappeared, but the mineral coloring still adheres to the rock and the paintings remain preserved in astonishing detail.

The "Holy Ghost", Great Gallery pictograph panel, Horseshoe Canyon

Geology of Canyonlands

...a whole landscape of naked rock with giant forms carved on it, cathedral-shaped buttes towering hundreds or thousands of feet, cliffs that cannot be scaled, and canyon walls that make the river shrink into insignificance.

John Wesley Powell, 1869

The first scientifically significant exploration of Canyonlands National Park was done by John Wesley Powell, a self-trained geologist who led an expedition down the Green and Colorado Rivers in 1869. Powell was greatly impressed by the massive layers of exposed rock he saw along the rivers. The formations are all sedimentary deposits that have been laid down in sequence over the last 300 million years, and fourteen distinct layers are visible. When viewed from the canyon rims the scene is reminiscent of a vast layer cake that has been sliced into thirds by the two great rivers.

The Jurassic Period
(144 to 208 million years ago)

The youngest layer of rock in Canyonlands National Park is the Jurassic **Morrison Formation** that was deposited some 144-150 million years ago. This formation has been almost completely eroded away within the boundaries of the national park; however some brown siltstones and mudstones of the Morrison Formation can still be seen on the mesa tops along the park's eastern side. The road to the Island in the Sky District also passes over a short section of the Morrison Formation a few miles before it reaches the park boundary. None of the trails described in this book pass through the Morrison Formation.

Beneath the Morrison lies the pinkish **Entrada Sandstone** that was laid down in this area about 160 million years ago. The Entrada is easily recognizable as the smooth, uniform, fracture-free slickrock that underlies a few of the trails on the mesa tops, particularly in the Island in the Sky District. It is also the material from which most of the sandstone arches in the nearby Arches National Park were formed.

The Entrada Sandstone is a remnant of the vast Sahara-like deserts that dominated the Colorado Plateau during the Jurassic Period. Where all of the sand came from is a mystery that has long puzzled geologists, but it is apparent that there were several long episodes of time when dry northwesterly winds blew across the land piling sand into huge shifting dunes, hundreds of feet thick. The desert environment was not a continuous phenomenon, however. Sixty million years of Jurassic time is a long enough span for many climatic interuptions and, among other things, the land was periodically invaded by the sea.

The somewhat thinner layer of reddish-brown rock immediately below the Entrada Sandstone, called the **Carmel Formation**, was deposited about 170 million years ago at the bottom of a shallow sea. The layer is composed of siltstones and mudstones that tend to erode into strange, contorted shapes. The "goblins" of Goblin Valley, just west of Canyonlands lie within the Carmel Formation.

Both the Carmel Formation and the Entrada Sandstone have been almost entirely eroded away within the boundaries of Canyonlands National Park, however immediately below them lies another thick layer of wind-deposited sandstone that is ubiquitous on the mesa tops of Canyonlands. This is the well known **Navajo Sandstone**. The Navajo Sandstone formation is extremely widespread in the American Southwest, stretching from Colorado into Nevada and from Wyoming all the way to Southern Arizona. The vast desert of windblown sand from which it was formed in the middle of the Jurassic Period was one of the largest deposits of sand the earth has ever known. And again, geologists have no idea where all of the sand came from.

The sand was drifted by the wind into huge white dunes, which even today still display the intricate cross bedding patterns typical of shifting sand. Much later, when the sand was overlaid by marine deposits the grains became loosely cemented together by the lime in the invading seawater, and today the Navajo Sandstone formation is still very much reminiscent of a vast desert of white, rolling sand dunes.

Perhaps the most interesting characteristic of the Navajo Sandstone is that it is not completely solid. There was never enough minerals in the water percolating through it to completely fill the voids between the sand; consequently the stone is still slightly porous. Although the Navajo slickrock appears as solid and impenetrable as any other rock, some of the water that falls on its surface actually soaks down into the stone and may appear years later at the bottom of the formation. The Navajo Formation is, in essence, a vast water storage tank under the southwestern desert.

The next older layer of rock beneath the Navajo Sandstone is the **Kayenta Formation**, a layer of stream-deposited sand and clay that represents a brief interval of much wetter climates in the history of Canyonlands. The land during that time was crisscrossed with streams, generally flowing west, and there were numerous lakes. There was also abundant life in the hospitable environment, as evidenced by the presence of numerous dinosaur tracks.

Although the Kayenta Sandstone appears more crumbly that the other layers of sandstone above and below it, the clay content renders it more resistant to water erosion. Furthermore it is relatively impermeable to water, and acts as a barrier to the moisture percolating down through the Navajo Sandstone above it. For this reason it is common to find springs and seeps at the boundary between the Navajo and Kayenta Formations. Indians, cattle ranchers, and other past residents of Canyonlands were well acquainted with the fact that water can sometimes be found in the alcoves just below the upper rim of the canyons, where the white Navajo Sandstone meets the darker reddish-brown Kayenta.

Probably the most recognizable geologic feature in Canyonlands, particularly in the Island in the Sky District, is the massive cliffs of the **Wingate Formation** that lies below the Kayenta Sandstone. The Wingate, like the Navajo Sandstone, was generally formed from windblown sand that drifted across the land at the beginning of Jurassic time. However the difference in appearance between these two formations is striking. There is no other sandstone formation on the Colorado Plateau quite as unique in appearance as the Wingate Sandstone.

The Wingate Sandstone is a much deeper red color than the Navajo, and, perhaps because of its mineral content, it tends to form a deep blue-black patina of desert varnish. Also the cross bedding in the Wingate Sandstone is not as pronounced as it is in the Navajo, and the surface of the formation does not display the large dome-shaped dunes that are common in the Navajo Formation. But the most notable characteristic

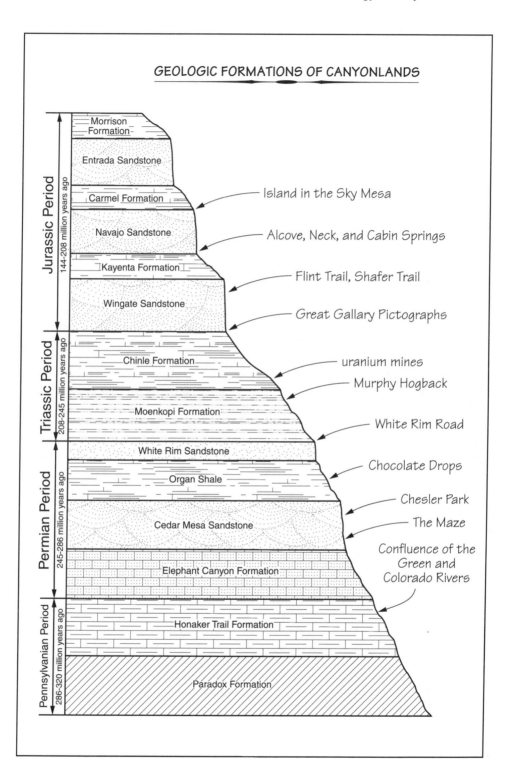

GEOLOGIC FORMATIONS OF CANYONLANDS

Period		Formation	Feature

Jurassic Period — 144-208 million years ago
- Morrison Formation
- Entrada Sandstone
- Carmel Formation — Island in the Sky Mesa
- Navajo Sandstone — Alcove, Neck, and Cabin Springs
- Kayenta Formation — Flint Trail, Shafer Trail
- Wingate Sandstone — Great Gallary Pictographs

Triassic Period — 208-245 million years ago
- Chinle Formation — uranium mines
- Moenkopi Formation — Murphy Hogback

Permian Period — 245-286 million years ago
- White Rim Sandstone — White Rim Road
- Organ Shale — Chocolate Drops
- Cedar Mesa Sandstone — Chesler Park / The Maze
- Elephant Canyon Formation — Confluence of the Green and Colorado Rivers

Pennsylvanian Period — 286-320 million years ago
- Honaker Trail Formation
- Paradox Formation

of the Wingate Sandstone is its propensity to sheer along vertical planes and form precipitous cliffs wherever the formation is exposed to the forces of erosion. These formidable cliffs often reach a height of 500 feet, forming daunting vertical walls around the buttes and mesas of the national park.

The Triassic Period
(208-245 million years ago)

Years of semantic controversy have blurred the boundary line between the end of the Triassic Period and the beginning of the Jurassic Period of geologic time. Previously, many scientists defined the beginning of the Jurassic Period to be about 195 million years ago, which meant that the Wingate Formation would have been laid down during the Triassic Period. Now, however, there seems to be general agreement that the Jurassic Period began about 13 million years earlier, so that in Utah the geologic boundary between the two periods lies at the bottom of the Wingate Formation.

Immediately below the stately cliffs of Wingate Sandstone lies a confusing multicolored mixture of sedimentary rock called the **Chinle Formation**. 220 million years ago, while the Chinle sediments were being deposited, the land was subjected to a wide variety of changing climatic and ecological conditions; consequently the formation is now very inhomogeneous. It is striped with thin layers of shale, siltstone, sandstone, volcanic ash, and limestone that vary in color form grayish green and purple to reds and browns. Most of deposits in the Chinle Formation were brought into the area by running water and, along with the mud, sand, and gravel, the rivers and streams also brought a significant amount of organic material. Consequently there is now a fair amount of petrified wood in the formation.

There is also a significant amount of uranium ore in the Chinle and, interestingly, it is frequently found in association with the petrified wood and other plant fossils. Scientists theorize that mildly acidic water percolating down through the formation leached uranium compounds out of a deposit of volcanic ash. Then when the uranium bearing water came into contact with buried organic matter the pH of the solution changed from acidic to basic, causing the precipitation of yellow uranium oxide.

The yellow uranium ore is particularly prevalent at the bottom of the Chinle in the Moss Back and Shinarump Members. These members of the formation consist of hard conglomerate sandstones that were formed from stream gravel, sand, plant debris, and other deposits that were washed into the area at the beginning of the Chinle time about 240 million years ago. The layers are less resistant to erosion than the overlaying Chinle deposits, and they tend to form ledges over the top of the slopes below.

Beneath the Chinle Formation lies the chocolate brown **Moenkopi Formation**, the oldest rock of the Triassic Period and one of the most interesting formations in Canyonlands. The Moenkopi is the result of a huge mud flat that extended inland for several hundred miles from an ancient seashore in western Utah between 240 and 245 million years ago. Layer upon layer of clay mud was deposited on the flat during that time, and hundreds, even thousands, of the thin layers of mudstone are still visible today. Many of the flat, horizontal layers are less than a millimeter thick, piled high up the sides of the gullies and arroyos like a stacks of brown wrapping paper.

But the thing that makes the Moenkopi Formation so interesting is that it is so well preserved. Since the rock contains so much clay it is almost insoluble in water, and as a result the flat tablet-like layers have preserved in exquisite detail a fascinating record of their ancient environment. Cracks in the mud, imprints of tiny animals, ripple marks, even small craters left by rain drops appear frozen in the layers of brown stone as if they were made only yesterday.

The Permian Period
(245 to 286 years ago)

Beneath the oldest rock of the Triassic geological period lies the **White Rim Sandstone**, which on the geologic calendar dates back to the earlier Permian Period. This easily recognizable boundary also marks the beginning of the of the Mesozoic Era when flowering plants, birds, dinosaurs and mammals first appeared on earth. There are no fossils of large animals in or below the White Rim Formation.

The White Rim Sandstone probably formed on the shore of an ancient sea about 240 million years ago. Cross-bedding in the layer indicates that the sand was deposited by the wind east of the park, but its western extremity was definitely a marine deposit. The hard, flat layer is generally quite thin, reaching a maximum thickness of 250 feet near Elaterite Butte in the Maze District and eventually pinching off to nothing below Dead Horse Point.

The White Rim Sandstone has also played an important role in the human history of Canyonlands—particularly in the Island in the Sky District. The thin layer of stark white rock is much harder that most of the other rock formations in the canyons, and with the erosion of the softer layers above it a wide, flat bench has been formed below the Island in the Sky Mesa. Before the 1960s this bench was an important summer pasture for sheep and cattle ranchers, and in the early 1950s the bench was used by uranium miners for building access roads to mines in the uranium-rich Chinle Formation above it. If you peer into the canyons from any of the viewpoints on the Island in the Sky you can easily see the old jeep roads

threading their way across the White Rim Plateau a thousand feet below. The best known of these roads is called, appropriately enough, the White Rim Road.

Below the White Rim Sandstone it is back to the red and reddish brown rocks of a shale and siltstone deposit again—this time it is called the **Organ Rock Formation**. The soft, crumbly Organ Rock Shale would be almost completely washed away throughout Canyonlands by now were it not for the more durable White Rim Sandstone above it. The sandstone acts like a capstone, protecting the underlying material from the rain and packing it together with compressive force. There are many places in the park where all that is left of the Organ Rock are tall, isolated pinnacles of deep red shale protruding upward for 200 feet or more. Each one is invariably capped with a large block of precariously balanced White Rim Sandstone.

And below the Organ Rock Shale, more sand in the form of the **Cedar Mesa Formation**. This huge layer of subterranean sandstone extends all the way across Southern Utah, from the four corners area to Nevada, and it resurfaces again in the Grand Canyon where it is called the Esplanade Sandstone. A large part of the formation appears to have been deposited underwater; hence some or all off Southern Utah must have been submerged below a shallow sea at that time.

The Cedar Mesa Sandstone makes a dramatic appearance in the Needles District of Canyonlands, where it has been sculpted by erosional forces into thousands of picturesque spires, or "needles", that cover the landscape. The scene is made even more appealing by the fact that the Cedar Mesa Sandstone undergoes a facies change in this area, causing the odd formations to be striped with alternating bands of red and white. The Cedar Mesa Sandstone is also widespread in the Maze District of Canyonlands National Park, however the red bands that make it so attractive on the east side of the Colorado River are not as prominent there.

The oldest layer of Permian rock in Canyonlands is the **Elephant Canyon Formation**, but it is buried so deeply that the only place it can be seen is along the Colorado River and in the depths of Stillwater Canyon above the Green River. It was named after a tributary of the Green that joins Stillwater Canyon a few miles above the confluence.

The Elephant Canyon Formation consists of alternating layers of sandstone and limestone that were deposited some 275-285 million years ago. Near the top of the formation the sandstone predominates, while at the bottom the structure is composed almost entirely of limestone. It is reasonable to conclude that at that time the area was entirely under the ocean, but then as time went on the land rose above sea level. Following that, the land was again reclaimed many times by the sea—a pattern that has been and most likely will be repeated as long as there are oceans on the earth.

The Pennsylvanian Period
(286 to 320 million years ago)

Rock layers older than 280 million years old in Canyonlands are usually buried far beneath the surface and are rarely seen; consequently there are few visible remnants of the Pennsylvanian Period. The youngest rock from this time is the **Honaker Trail Formation**, which lies directly under the Elephant Canyon Formation. The only ones privileged to see this layer of rock, though, are those who have floated or hiked along the Colorado River below its confluence with the Green, and even then it is difficult to tell from a casual inspection which layer is which. To the untrained eye the Honaker Trail Formation looks very similar to the overlying Elephant Canyon Formation, especially when all you can see is a vertical cross section on a canyon wall. The most significant difference between the two layers is in the fossils they contain.

Beneath the Honaker Trail Formation is a layer of rock that must be mentioned even though it is rarely seen. This one is called the **Paradox Formation**, and although it was deposited over 300 million years ago no other formation has played a greater role in the geological history of Canyonlands. The Paradox Formation contains several vast beds of salt that were deposited during Pennsylvanian time when seawater engulfed the area at various times and then evaporated. The geologic record indicates that this invasion of saltwater occurred at least 29 times, resulting in a layer of salt that is in places nearly a half-mile thick.

Although the Paradox salt beds are not exposed, their presence has had a great influence on the landscape in Canyonlands. The reason is that, as odd as it may seem, salt tends to flow like wet mud when it is under pressure. It oozes into cracks, it lubricates faults, and it bulges up toward the surface in areas wherever erosion has reduced the pressure of the overburden. Many of the bulges, depressions, ridges, and folds in Canyonlands' landscape have been caused by movements in the salt beds that underlay the area. The salt deposits are also of commercial importance. Potash, a salt of potassium that is used in the manufacture of fertilizer, is being mined just outside Canyonlands National Park near Moab.

Index

X, Y, Z

David Day grew up in a small desert town south of the Grand Canyon. His family subscribed to Arizona Highways magazine, and as a teenager he spent many hours studying the works of his favorite photographers, Joseph and David Muench. When he was 17 he landed a summer job in a photo shop at the Grand Canyon, and after 3 months of hiking and photographing the canyon his lifelong passion was firmly established.

Today he lives in Provo, Utah, where his love of wild places has led to the publication of three books about Utah's backcountry. *Canyonlands* covers an area that is particularly dear to his heart, perhaps because it brings back memories of his childhood experiences in the Grand Canyon.